RETREATS THAT WORK

*Designing and Conducting Effective Offsites
for Groups and Organizations*

Sheila Campbell • Merianne Liteman
with Steve Sugar

JOSSEY-BASS/PFEIFFER
A Wiley Imprint
www.pfeiffer.com

Published by Jossey-Bass/Pfeiffer
A Wiley Imprint
989 Market Street, San Francisco, CA94103-1741   www.pfeiffer.com

ISBN: 0-7879-6444-1

Library of Congress Cataloging-in-Publication Data
Campbell, Sheila
Retreats that work: designing and conducting effective offsites for
groups and organizations / Sheila Campbell, Merianne Liteman, with Steve Sugar.
p. cm.
Includes bibliographical references and index.
ISBN 0-7879-6444-1 (alk. paper)
1. Management retreats—Handbooks, manuals, etc. I. Liteman,
Merianne. II. Sugar, Steve. III. Title.
HD30.4 .C355 2003
658.4'56—dc21
2002008568

Jossey-Bass/Pfeiffer books and products are available through most bookstores. To contact Jossey-Bass/Pfeiffer directly, call our Customer Care Department within the U.S. at 800-274-4434, outside the U.S. at 317-572-3985 or fax 317-572-4002.

Jossey-Bass/Pfeiffer also publishes its books in a variety of electronic formats. Some content that appears in print may not be available in electronic books.

Printed in the United States of America

Acquiring Editor: Josh Blatter
Director of Development: Kathleen Dolan Davies
Developmental Editor: Janis Chan
Editor: Rebecca Taff
Senior Production Editor: Dawn Kilgore
Manufacturing Supervisor: Becky Carreño
Interior Design: Gene Crofts
Cover Design: Bruce Lundquist
Illustrations: Lotus Art

Printing 10   9   8   7   6   5   4   3   2   1

Contents

Acknowledgments   ix

Introduction   xi

SECTION ONE   *The Convenor's Guide to Ensuring a Successful Retreat*

Chapter 1   So You're Thinking of Holding a Retreat   3

    Nine Reasons to Hold a Retreat   5

    Guiding Principles for Retreat Design   7

    Ten Reasons Not to Hold a Retreat   9

    Kinds of Retreats   12

    Who's Who in Planning a Retreat   15

Chapter 2   Setting the Goals, Deciding the Format,
and Inviting the Participants   21

    Last Things First—What Do You Want to Be Different? 21

    Who Should Facilitate?   22

    Whom Should You Invite?   25

    Using a Specialized Retreat Format   30

    Involving Participants in Retreat Planning   37

Chapter 3   Planning Retreat Logistics   39

    How Long Should a Retreat Last?   40

    When Should You Schedule Your Retreat?   42

    Where Should You Hold Your Retreat?   45

    Sleeping Rooms and Meals   47

Sports and Recreation   48
Notifying Participants   48

Chapter 4   The Role of Leaders at the Retreat   51

Reaching an Understanding About Participants' Authority   51
Leadership Behavior During the Retreat   53
A Common Post-Retreat Concern   59

SECTION TWO   *The Facilitator's Guide to Designing and Planning the Retreat*

Chapter 5   Retreat Design Issues   63

Aligning Yourself with the Convenor   63
Pre-Retreat Interviews with Participants   66
Identifying the Scope of Issues and
      Creating the Retreat Plan   70
Capturing the Work Product   70
Using Behavioral Assessments   72
Pre-Work for Retreat Participants   76
Using "White Space"   77
Thinking About Logistics   78
Sins of Omission: The Top Ten Retreat Design Mistakes   80
Special Design Considerations for Board Retreats   83
Design Issues for a Series of Retreats   87

Chapter 6   Retreat Design Components   91

Introduction   92
Ground Rules   93
Individual Check-In   95
Giving Feedback to the Group   97
Content Segments   100
Decision Making   111
Action Planning   112
Closing   112

SECTION THREE *The Facilitator's Guide to Leading the Retreat*

Chapter 7 Leading the Retreat   115

  Process or Content Facilitator?   117
  When Should the Facilitator Intervene?   120
  Giving Feedback to Retreat Participants   122
  Working with Co-Facilitators   123
  For Internal Facilitators: Partnering with Another Facilitator   125
  Diversity Issues at the Retreat   126
  Encouraging Participation   132
  Changing the Plan   134

Chapter 8 Helping Participants Make Decisions and Plan for Action   137

  Methods of Decision Making   137
  Types of Retreat Decisions   142
  The Nub: Action Planning   146

Chapter 9 How to Recover When Things Go Awry   155

  A Few Participants Dominate the Discussions   156
  The Group Keeps Wandering Off Task   156
  The Group's Energy Is Flagging   158
  A Participant Keeps Plowing the Same Ground   158
  A Participant Repeatedly Disrupts the Conversations   159
  A Senior Manager Violates the Ground Rules   159
  People Are Misusing Humor   160
  A Participant Is Overtly Hostile or Refuses to Participate   161
  "I'm Outta Here": A Participant Walks Out   163
  The Boss Gets Furious or Bursts into Tears   164
  Participants Are Resisting New Ideas   165
  An Intense Conflict Breaks Out   168
  A Participant Breaches Another's Confidence   170

SECTION FOUR   *The Facilitator's Activity Manual*

Chapter 10   Leading a Strategic Planning Retreat   173

Elements of Organization Strategy   174
Mission, Vision, or Purpose?   178
Activity: Exploring Strategic Purpose   180
Discerning the Organization's Values   182
Activity: Looking at Our Values   183
Understanding the Environment   185
Activity: Glimpses into the Future   186
Activity: Rating Resources   189
Activity: Our Stable of Clients or Resources   191
Activity: Prioritizing Constituencies   194
Activity: Distinctive Competencies   196
Evaluating Work Processes   198
Planning for Action   200
Prioritizing Among Goals   203
Activity: Targeting Core Priorities   204
Checking Against Resources   206
Activity: Resource/Impact Matrix   207
Devising Strategies   209
Testing Strategies   210

Chapter 11   Leading a Culture Change Retreat   213

Great Expectations: What Can Realistically
    Be Accomplished at a Retreat   214
Activity: Visit Our Village   216
Activity: Timeline of Our History   221
Activity: Significant Stories   223
Working with Sensitive or Controversial Issues   224
Activity: Silent Dialogue   225
Reward Structures Help Shape Culture   228
Activity: What Gets Rewarded Here?   229

How Individuals Foster Cultural Change 230

Recognizing and Removing Obstacles to Change 231

Activity: Obstacle Busters 232

Feedback for Senior Executives (and Others) 234

Activity: Metaphorical Management 235

Chapter 12   Leading a Relationship–Building and Teamwork Retreat 239

If You're Asked to Lead a "Teamwork" Retreat 239

Exploring How Things Are and How Participants
     Would Like Them to Be 241

Activity: Vehicle for Change 242

Clarifying Individuals' Roles and Responsibilities 245

Improving Work Processes 245

Activity: Decorations Factory 247

Strengthening Communication 253

Activity: How We Communicate 254

Exploring the Importance of Feedback 256

Activity: Snowball 257

Probing for Sources of Conflict 259

Activity: How Conflict Affects Us 260

Activity: Taking Responsibility 261

Exploring How Individuals Can Change Their Own Behaviors 262

Activity: Star Performers 263

A Special Case: A Peers-Only Retreat to Call a Cease Fire
     in Interdepartmental Turf Battles 266

Chapter 13   Leading a Creativity and Innovation Retreat 269

Activity: Wide Open Thinking 271

Activity: Really Bad Ideas 275

Minimizing "Groupthink" 276

Activity: Impressions 277

Cultivating the Creativity Habit 279

Activity: Isolated Words 280

Activity: Multiple Perspectives 282

	Activity: Expert Opinion	284
	Letting Go of Judgment	285
	Activity: Considering Risk	286
Chapter 14	Closing the Retreat	289
	Activity: The Messy Room	290
	Activity: Top Priorities	293
	Activity: Closing Thoughts	294
	Activity: Letter to Myself	295
	Activity: Appreciation	296
	Activity: Expectations and Outcomes	298
	Activity: The Road We've Traveled	300
	Writing the Follow-Up Report	301
EPILOGUE	*The Convenor's Guide to Keeping the Work of the Retreat Alive*	
Chapter 15	Assuring That the Action Plan Is Implemented	305
	Announcing Retreat Outcomes	307
	Translating Decisions into Action	308
	Avoiding Post-Retreat Letdown	309
	The Role of Senior Management	310
	Changing Cynicism to Support	311
	Making the Plan Stick	312
	Look Ahead, Plan Ahead	314
	Afterword	317
	Appendix	319
	References	325
	About the Authors	329
	Index	331

Acknowledgments

This book would not have been possible without the care and support of our families, friends, and colleagues. In particular, we would like to thank. . .

- Jeffrey Liteman, husband, friend, business partner, and consultant, who took part in endless hours of discussion and debate about the contents of the book, gave us honest opinions and useful feedback throughout the process, shared many meals given over to book talk, and helped us polish the rough edges.
- Steve Sugar, who believed in this project, guided us through the publishing process, and gave us sound advice on how to make the exercises more reader-friendly.
- Kathleen Dolan Davies, our developmental director, Janis Chan, our developmental editor, and Dawn Kilgore, our production editor, who were so encouraging in their comments and so skilled in helping clarify our intent, and Josh Blatter, our acquiring editor, who saw the potential in this book.
- The Center for Creative Leadership's Leading Creatively Program and Airlie Conferences, which nourish our creative spirits and keep us learning.
- Our families and friends whose love and encouragement sustained us throughout the challenging process of creating this book.
- Our classmates and professors in American University's AU/NTL OD program, who years ago gave us a lab in which to try out many of our ideas.

And we're deeply grateful to all our clients, who have invited us into their organizations and openly shared their issues and insights. You inspire and challenge us daily.

Merianne Liteman and Sheila Campbell

Introduction

This book is for anyone who has ever had to plan an offsite retreat and wondered, "Where do I start?" It's for anyone who has convened a retreat and watched, stunned, as it careened off in unforeseen directions. And it's for anyone who is planning to convene a retreat or design and facilitate one.

At their best, retreats are a powerful means to bring about positive change. They provide a space where people are freed up from their day-to-day flurry of activities so they can think in fresh ways. The casual dress and informal structures of a retreat create an environment where participants can get to know and learn to trust one another, explore issues more openly, and generate new ideas more creatively.

Retreats give people time to dig deeply into their organization's issues and develop appropriate strategies to address them. As a result, key decisions and plans made at retreats often have more solid and lasting support than those made in more hierarchical meetings.

We've written this book because we love retreats that work—designing and leading them and also taking part in them—and because we've seen retreats fail when they might have succeeded.

Too many retreats have had no effect when people get back to their everyday work. You only have to experience one or two of these time-wasting affairs to flinch the next time somebody says, "Let's have a retreat."

We want to help experienced professionals and first-time retreat planners alike lead offsites that will make a difference long after the participants are back in their organizations.

About This Book

This book is full of information about retreats, gleaned from our experience as designers and leaders of hundreds of offsites and from the stories related to us by our colleagues in the field. We hope you will find this information helpful whether you are the person who has decided to hold an offsite or the facilitator who is preparing to design and lead one. Chapters 1 through 4 and 15 are addressed specifically to the convenor and the rest of the book is addressed to the facilitator, but you'll get the most out of the book if you read all the chapters, whether you read them in order or skip around to explore the issues that are most on your mind.

If you are the convenor, the first chapters will help you establish the conditions for making your retreat a success. The chapters on facilitating the retreat are valuable also, however, because they will give you a deeper understanding of why the facilitator makes the choices he or she does.

If you are an internal or external consultant, professional facilitator, or human resources manager, or if you are facilitating a retreat for the first time, all the elements you need to plan and design a retreat that works are in Chapters 5 through 14.

We especially want to call your attention to Chapters 10 through 14, which contain dozens of practical, tested retreat activities.

Here's an overview:

Section One: The Convenor's Guide to Ensuring a Successful Retreat

- *Chapter 1. Deciding Whether to Hold a Retreat.* We cover what a retreat might achieve and outline the circumstances under which it would be better *not* to convene one.
- *Chapter 2. Setting Goals for the Retreat.* We discuss what can reasonably be accomplished within the limited time frame of a retreat and how you can focus the offsite so it addresses your primary goals. We help you decide who should facilitate the retreat and who from your organization should attend. We also lay out various retreat formats for you to consider.

- *Chapter 3. Thinking About Logistics.* We explore the role that the site, setting, seating arrangements, out-of-session time, and even the food and accommodations play in creating the right retreat ambiance.
- *Chapter 4. Creating an Environment for Change.* We provide guidance on how to establish and sustain a positive environment during the retreat and what to avoid so that the offsite doesn't derail.

Section Two: The Facilitator's Guide to Designing and Planning the Retreat

- *Chapter 5. Ensuring That the Facilitator and Convenor Share Expectations.* We discuss how to involve participants in the design process so they feel ownership of the retreat. We explore how you might use assessments, and we talk about special considerations for board and multi-session retreats. We also include "Sins of Omission," the most common mistakes people make in planning retreats.
- *Chapter 6. Designing the Retreat.* We look at the actual architecture of an offsite—the elements that go into the design—and explain design issues in some depth. We help you choose the most appropriate content segments to keep the retreat varied and engaging while moving the participants steadily toward their goals. We show you how to develop an hour-by-hour plan, but—since no retreat flows exactly as scheduled—we also explore ways to build flexibility into your design.

Section Three: The Facilitator's Guide to Leading the Retreat

- *Chapter 7. Facilitating the Retreat.* It takes skill and practice to create a safe working environment, keep the group focused, constantly scan for what's happening in the room, and sense when to push for decisions and when to hold back. We explore the facilitator's role and discuss how to work with co-facilitators. We also look at how to manage the diversity issues that are likely to emerge.
- *Chapter 8. Helping Participants Make Decisions and Plan for Action.* We cover the kinds of decisions that typically are made at retreats and explore

the advantages and disadvantages of various decision-making techniques. We also talk about how to help retreat participants develop action plans that are likely to be implemented.

- *Chapter 9. Recovering When Something Goes Wrong.* People sometimes get angry, burst into tears, or refuse to participate. We suggest strategies to manage those awkward situations. At the end of the chapter, we also talk about how to deal with resistance to change among retreat participants.

Section Four: The Facilitator's Activity Manual

- *Chapters 10 through 13. Choosing Retreat Activities.* These chapters contain many activities you can use to help increase staff alignment, foster improved cooperation and collaboration, recover from a crisis, chart your future course, or think more creatively about your policies, procedures, products, and services. We provide step-by-step instructions, suggest scripts for the facilitator, and recommend questions for debriefing each activity. In addition, we indicate the level of experience a facilitator would need to lead each one successfully.
- *Chapter 14. Closing the Retreat.* All too often, the end of an offsite is a rushed affair that doesn't help participants make the transition from the retreat to the workplace. This chapter includes specific activities that help elicit commitment from participants and set the stage for follow-up action back at the office. We also explore the all-important issue of how to report to non-participants what happened at the retreat and what changes are anticipated as a result.

Epilogue: The Convenor's Guide to Keeping the Work of the Retreat Alive

- *Chapter 15. Ensuring That the Retreat Plan Is Implemented.* The success of the retreat will ultimately depend on what actually happens once everyone returns to the workplace. We suggest follow-up activities and outline what senior management's role is (and is not) in maintaining the momentum for change.

Appendix: Retreat Checklists

We include checklists that both the convenor and the facilitator can use to make sure they haven't forgotten anything that could jeopardize the offsite.

We wrote this book because there was no manual for us when we started leading retreats many years ago. We hope it will be a useful reference tool that you will come back to again and again in convening, designing, and facilitating your own retreats that work!

SECTION ONE

The Convenor's Guide to Ensuring a Successful Retreat

Chapter 1

So You're Thinking of Holding a Retreat

Chances are you were in a meeting today. Much of the daily work of organizations takes place in meetings. But what if your organization needs to examine fundamental issues or make a major change in its strategy or operations? Since the structure of standard meetings doesn't encourage the deep focus and thoughtful approach that such decisions require, maybe you're thinking of convening an offsite retreat. We've summarized some of the differences between retreats and meetings in Table 1.1 at the end of this chapter. Meanwhile, here are some things to consider.

Your memo announcing, "We're having a retreat," will likely trigger a variety of reactions among the staff. Some will love the idea of dedicating time to talk about new ideas and maybe hang out with more senior leaders. Others will dread the very same things. Some will recall successful retreats they've attended, while others will remember bad experiences.

Retreats can make people feel vulnerable. You say, "We want to hear the truth," but not every participant will take you at your word. Some may remember that a month after Elise spoke out about a concern, she was abruptly dismissed for reasons that were never disclosed.

Retreats are places where emotions can be exposed and expectations can be dashed. "Just let me get through these two days without getting angry," a reluctant participant might think, while another—eager but naïve—might believe, "At last I'm going to convince people to do what I've been proposing for the last six months."

Retreats often require an overnight stay; managing the logistics of being away from home can be difficult for some people. And retreats are expensive. In addition to the costs of a site, transportation, meals and lodging, and perhaps hiring a facilitator, organizations must tap their most valuable asset, staff time.

Moreover, retreats require a commitment to follow through after the participants return to work. The seeds planted at a retreat must be nurtured before the fruit can be harvested.

Finally, retreats are risky. An ill-conceived, badly prepared, poorly designed, or ineptly led retreat can make things worse and take your organization backward. Think of everything that can go wrong in a meeting, magnify it in intensity and duration, and that merely scratches the surface of what can go wrong at a retreat.

So why incur the costs and take the risks?

Well, why invest in real estate or the stock market when a savings account at a bank is insured and gives you a predictable, albeit low, rate of return? Retreats are investments in your organization's future. Unlike meetings, which typically focus on current issues and concerns, retreats take a longer view and focus on deeper issues. Thus, while some up-front investment is required, the potential payoff of retreats is considerable.

Definitions

- For the sake of simplicity, clarity, and good grammar, we often use "he" and "she" when referring to the convenor, facilitator, and others. Our use of these personal pronouns is completely arbitrary, and readers should understand that men and women can and do play all roles in retreats.

- We use the terms "retreat," "offsite," and "offsite retreat" interchangeably.

- All the stories in this book are real, but names of individuals and companies and other identifying data have been changed to preserve our clients' confidentiality.

Nine Reasons to Hold a Retreat

1. To Explore Fundamental Concerns

Suppose turnover is exceptionally high or staff morale low. Or you have seen a significant drop-off in customers or increase in their complaints. A retreat can be the ideal forum to explore and address the underlying causes.

2. To Harness the Collective Creativity of the Group

When it's important to generate ideas for new products, services, or work processes, typical brainstorming sessions often fail to produce significant results. Retreats, free of routine workplace demands, have fewer barriers to imagination and creative thinking. The offsite setting can help innovative solutions emerge.

3. To Foster Change

A retreat can promote new approaches to strategic planning, product design, service delivery, or marketing. The open discussion that characterizes well-run retreats promotes understanding of and commitment to new directions.

4. To Change Perceptions, Attitudes, and Behavior

In every organization, people make up stories to account for things they don't understand. These stories lead to attitudes and actions that can be harmful to the organization. A retreat can be a great setting for participants to raise concerns and ask questions. They can provide more information, clear up misunderstandings, discuss the impact of past decisions, and modify those decisions if priorities have changed or if prior decisions failed to achieve their purpose.

5. To Correct Course when Things Are Going Wrong

You can't turn an organization around by executive fiat. People will change only when they see that it's important to do so. Retreats provide a forum for discussions about the reasons for and the urgency of a desired change. When people play a role in deciding what needs to be changed, they are more committed to ensuring that the change effort succeeds.

6. To Change Your Organization's Culture or Improve Relationships That Are Hindering Its Effectiveness

Suppose members of a team or division are having difficulty communicating effectively with one another. Or two departments seem unable to work together. Or people are afraid to tell you what they think you might not want to hear. Retreats can help people open up to one another and create a climate of trust.

7. To Create a Collective Vision for the Organization

Much of the tension that exists in organizations does not stem from inherent personality conflicts, but rather from individuals pursuing their own visions of what is best for the organization. These visions often clash with one another because none of them necessarily represents the full picture of an organization's circumstances.

Retreats can help participants understand and build commitment to the organization's overall priorities. This understanding and commitment can encourage individuals to hold themselves accountable for the organization's success, not just the success of their own work group.

8. To Accomplish Something That Cannot Be Done by the Leader Alone

No matter how experienced and competent leaders are, they can't do everything on their own. Retreats provide an environment in which everyone can contribute knowledge, expertise, and skills to address issues that often plague and confound busy executives.

9. To Make Tough Decisions

Leaders often confront very tough decisions: to eliminate a signature product or service, to close down a particular operation, to reduce staff, or to change the nature of a long-standing alliance. Imagine how much more commitment there would be if many people from different levels in your organization participated in deciding what to eliminate or change and how to go about doing so, rather than simply being told what to do by the leaders.

At a retreat, leaders receive the benefit not only of broad participation in idea generation, but also of better decisions, because the group collectively will have a wider perspective and a greater number of ideas than the leader alone.

Guiding Principles for Retreat Design

Pick up an issue of *Business Week, Fast Company,* or *The Wall Street Journal* and you'll frequently read, "At a retreat Company X decided. . ." as a way of introducing a significant new strategy. But the articles don't say what participants in that retreat did that led them to adopt that new strategy. That's what we want to help you figure out: how to use retreats to help your organization make strategic decisions and lay the foundation required to implement them back at work. That brings us to our first guiding principle of retreat planning:

- A retreat should be designed to result in action for change.

Executives don't usually call for retreats because they're delighted with the *status quo.* They convene retreats because they want something to be different in their companies, departments, teams, or organizations. Everything in the retreat should lead participants toward the development of well-thought-out action plans that are likely to produce change for the better.

Of course, we all know that decisions are implemented only when there is strong commitment from the people who will have to take action on them. Offsite retreats provide an excellent forum for getting everyone's input into important decisions, thus increasing the chances that decisions will be widely supported.

But too often participants are skeptical. They suspect that management has already made the decisions and that the retreat is just a smokescreen to make them think they had a say in the issue. The need to allay those suspicions has led to our second guiding principle of retreat planning:

- At least some of the participants should contribute to formulating the goals of the retreat.

There are many ways to do this. Outside consultants often interview participants before committing to a retreat design. The convenor can hold internal meetings or focus groups to discuss hopes and fears for the retreat. But however it is done, it's critical for participants to understand that the retreat is not the exclusive tool of management. Unless participants believe that they can influence the outcome, they'll simply say what they think executives want to hear, rather than speaking honestly about how they see things.

Which leads to our third guiding principle of retreat design:

- What happens at the retreat must relate to what happens in the day-to-day work of the organization.

One of the great things about retreats is that people can test new ideas and try out new approaches in a non-workplace environment. But the participants still have to be able to see how what they do at the retreat is pertinent to their work. Otherwise, the offsite feels disconnected from reality, and people will not be motivated to change their behavior when they return to the office.

One more important point: The open nature of retreats can create a sense of false security. Some people may imagine that it's safe to say or do anything, from telling sexist jokes after drinking too much at the bar to finally telling off that so-and-so. They forget that they are with colleagues with whom they will have to interact when the retreat is over.

It's important to work with the facilitator to make the behavioral boundaries very clear. A retreat is not a free-for-all.

Principles for Effective Retreats

- A retreat should be designed to result in action for change.
- At least some of the participants (the more, as practical, the better) should contribute to formulating the goals of the retreat.
- What happens at the retreat must relate to what happens in the day-to-day work of the organization.
- The need to respect other participants must be clearly understood by all.

Ten Reasons Not to Hold a Retreat

Holding a retreat isn't the best means of responding to every situation and addressing every concern you might have. Don't convene a retreat if:

1. *All You Want to Do Is Improve Morale*

While taking positive action based on the recommendations made at a retreat can increase participants' commitment to the organization, don't expect that simply holding a retreat will improve morale. In fact, just the opposite can happen. A retreat can have a negative impact if the issues that come up aren't dealt with appropriately, if people feel that their concerns are not taken seriously, if conflict is not managed successfully, if trust is violated, or if participants feel that it was a waste of their time.

2. *You Want to Use the Retreat to Reward People for Their Hard Work*

Participants rarely see retreats as rewards. They're likely to have even more work waiting for them when they return; juggling family needs can be difficult; and many would find time off with family and friends more rewarding than attending an offsite.

3. *You Want to Discover and Punish Non-Team Players*

This is a terrible reason to have a retreat. If people sense that your purpose in bringing them together is to find out who is loyal and who is not, you will erode trust and do great—if not irreparable—harm to your organization's culture.

4. *You Have a Covert Agenda That You Want to Advance*

If you try to pursue an agenda that is different from the retreat's stated purpose, you will undermine trust in you personally and in your organization. It is far better to tell participants that you have decided, for example, to cut a department's head count and ask for their help in determining the best way to handle layoffs than to try to manipulate them during the retreat into thinking that it was their idea all along. When people figure out what you're up to (and they will!), you will have fostered resentment and engendered much more resistance to your ideas than if you had been truthful all along.

5. You Want to Control the Conversation

It's counterproductive to try to control what is said or who is authorized to say what. Just because something isn't said out loud doesn't mean that people don't believe it to be true. Trying to direct what participants talk about deprives you of strategic information you need to make informed decisions. Putting everything out on the table and having a candid dialogue about participants' perceptions and misperceptions is better than trying to stop them from saying what's on their minds.

6. You Want to Avoid Conflict

Concern about the difficulty of managing conflict is a principal and legitimate reason that many retreat convenors decide to hire outside facilitators. Chapters 7 and 9 include strategies for dealing effectively with any conflict that might emerge.

Some people relish conflict, but most dread it. Typically, the more people care about each other, the more averse they are to getting into conflict situations. But aiming to avoid conflict at all costs will practically guarantee that it will crop up and that it won't be managed effectively.

Successful retreats almost always involve surfacing and dealing with some disagreement, dispute, or difference of opinion. If no conflict emerges, chances are participants aren't being honest with themselves or with others or that the retreat has focused on issues that aren't of great concern to them. Conflict is inevitable (and actually healthy) when people care about something. We urge you not to ignore it or dismiss it. Instead, take advantage of your facilitator's expertise to find ways to manage conflict so that it can be explored openly.

7. You Merely Want a Platform for Your Own Ideas

Retreats provide a valuable opportunity for you to hear from others. Don't squander it by doing too much of the talking. As the convenor, it is best for you mostly to listen to what others have to say and repress your inclination to lead discussions and resolve disputes.

8. *You Do Not Intend to Act On What Participants Recommend*

There is nothing more demoralizing to participants than being led to believe that they have a role in the decision-making process, only to learn that the decision was pre-determined. Participants naturally will expect that you will take their advice into consideration before reaching a decision, and that if you don't accept their recommendations you will explain why. If you ask participants to rubber-stamp decisions that you have already made, or if after the retreat you announce and attribute to them decisions they didn't make or ideas they didn't generate, the effect is likely to be very destructive.

9. *You Want to Defend Your Point of View, Promote Your Position, or Maintain the Status Quo*

Retreats are associated with change in most people's minds. If you want things to stay the same, have a meeting to encourage everyone to keep up the good work. Reserve retreats for when you'd like things to be different. And remember, the first person who is likely to have to change is you. Your willingness to explore more productive leadership practices will signal to participants how open they should be to trying new things.

10. *You Merely Want to Keep Up the Tradition of Having Annual Retreats*

Many people think that having a retreat with no other purpose than to bring everyone together on some regular basis is a good practice at best and at worst is harmless. It is neither. A retreat is not a company picnic. Don't plan a retreat if you don't have a serious purpose in mind. Such an event will communicate to participants that you don't value their time.

And don't confuse a retreat with a conference. Presentations by in-house or outside experts can provide valuable information or training, but they don't

- Improve morale

- Reward people for their hard work

- Punish non-team players

- Advance a covert agenda

- Control the conversation

- Avoid conflict

- Disregard what participants recommend

- Defend your point of view, promote your position, or maintain the *status quo*

- Keep up the tradition of having annual retreats

constitute a retreat. It's certainly important that people be well-informed, but a retreat—at least in the way we are using the term in this book—is about sparking change, not just absorbing or exchanging information.

On the other hand, you might be able to take advantage of a tradition of holding regular retreats to accomplish some important things. However retreats may have been conducted in the past, structure the next one to address key issues that are of genuine concern to you and to the participants. Involve people in identifying those issues and in planning the event.

Kinds of Retreats

There are many kinds of retreats, each with its own characteristics and special planning concerns. Some of the most common are described below.

Executive

In an executive retreat, top management gets together without other employees, usually to chart strategic direction, measure progress against goals, foster teamwork within their group, establish new priorities, or make key decisions. The CEO frequently takes the lead in setting the retreat agenda.

Board

Board retreats typically are used to align the actions of the staff with the priorities set by the board or to help the board understand strategic and operational issues faced by the staff. Because of this board-staff interrelationship, such retreats usually include some of the organization's senior staff as well as the board members themselves.

Single Department

Retreats for a single department are often scheduled when a new department head arrives, when the organization's leaders have mandated performance improvements, or when the department needs to measure progress against goals and establish a strategy and priorities for the coming year. Such retreats can be very helpful in focusing everyone on the new goals and involving them in determining the best ways to meet them.

Interdepartmental

Occasionally people from two or more departments in the same organization jointly convene a retreat to devise better ways of working together. Because there's no hierarchical relationship between the departments, one challenge for participants in such retreats is to maintain the course decided on when everyone goes back to the pressures of the everyday work environment.

Teamwork

Managers frequently want to convene retreats to improve teamwork. The casual nature of retreats encourages people to get to know and understand each other better. We believe that the best way to build teamwork at the retreat is not through team-building exercises *per se,* but to have participants work on solving real workplace dilemmas and enhancing skills that transfer back to the office.

Associations and Member Organizations

Because people in key positions in nonprofit associations and membership organizations are often volunteers who don't work together every day, retreats can be a highly effective way of gathering the paid and unpaid leadership in one place to address broad issues.

Customer or Vendor

Organizations sometimes wish to bring together important shareholders, customers, vendors, or clients. Such retreats can help start a new partnership on the right foot or strengthen an existing relationship.

Whole System

At times organizations want to bring their entire workforce or even all their stakeholders, including customers, vendors, regulators, or community activists, together at an offsite. The goal of such a retreat is usually to reach a common understanding of key issues and foster better working relationships.

Creativity

Organizations are increasingly using retreats to spark creative thinking about their products, services, and processes. Specialists in creativity often lead these retreats, sometimes at facilities designed for that purpose. A creativity segment may also be a component of another kind of retreat, for example, a strategic planning exercise in which participants can immediately apply newly learned techniques and sharpened creative skills to solving real problems.

Fixed Format

See Chapter 2, "Using a Specialized Retreat Format," p. 30, for more information on these specialized retreats.

Certain retreats follow a fixed framework that serves specific purposes. These formats include large systems interventions such as Future Search® and Open Space®; real-time simulations; and General Electric's Work-Out™ program, which has been used by many organizations to focus their managers on performance and change issues.

Who's Who in Planning a Retreat

To call a meeting, you send out a memo or e-mail, reserve a conference room, distribute an agenda, and perhaps make arrangements for refreshments. A good meeting takes planning, but the process of organizing one is fairly routine.

A retreat isn't so easy; it often takes weeks or even months to plan and organize. And there are very specific roles different individuals must play. Even people who don't attend have a part in determining whether the retreat will be successful. An individual may assume more than one role, but it is critical to ensure that each role is filled and carried out properly.

Convenor

This is the person who decides whether to hold a retreat. He or she might be the board chair, the CEO, a department head, or a team leader. Almost always, the convenor is someone who is senior (or at least equal) in title to most of the people who will participate. In fact, this relative position matters. People are more likely to see a retreat as important if the convenor is a senior executive.

Sometimes the convenor is a group of people—the board of directors, the membership committee, the new markets task force—who jointly agree they need to hold an offsite. It would be unwieldy, however, for the whole group to plan and design the retreat. We recommend a team of no more than three or four be formed to carry out these functions.

The convenor is not just the initiator of the retreat, but must also oversee the action plan that comes out of it. No matter what the participants agree to, the convenor will want to ensure that the plan is implemented, or the whole retreat effort and expense will have been wasted. This process, which we discuss in Chapter 15, can last for several months after the retreat.

Facilitator

The facilitator designs and leads the retreat. He or she might be an external consultant, an internal consultant from the company's human resources or organization development department, or a staff member from another department. In rare cases, the convenor might take on this role.

The facilitator plans the flow of the event. Her design focuses on "What will we do?" and "How will we do it?" She considers which exercises will most likely move the group to the desired outcome and allocates time for each. She creates a plan for the retreat from beginning to end, as well as for what has to be done in advance, such as surveys, interviews, or pre-retreat reading and other assignments.

For more information on choosing a facilitator, see Chapter 2, "Who Should Facilitate?" pp. 22.

Sometimes convenors want the design and facilitation functions performed by different people. For instance, you might hire an external consultant to design a retreat and have an internal facilitator lead it. Or you might create the agenda, alone or in concert with some of the retreat participants, and hire an external consultant to lead the retreat. Neither of these scenarios is ideal, in our experience. Carrying out someone else's design isn't like an actor reading the playwright's words. The facilitator must understand the designer's vision and intentions, and this is an extraordinarily difficult thing to do.

Administrator

The administrator is responsible for the retreat logistics, finding a place to hold the offsite, determining a date that's convenient for most intended participants, arranging for rooms and travel, planning meals and breaks, ordering audiovisual equipment, and so on. The administrator works with the convenor to establish a retreat budget, negotiate prices with the retreat site, and advise the facilitator of any unique opportunities or challenges the site might offer.

The administrator and facilitator must work together closely, because logistical details contribute greatly to the success or failure of a retreat. The facilitator may have some special needs, such as extra breakout rooms, non-intrusive morning and afternoon breaks, an overhead projector, or so many flip charts. For overnight retreats, the administrator may have to assign sleeping rooms, coordinate evening social and recreational activities, and maintain a list of emergency contact numbers.

The administrator should be present during the retreat if at all possible to handle any last-minute glitches. This will allow the convenor to be a full-time participant and will keep the facilitator free of extraneous distractions. There is only a limited amount of time to accomplish the work of the retreat, and the administrator can keep seemingly minor but actually very important details like a sudden need for more markers or a misunderstanding about how many seats are needed in the breakout rooms from holding up progress.

In small organizations, the convenor or an internal facilitator might handle the administrator role, but avoid this arrangement if you can. It is very frustrating to participants to interrupt their discussions because someone has to deal with a mix-up over when lunch is supposed to be served.

Reporter

For a retreat to be successful, there must be a record of what is discussed, what is decided, and what action steps are agreed on. This is important for participants as well as for those who were not present at the retreat but who will be affected by the outcome.

There are several ways to capture what went on at a retreat. One is to save all relevant flip charts. Most commonly, someone transcribes the charts after the retreat and distributes copies to the participants and others who might be involved in implementing the action plan. Some organizations even take the key charts back to the office and display them in prominent locations.

There is more information on how to collect and report the results of the retreat in Chapter 5, "Capturing the Work Product," pp. 70–72.

In addition, some convenors like to have someone take notes of the proceedings to distribute after the retreat. Sometimes a non-participating employee is assigned to take and distribute the notes, but having a non-participant write everything down can be inhibiting to the spirit of the retreat. For that reason, we suggest that one or more of the participants keep the notes of the key discussions, decisions, and action plan elements.

Ideally, reporters should be volunteers. If people must be designated to fill this responsibility, it's important to remember that note taking is not a secretarial function and should not routinely be assigned to administrative assistants who might be among the participants.

Participants

In the next chapter we'll discuss different ways of deciding who should take part in the retreat. Whoever the participants are, however, they have to understand that, despite the casual atmosphere, a retreat is real work and each person is expected to make an active contribution to that work. No one should be present as a mere observer, critic, or judge.

The Uninvited

When you convene a retreat, you also assume responsibility for the people who won't be there. Make no mistake: Unless the retreat consists of an intact work group, someone is going to feel left out. It's going to be vividly noticeable to those who weren't invited that some people are out of the office and, as one person told us, "The rest of us are stuck here covering their work." You can't prevent those feelings, but you can minimize them by communicating to participants and non-participants the goals of the retreat and why you invited the people you did. If appropriate, you might seek non-participants' input on

What can a retreat achieve?

A well-conceived, well-designed, well-run retreat can

- Help change your organization's strategic direction

- Generate new solutions for old problems

- Get everyone pulling in the same direction

- Help people feel heard about issues that matter to them

- Deal with sources of overt or buried conflict

- Allow colleagues to get to know and come to trust one another

- Foster new ways of working together

- Help people see things in new ways and envision new possibilities for themselves and the organization

- Create a common frame of reference on past events and future expectations

- Contribute to creating a new and healthier culture for the organization

- Encourage people to take risks that are necessary for the organization to thrive

the issues before the retreat, so their concerns are represented even if they are absent.

It's only human nature for the people who aren't present to speculate about what's being discussed. Naturally, they are going to have questions, so you should devise a plan, either in advance or at the retreat itself, to communicate as much as possible as soon as possible after the retreat. Think about how to involve those who didn't attend in carrying out the decisions that were made.

Table 1.1   Differences Between Retreats and Meetings

	Meetings	Retreats
Setting	Usually onsite	Conducted offsite
Attendance	Often includes people who do not work together closely	Generally people from the same department or work group, or management level
Dress	Business or business casual	Casual
Length	Less than a day; often only an hour or so	Day-long or longer; often include down-time for participants
Discussion Size	Whole group discussion	Mix of whole and small group discussions
Purpose	Convey/exchange information or make a specific decision	Explore issues or ideas and plan for the future
Structure	Hierarchical by nature; led by one person	Participative by nature; participants talk with one another
Outcomes	Generally predictable	Generally unpredictable
Risk	Low	Potentially high
Capacity to drive change	Generally low	Potentially high
Emotional involvement	Emotions not usually in open play	Can be emotionally intense

Although the people you don't invite won't be physically present, you should still consider their interests and concerns. For example, are you coming up with more work for them, but not for the retreat participants? An old Southern saying goes, "Don't let your mouth write a check that my body's gotta cash." That may be how the people back at the office will feel if you return from the retreat with an action plan . . . for *them*.

We've discussed the challenges associated with convening a retreat; looked at reasons for holding (and for not holding) one; explored different kinds of retreats; defined the roles and responsibilities of the convenor, facilitator, administrator, reporter, and participants; and outlined what a retreat might achieve. In the next chapter, we'll help you determine where you want the retreat to take you, how it will get you there, and whom you want to take along on the journey.

Chapter 2

Setting the Goals, Deciding the Format, and Inviting the Participants

Retreats, by definition, are distinct from people's everyday work lives. That's good, because it means participants will not be distracted by ringing phones and pinging e-mail notices. They are going to devote hours—perhaps even days—of focused, uninterrupted attention to exploring problems and opportunities.

The informality of retreats is designed to loosen people up so they can talk openly and do some real work. But the separation from everyday work life can also be a problem. It's easy to come up with strategies and action plans while cocooned from the outside world. It's much harder to go back to the office and actually carry them out.

That's why every retreat should be conceived backwards—starting with a vision of what you want to be different *in the workplace*.

Last Things First—What Do You Want to Be Different?

Your first step—long before selecting a date—is to ask, "What do we want to be different after this retreat?" The point is not to specify the ideas you want the retreat to generate—the "how"—but to identify clearly the organizational goals for holding the retreat—the "why."

To the question, "What do we want to be different?," the senior leadership team of a rapidly growing high-tech firm might answer, "We want to revolutionize our customer service while still maintaining high profitability." The retreat might then center on finding high-impact, low-expense ways to improve the customer service function. An association board might say, "We want a more diverse membership base"; their retreat might focus on membership outreach strategies to achieve that goal. A government agency might declare, "We want to serve the taxpayers who require our services more quickly and accurately (and incidentally convince elected officials to increase our funding)"; their retreat might focus on process improvement.

Before convening a retreat, you should be very clear about your answer to the "What do we want to be different?" question. Then make sure that a retreat is the best means to accomplish your goals.

Your answer should be pretty simple. Retreats typically last only a few days at most, so you're not likely to be able to redesign the whole organization.

Just as a traveler must be prepared for road detours or flight delays, you should expect surprises along the way. The promotion department of a television production company, for example, held a retreat to address the "What do we want to be different?" question this way: "We feel unappreciated by the rest of the company. We want them to listen to us and respect our opinions."

By the end of the retreat, however, the participants realized that they weren't giving the rest of the company the very things they desired for themselves—listening and respect. The action plan they devised focused on listening more closely to their internal clients and taking responsibility for improving those relationships—a strategy the participants couldn't have imagined in advance.

Who Should Facilitate?

Regardless of their skill or experience in running meetings, we don't recommend that convenors lead their own retreats. Here's why:

- It's critical that the facilitator be neutral—and be perceived as neutral—with no personal stake in the outcome. You, by definition, have a big stake in the outcome.
- The facilitator must focus on how participants are working together to achieve their goals. You, on the other hand, must be a fully engaged participant in achieving those goals. Playing both of these roles simultaneously is difficult at best.

So if not you, who? We recommend that you use an experienced facilitator, either someone from within your organization or an outside consultant, and that you work closely with the facilitator from as early in the process as possible. To ensure that the person you want is available, it's best to select the facilitator before you set the date for the retreat. The facilitator can make or break your event, so don't underestimate the importance of finding the right person.

Not everyone has the temperament to lead a retreat. Good facilitators are able to:

- Listen accurately to what others are saying without injecting their own biases
- Be neutral (and be perceived to be neutral) about the outcome of the discussions
- Suspend judgment of retreat participants
- Understand multiple perspectives, help bring them to the surface, and resist colluding with the group in avoiding thorny issues

Understanding What You're Paying For

If you're working with an outside facilitator, make certain you understand exactly how that person charges. Some consultants charge fixed inclusive fees, and others price each service separately. You should know which of the following are included in the price: preparation, design and facilitation fees (usually quoted per day, but sometimes per hour); interviewing charges; reimbursement for out-of-pocket expenses such as travel and long-distance calling; costs of materials used in the retreat; fee for writing the retreat report; and rates for post-retreat follow-up.

- Encourage participants whose viewpoints may not be popular to speak out and encourage others to listen
- Help retreat participants recognize and deal with any behavior that might be hampering the group's work
- Deal skillfully with the members of the group who might not want to accept their guidance
- Empathize with others
- Analyze and summarize key issues
- Remain comfortable with ambiguous situations and those circumstances they do not control
- Recognize and manage differences that may stem from the diversity (cultural, racial, gender, age, sexual orientation, and so forth) of the participants
- Hear feedback from the participants without becoming defensive
- Adjust their approach, acknowledge missteps, and ask for help when they need it

Once you've decided who will lead your retreat, you and that person must agree on what your respective roles will be. Ideally, once the retreat begins you will "forget" you're the convenor and will behave as any retreat participant—albeit an especially key one. This means letting the facilitator run the show. You will undermine the facilitator's credibility and effectiveness if you compete with him or her for control of the agenda.

Most facilitators conduct interviews prior to the retreat to assess organizational issues. We urge you to take advantage of this opportunity to learn more

We worked with a large department of an international bank whose director, Judy, said she wanted feedback on what wasn't working well in the department. Judy repeatedly said that she welcomed comments, even critical ones, and assured participants that there would be no repercussions for speaking out. At a break, a participant asked us to raise a particular issue that he felt strongly Judy should hear. We declined, explaining to the participant that if we, rather than a member of the group, brought up the issue we would be colluding in the myth that it was not safe to speak out. (The participant did raise his concern and Judy thanked him publicly for doing so.)

about the impact of your leadership style by asking the facilitator to give you feedback—anonymously, of course—from those interviews he or she conducts.

Prior to choosing the facilitator, make sure that you have confidence in his or her judgment, skills, and personal integrity. Then be prepared to allow him or her to work without undue interference from you.

For more discussion on the importance of conducting participant interviews before the retreat is designed, see Chapter 5, "Pre-Retreat Interviews with Participants," pp. 66–69.

Whom Should You Invite?

Sometimes there's no question about who will participate in the retreat. For example, a retreat might involve a relatively small and clearly defined work group—a team, a department, or a board. Often, however, you and other key people will have to determine who will be invited and who will not.

Size matters in retreats. By their nature, retreats should be limited to reasonably small groups if you want to accomplish serious work. If your goal is to make tough decisions, such as how to handle redundant functions after a merger, you'll have to discuss highly sensitive information. Make the group too large and there are bound to be people who don't normally have (and don't need to have) access to that information.

On the other hand, inclusiveness is often important. The group can be larger if your retreat focuses on overarching cultural or teamwork issues. In addition, for some issues it can be invaluable to have the broader perspective that a larger group provides.

We've seen successful retreats with as few as three participants and as many as one hundred, but be aware that if your group grows larger than about forty people, it will take longer to discuss every topic and you won't be able to make many strategic decisions. While some excellent work can take place in breakout groups, large numbers make it very difficult for everyone to hear all the comments and reach consensus.

See "Using a Specialized Retreat Format" later in this chapter for a more detailed discussion of retreats expressly designed for large groups.

Although as the convenor you may have a clear idea of who should attend the retreat, the criteria for deciding who is included or left out should be made clear to the people who were invited to attend as well as those who were not. Here's an example of why.

The vice president of "Greenleaf Insurance Company," Mavis, convened a retreat designed to improve communications and collaboration among senior managers. Mavis decided that the retreat should be expanded to include the supervisors from one of the larger departments. Then she invited a few—but only a few—members of the support staff who had requested professional development opportunities. Neither the retreat participants nor those who had been excluded understood the basis of her decision. Many people at the retreat felt uncomfortable about making recommendations for change without consulting those who weren't in the room, and many who were excluded were resentful and resistant to implementing the ideas that came out of the retreat.

There are several methods you can use to decide who will attend a specific retreat. The most common are described below.

Retreat participants can be

- An intact work group

- Everyone with the same job title (such as all department heads)

- A representative cross section of the organization

- Anyone who has the capacity to help the organization make desired changes

- Anyone who wants to come

- People who compete to attend

- People who want to shake up the *status quo*

Intact Work Group

This is the simplest way to choose retreat participants. A board, task force, department, or small organization is having a retreat, and everyone is invited. Of course, it doesn't always work out that easily. If the department is large, you may still have to choose who will attend based on some other criteria.

Intact Work Group with Invited Outsiders

In some cases, an intact work group may want to involve selected outsiders (associates from elsewhere in the larger organization, for example) in its retreat. Take care not to expand the group too much, however, as too many outsiders can interfere with group cohesion.

Titles and Positions

If the retreat will include people from many departments, a traditional way to select participants is simply by job title: all the vice presidents or department heads, for instance, or all the board committee chairs. This is a safe way to choose; no one can criticize you for playing favorites or leaving someone out. But it is not uncommon for peers to share many experiences, attitudes, and ways of seeing things, so you may not have the breadth of perspectives that would be most useful for the group's discussions.

Cross Section Representatives

When an issue cuts broadly across the organization, a retreat might be composed of a cross section of people from different disciplines and various levels on the organization chart. But how do you decide whom specifically to include? You might make the decision alone or with the advice of colleagues. Department heads may decide who will represent their departments, or employees themselves may choose their own representatives. Whatever method you employ, take care that the staff doesn't perceive management bias in the selections.

The Right Stuff

This is a less common way to choose retreat participants, yet it can achieve powerful results. Here the convenor—usually the CEO or a very senior leader—asks, "Who are the people who can best help us get where we want to go?" She then invites the people most likely to have the expertise and experience necessary to address the issue most effectively.

One danger of selecting participants in this way is that there will always be people who weren't invited who feel that they should have been. Those who were not invited—and their supporters in the organization—may feel resentful and resist the decisions that come out of the retreat.

There is another danger as well: Executives may believe that the people who have the "right stuff" are those who think as they do. They may thus inadvertently exclude divergent thinkers who could help move the organization forward.

Open Offer

Sometimes everyone who wants to attend the retreat is welcomed. The assumption behind an open offer is that anyone who is willing to put the time and effort into the retreat is interested in the issues and committed to getting things done. One potential downside, however, is that the group could become too large, although you can prevent this by limiting the number of slots. Another possible pitfall is that the volunteers are likely to be employees with strong biases regarding the issues to be discussed, which could skew the results. Yet another concern is that some of the people you would most want to attend might choose not to take part.

Competition

This is a variant on the open offer. People who want to come to the retreat compete for one of, say, twenty slots. All who are interested write their cases to the convenor, laying out why they should be included. They describe what they can contribute to the success of the event and what they would do to involve others who did not attend in the decisions that might be made.

This method creates highly motivated participants who feel it is a privilege to participate and who will work hard to make the retreat successful. The challenge is to make the offsite compelling enough that people will *want* to compete for a slot.

Revolutionaries Inside the Palace Walls

In his book *Leading the Revolution,* Gary Hamel wrote, "If senior management wants revolutionary strategies, it must learn to listen to revolutionary voices"(2000). It takes courage to invite non-traditional participants to a retreat. They tend to rock the boat (which is why you invite them, of course), and their selection can generate resentment among loyal pillars of the establishment in your organization.

Revolutionary thinkers can be a challenge to work with during the retreat. If they're not part of the usual group, they may not know the unspoken rules and rituals that guide communications. They ask questions that everyone else knows the answers to (or at least everyone thinks they do). They come up with "weird" ideas. But by raising issues in new and challenging ways, they can stimulate creative thinking among all the participants.

Part–Time Participants

Occasionally we're asked whether some people can be invited for just part of the day or a portion of the retreat, to make the offsite more inclusive. This may

"Elektrixx," an interactive communications company, invited several young web designers to help them formulate a new strategy for the firm. Eyes rolled when one young woman, Kris, suggested, "Why don't we just give away our work? Let's do it for free!" The initial reaction to Kris' suggestion was dismissal: "She can't be serious." Then someone said, "Wait a minute; let's look at this. It might not be so crazy after all." In the ensuing discussion, participants came up with several advantages of giving away some of their product. They saw how this might help the company attract potential customers, build goodwill, and sell other highly profitable services. The result was a bold new approach to marketing the company.

sound like a good idea, but in our experience it usually does not work very well. The presence of part-time participants often diffuses the focus of the larger group and alters the dynamics of the interactions. Moreover, when some people arrive after the retreat has begun or leave before it ends, there is a sharp delineation between the "ins" and the "outs," even though the intention may be just the opposite.

Using a Specialized Retreat Format

A specialized retreat format is a pre-packaged methodology designed to address issues that are common to most organizations. Typically, such a specialized format can be used either by itself or in conjunction with custom-designed segments.

We believe that the best retreats are tailor-made to fit an organization's specific needs, and in Chapters 5 and 6 we'll walk you step-by-step through the process of custom designing a retreat that will get results.

We have, however, successfully integrated specialized retreat formats into longer retreats when we felt that this would be the best means of addressing the organization's concerns.

Specialized Retreat Formats

- *Large System Interventions*—One hundred or more participants representing a broad range of stakeholders work through a pre-designed methodology

- *Open Space Technology*—Participants design their own agenda at the retreat itself

- *Simulations*—Participants engage in highly realistic exercises that provide a springboard for assessing organizational issues

- *Appreciative Inquiry*—Participants build on past successes to create plans for the future

- *Outdoor Experiences*—Participants engage in exercises that require them to work as a team

- *Work-Out*™—A structured process that guides participants to suggest performance improvements

Certain specialized retreat formats require that the facilitators be trained and certified in those methodologies. Thus, if you are interested in using one of those, you will have to find a facilitator who is qualified to lead it.

What follows is not a comprehensive list of the available formats, but it will give you an idea of what is available for you to consider.

Large System Interventions

Large system interventions are sessions in which many people—often more than one hundred—representing many different segments of an organizational system gather to explore and plan for change.

One of the best-known large system interventions is the three-day Future Search® conference developed by Marvin Weisbord and Sandra Janoff. While the originators describe Future Search as a conference or meeting, its highly experiential approach makes it very similar to a retreat. "A future search is a large group planning meeting that brings a 'whole system' into the room to work on a task-focused agenda," say Weisbord and Janoff in their book, *Future Search*.

What is unusual about a Future Search conference is that stakeholders from all segments affected by the organization participate. For a nonprofit health clinic, for instance, participants might include not only the organization's leadership, but also the board, employees, clients (including former clients and potential clients), referral sources, government health officials, volunteers, individual donors, charitable foundations, complementary services such as food banks and housing agencies, media, vendors, clinic neighbors, churches, and other organizations that serve the same constituency. Having all these voices in one room for a concentrated focus can have a major impact on the organizations involved, helping them find common ground and new ways to support one another's work.

Although Weisbord and Janoff have published a book describing their methodology, *Future Search: An Action Guide to Finding Common Ground in Organizations and Communities,* we recommend that you use a facilitator who was trained by one of the founders if you decide to convene a Future Search conference.

Open Space Technology

Open Space is a method developed by organization consultant Harrison Owen. In Open Space, the convenor and facilitator help set up the conditions for the participants to design and conduct their own retreat sessions as part of the retreat itself. Open Space is particularly appropriate for retreats where, as Owen (1997b) says in his book, *Open Space Technology,* "A diverse group of people must deal with complex and potentially conflicting material in innovative and productive ways. It is particularly powerful when nobody knows the answer and the ongoing participation of a number of people is required to deal with the questions."

At the beginning of an Open Space session, the participants themselves determine the topics they would like to address and who will convene various subgroups to discuss each topic. Then they decide which subgroups they will take part in to discuss the issues that are most important to them. This sounds (and sometimes seems) chaotic, but it takes place in a well-structured environment. There is a formal process for involving the entire group in the work that has taken place in the individual sessions, so all participants have the opportunity to discuss any topic.

Open Space is not suitable for every situation. It will definitely not work in an organization where top management desires to maintain high control. It yields a different kind of result than tightly structured retreats, one that often can't be foreseen in advance, but that very accurately reflects the group's concerns.

> Owen does not certify facilitators. He offers his methodology for anyone who cares to learn it by reading *Open Space Technology: A User's Guide, Tales from Open Space,* and *Expanding Our Now: The Story of Open Space Technology.* Nevertheless, Open Space requires a specific set of conditions for success. If you decide to hold an Open Space retreat, you would be wise to use a facilitator skilled in the technique.

Simulations

A simulation is a structured activity in which participants must confront problems and solve them. Simulations are usually built around a realistic narrative that challenges participants to respond to changing circumstances or new information. The best are interactive and engaging and can be adapted to address a multiplicity of issues that most organizations encounter.

Simulations are most commonly employed as training tools, but some can be used to great effect to help participants recognize patterns that characterize their workplace interactions. In addition, they can help participants gain specific insights or skills they need to accomplish their goals for the retreat. Be aware, however, that most simulations take several hours to run and debrief, so you'll only want to use them for retreats that last longer than a day.

A number of companies produce off-the-shelf simulations that can provide a framework around which to build an offsite retreat. One of our favorites is The Organization Workshop: Creating Partnership®, developed by Barry Oshry of Power & Systems.* The Organization Workshop takes a minimum of half a day to facilitate and debrief, but can provide an extremely useful framework for addressing communications, cooperation, and teamwork issues in an experiential way. We particularly recommend this simulation in retreats for organizations that are struggling with turf battles or lack of cooperation and coordination between departments.

Barry Oshry's perspectives on organizations are outlined in *Seeing Systems: Unlocking the Mysteries of Organizational Life* and *Leading Systems: Lessons from the Power Lab*, books that come out of his experience leading a very intense six-day residential program called the Power Lab. Only a facilitator who has been trained and certified by Power & Systems may lead an Organization Workshop.

This highly engaging simulation centers on an organization exercise in which participants are randomly selected to be top executives, middle managers, workers, or customers and who must interact in a rapidly changing, high-pressure environment. The simulation is interrupted at key points to provide practical strategic frameworks that help participants understand what they're experiencing and apply these learnings to what goes on in their own organizations.

The Center for Creative Leadership and Discovery Learning have co-created an excellent and highly flexible simulation called EdgeWork® that can be run in four to six hours. Participants start the simulation "day" with an in-basket of internal memos, newspaper articles, and reports, but are quickly drawn into a breaking crisis. EdgeWork can help an organization examine its habitual ways of managing both its everyday work and the critical problems that it must address.

One interesting dimension of the EdgeWork scenario is that it not only explores internal issues but also the relationship between two companies, one a manufacturer of a high-tech product and the other a service company that uses the manufactured product. For an organization engaged in strategic alliances, EdgeWork can draw attention to how these critical relationships work.

Another often-used simulation on teamwork and re-thinking processes is Paper Planes, Inc.® Participants work together to manufacture paper planes; as

*For more information on The Organization Workshop, go to www.retreatsthatwork.com or www.powerandsystems.com.

Find out more about EdgeWork and Paper Planes, Inc., at www.discov-erylearning.com.

the simulation runs, people observe the impact of how they chose to organize their work and cooperate with each other.

Both the publishing house Jossey-Bass/Pfeiffer and consulting firm Human Synergistics offer one- to two-hour "survival" simulations in which groups must make individual and joint choices about items they will need to survive in dramatic situations such as being stranded in the Himalayas, escaping an Australian bush fire, or being marooned by a plane crash in the Arctic. These simulations empha-size the synergy obtained though joint effort. In addition, skilled facilitators can use these simulations to help groups explore organizational issues such as communica-tion, leadership, power and authority, decision making, and conflict management.

Appreciative Inquiry

Appreciative Inquiry is a methodology that, in the words of its primary origi-nator, David L. Cooperrider (1995), uses "the best of the past and present" to "ignite the collective imagination of what might be."

Essentially, Appreciative Inquiry flips traditional problem solving on its head. Rather than identifying problems, finding their causes, deciding on pos-sible solutions, and taking action, groups following the Appreciative Inquiry approach look at what they do well, envision possible scenarios for the future, discuss what they'd like to see happen, and come up with innovative solutions that are grounded in current successes. Appre-ciative Inquiry has been combined very successfully with Future Search conferences when applied to large systems.

If you are interested in learning more about Appreciative Inquiry, there are several books and arti-cles to chose from. We recom-mend *Introduction to Appreciative Inquiry* by David L. Cooperrider and *Lessons from the Field: Applying Appreciative Inquiry,* edited by Sue Annis Hammond and Cathy Royal.

When skillfully facilitated, Appreciative Inquiry works particu-larly well in organizations that have undergone difficult transitions. We used it to stunning effect in a retreat for an organization that had gone through a poorly managed downsizing. For the first time, employees who were frightened, cynical, and burned out were able to talk about what they did best and what they aspired to for the future. This was the beginning of a process that allowed a healthier organization to emerge, something that had eluded the executives in the post-downsizing problem-solving sessions they had convened.

There is no formal training required to lead an Appreciative Inquiry retreat, but you will have best success with a facilitator who is skilled in this methodology.

Outdoor Experiences

Many companies offer outdoor experience programs that combine a physical experience, such as white-water rafting, ropes courses, rock climbing, horseback riding, obstacle courses, hiking, and so on, with facilitation in teamwork, risk taking, and leadership.

For many groups and individuals, an outdoor adventure can be a memorable and exhilarating event. On the other hand, a company-mandated experience to deal with one's physical fears can be an extremely stressful—and unproductive—situation for some people. You should not make the assumption that everyone would benefit from participating in such a retreat. For that reason, we prefer outdoor experiences that are fairly accessible to all—a walk in the woods, for instance—rather than climbing up the sheer face of a rocky cliff. Any outdoor program should be selected carefully, keeping in mind the mental and physical abilities of all who will be there and making sure that the facilitators are licensed, bonded, and well insured.

Work-Out™

Work-Out sessions, which were developed by former General Electric CEO Jack Welch in the 1980s, provide a mechanism to involve management and employees in open dialogue about an organization's strategies. The aim of a Work-Out is to improve processes by eliminating bureaucracy and non-value-added work.

Typically, a Work-Out is a structured two- or three-day process for multi-level, cross-functional teams of twenty to fifty people. The teams participate in a progressive series of large-group and breakout discussions.

One premise of Work-Out is that the teams will get quick approval from decision makers about the recommendations they offer. At the end, the teams meet with top managers to report their conclusions. As described in *The GE Way Fieldbook* (Slater, 2000), "Work-Out reaches its peak of drama and tension in that final-day encounter between boss and employees. For two days the boss has

> Work-Out is a rigorous methodology for changing an organization's work processes. It is not typically used for a single retreat, but may form the framework for a series of sessions. General Electric uses academics and others trained in its system. If you are interesting in using it, we recommend that you work with a consultant who is experienced in the process.

been isolated from the employees who have been dissecting the business. This time the employees are the ones who have something to say to the boss."

The Pitfalls of Fixed-Format Retreats

As useful as fixed-format methodologies can be under the right conditions, we can't urge you strongly enough *not* to use one unless you are confident that it's the best way to address your organization's particular concerns. Here's an example of how a fixed-format retreat can go wrong.

A consultant we know, Steve, signed a contract to lead a fixed-format retreat for a company that had just undergone a radical downsizing. The convenor told Steve that the retreat would be a morale builder for the staff, and Steve took the convenor at his word.

About two hours into the retreat, a participant stood up and confronted Steve, "What the hell does this have to do with our circumstances? I've got twice as much work as I used to have. I don't see how any of what we're doing here is going to make it easier for me to do my job tomorrow."

If the format had been flexible rather than fixed, Steve might have been able to stop the action at that point and acknowledge that person's concerns. He could then have facilitated a candid discussion about what had changed in the company since the downsizing and how the group might be able to work together to relieve some of the pressure they were experiencing in its wake.

Instead, Steve was trapped into the fixed agenda he had agreed to with the convenor. He didn't have much information about the company, or the option to respond in the moment to what had come up. "I'm sorry," he said. "I don't really know anything about your circumstances. This is the retreat I was hired to lead." Of course, he lost the respect of the group, and the retreat just deepened employee cynicism.

To avoid such a disaster at your retreat, we encourage you to give the facilitator you hire maximum flexibility to custom-design a retreat that is right for your organization.

Involving Participants in Retreat Planning

Any change initiative generates some anxiety within an organization, and a retreat is no exception. Your actions prior to the retreat will have a good deal of influence on the level of anxiety generated and thus on the success of the event.

As the convenor, you may decide by yourself whether or not to hold a retreat and where and when it will take place. You may also decide on your own the retreat's purpose, and whether or not to hire outside facilitators. This approach has the obvious advantage of efficiency.

On the other hand, you can consult with others in your organization about any or all of these questions. This approach has the advantage of involving others who might have good ideas and important concerns about the retreat. It may also help squelch rumors, reduce anxieties, and generate broader support for the retreat. It demands busy people's time, however, and—because decisions typically take longer when many people contribute to them—requires more advance planning.

Most convenors employ a combination of these approaches. For example, you might decide on your own to convene a retreat and then solicit input about where and when it should take place and what participants would most like to see accomplished.

Whichever approach you use, it is of critical importance that everyone be kept in the loop as decisions are made. This helps set the stage for a successful retreat. Communicate the purpose of the retreat in writing to everyone in the organization—not just to those who will take part—at the earliest possible moment. As a practical matter, announce the dates and place of the retreat well in advance so participants can arrange their personal and business commitments.

If the retreat will be designed and led by an outside facilitator, send a memo to participants and non-participants alike introducing the facilitator and describing the retreat planning process. This memo should make it clear that the facilitator will be working for the good of the entire organization, not just for you or the small group of retreat participants. It should outline the facilitator's role before, during, and possibly after the retreat. If the facilitator will be conducting interviews or surveys, the memo should emphasize his or her guarantee of anonymity and a promise from you (or the head of your organization as appropriate) that there will be no negative consequences for providing candid responses to the interview and survey questions or for speaking honestly at the retreat itself. See the sample announcement below.

Sample Retreat Announcement

I am pleased to announce that Mecha Rodriguez of the Theta Group will lead our upcoming retreat. The purpose of this retreat is to explore ways to make our operations more customer-friendly.

Mecha will help us perform a purposeful self-examination and make decisions about how best to meet the needs of our customers while improving the work processes for ourselves.

This initiative will build upon previous studies and efforts to improve our operational effectiveness. In the end, all employees—not just the department heads who will attend the retreat—will be asked to make recommendations for change. Therefore, I will be working with Mecha to design a process that includes everyone's perspectives.

Mecha's work with us will consist of three phases: (1) assessment, (2) a two-day retreat for department heads, and (3) support for staff, as needed, to implement the changes that we decide to make as a result of the retreat. [Note: Such a third phase may or may not be included in your initial agreement with the facilitator.]

During the assessment phase, Mecha will be interviewing everyone who will be attending the retreat and a cross section of other staff members. If you are called for an interview, please respond candidly to her questions.

Mecha will respect your confidence and will not disclose to anyone—not even to me—any comments that could be attributed to a specific individual. She will share her findings with us, but in summary only and without attribution.

The second phase of this initiative will be a two-day offsite retreat for department heads that will take place October 6 and 7 at the Berkeley Center, about an hour and a half from here. Retreat participants will receive the logistical details soon.

Candor and openness are key to the success of this initiative, and there will be no repercussions for anyone speaking his or her mind to the facilitator during the interviews or publicly at the retreat itself.

I expect that we will use this retreat to address the most pressing concerns facing our staff as we seek to redesign our customer relationships and operating procedures. I hope everyone will take part in this initiative with open minds and a commitment to making our company the best it can be.

We've explored first steps in this chapter: setting goals for the retreat by envisioning what you want to be different; determining who should facilitate your retreat—you, an internal consultant, or an external consultant; and deciding whom to invite. We've looked at several specialized retreat formats and discussed their advantages and disadvantages, and we emphasized the importance of involving participants and others in the initial planning.

Now let's turn our attention to the seemingly more mundane but very important questions of logistics, attending to the details that can make or break your offsite.

Chapter 3

Planning Retreat Logistics

You're attending a retreat in a hotel ballroom. It's divided into smaller rooms by sliding air walls, but you are distracted by the applause you're hearing from the group next door. No daylight filters in; there are no windows. People are shifting uncomfortably on narrow armless chairs, sitting around a formal U-shaped table covered with white tablecloths. At 10:30 and 2:00, a waiter trundles in the coffee break; lunch is set up buffet-style in a corner of the room at noon. Promptly at 5:00, the hotel's banquet staff appears at the door, ready to break down the room for the next event. While the participants gather up their belongings, the facilitator rushes to grab flip chart pages off the walls, and Post-it® Notes float to the floor unnoticed. Your one-day retreat is over.

Far more than those for a regular meeting, the logistical details for a retreat play a vital role in determining the event's success. In this chapter, we discuss the key logistics to consider when planning your retreat: length of the retreat, scheduling, site selection, sleeping rooms, meals, recreational options, and notifying the participants of the details.

How Long Should a Retreat Last?

The length of a retreat will be constrained by several factors. They include the nature and complexity of the issues to be addressed, when key employees are available, and the funds that can be dedicated to the offsite. By the same token, there is a practical upper limit to how long a retreat can continue to yield good results, after which the law of diminishing returns kicks in. Participating actively in a retreat requires effort, and people can give their full attention and energy for only so long before mental fatigue sets in and focus begins to blur.

But the key factor in determining length is the purpose, the answer to the question posed in Chapter 2: "What do you want to be different?" If you'll need three days to address the issues, don't schedule a one-day retreat because that's all the budget will allow or busy employees can't get away for longer than a day. You may actually be making things worse by raising expectations that cannot be met in the time allotted.

In our experience, the most effective retreats are usually two- or two-and-a-half-day events. Retreats of this length allow participants time to create the climate of trust necessary to make genuine progress. There's time to explore issues thoroughly and to build commitment to change. Yet it isn't so long that participants' energy flags and momentum dissipates.

Although there are many variations, the ideal "two-day" retreat begins in the evening of Day One. Participants arrive at a reasonable hour, enjoy an informal dinner, get to know each other if they're not already well-acquainted, and get a good night's sleep before convening early the next morning. They have a full first day,

What Is a "Two-Day" Retreat?

What is a "two-day" retreat? Does it begin, say, mid-morning on Tuesday, after employees have traveled to the remote site, and end Wednesday right after lunch so employees can get home without getting stuck in rush hour traffic? No, that's actually a one-day overnight retreat when you add up the number of hours participants will actually be engaged in serious work. A two-day retreat allows two full working days to focus on the issues of concern. A two-and-a-half-day retreat adds an extra afternoon on the first day or a morning on the last day. Some examples of formats are given in Figure 3.1.

Figure 3.1   Sample Retreat Formats

Two-Day Offsite, Two Nights

Monday	Tuesday	Wednesday
	Begin retreat	Resume retreat
	Day One—full day	Day Two—full day
		End retreat, depart late afternoon or evening
Arrive evening		
(Night One)	(Night Two)	

Two-Day Offsite, Two Nights

Monday	Tuesday	Wednesday
Arrive A.M. Begin retreat	Resume retreat	Resume retreat
Day One—half day	Day Two—full day	Day Three—half day
(Night One)	(Night Two)	End retreat, depart mid-afternoon or evening

Two-and-a-Half Day or Three-Day Offsite, Three Nights

Monday	Tuesday	Wednesday	Thursday
	Begin retreat	Resume retreat	Resume retreat
	Day One—full day	Day Two—full day	Day Three—full or half day
Arrive P.M.			End retreat, depart P.M.
(Night One)	(Night Two)	(Night Three)	

Nearly Two-Day Offsite, One Night (for offsite very near home)

Monday	Tuesday
Arrive A.M.	Resume retreat
Day One—most of day	Day Two—most of day
(Night One)	End retreat, depart P.M.

including breaks, lunch, dinner, and "down time," and still have energy for Day Two, which might run through mid-afternoon, depending on the circumstances.

If the issues justify it, and if the organization can afford it, staying over a third night and having a half-day session on Day Three for action planning can be a very effective format. What goes on outside the formal sessions, particularly during and after dinner, nearly always reinforces and amplifies what takes place during those sessions. Issues are discussed, problems are solved, and personal relationships are formed and strengthened. Moreover, "sleeping on it" often produces breakthrough ideas. Participants have time to reflect, envision different possibilities, come up with additional questions, and rethink their positions on the issues. The time can help participants focus their enthusiasm and deal with their anxieties. We've even seen instances when people came in the next morning declaring, "We didn't aim high enough yesterday when we set our goals. Let's be more ambitious today."

If staying two nights is prohibitively expensive, consider convening your retreat close enough to the office so participants can arrive in the morning of the first working day and stay until the late afternoon or early evening of the second day. In this case, you would have the option of holding an after-dinner session the first evening to make up for the loss of time that morning.

When Should You Schedule Your Retreat?

It's tempting to schedule a retreat over a weekend. People don't miss any of their regular work, and those who aren't included don't have to cover for the people

What Is the Ideal Length for a Retreat?

There's nothing sacred about a two-day retreat. A mini-retreat involving a small number of people and a limited number of issues can be successful in one day, without an overnight stay. And some highly successful retreats last longer than two or two and a half days.

And there are variations, such as a day-and-a-half retreat over a three-day stay at a resort, where meetings are interspersed with social activities and sports. (In such a setting, however, the convenor and facilitator have to work harder to ensure that participants are present and focused for the working sessions.)

who are away. The weekend option may be attractive to senior management but can present problems for employees who have family obligations or need their weekends to take care of their personal affairs. You might not hear it directly, but if you schedule a weekend retreat, there will likely be some grumbling in the halls. And resentful participants are less likely to be invested in the success of the offsite.

Some companies plan retreats over government holidays on which they don't traditionally close, such as Veterans Day or Columbus Day. On those days, phone and e-mail traffic may be lighter because government agencies, many banks, and some other companies are closed.

Although convening a retreat during the work week can make employees more enthusiastic about attending, they still may have scheduling problems. Moreover, they'll have to ensure that urgent matters are taken care of in their absence and be prepared to handle the extra work that will be waiting for them when they return to the office. There may be no perfect time for everyone, but it is helpful to consult with participants about when their workloads are heaviest before you set the dates.

In other words, be sensitive to people's needs, and give them plenty of time to make arrangements so they can attend. The longer in advance you can confirm dates for your retreat, the more likely you'll have full attendance.

> Be sure to confirm the availability of key participants and the facilitator before locking in dates with the retreat facility.

While everyone you invite is, by definition, important to the success of the retreat, some participants may be more critical than others. If so, be sure to gain a commitment from these key players before setting the dates. Who these key players are depends on the nature of the issues that will be addressed, but in nearly every case they include people who have the power to make decisions and commit resources. If decisions must be made, and you don't have the authority to make them, be sure that whoever does—the CEO, executive director, department head, board chair—agrees to take part and understands the importance of that commitment. Because senior executives' schedules are often filled many months in advance, the earlier you determine dates, the better.

There is no universal best season to schedule a retreat, but summer is usually a particularly bad time. Key participants might elect to skip a retreat that coincides with their family vacations or become resentful if vacations have to be cancelled or postponed. Even if everyone is able to participate, valuable momentum can be lost if some of the participants go on vacation shortly afterward. By the time everyone is back at the office, the retreat may be a dim memory. Also, it may be more difficult to cover the work of retreat participants if a number of their colleagues are on vacation at the same time the offsite is scheduled.

Many companies like to hold retreats in advance of their annual planning period. Since managers often have to find time for planning while still doing all their regular work, it's helpful to hold the retreat a month or two before the actual planning and budgeting work begins. This will give participants time to include the retreat outcomes in their thinking.

What if someone who has committed to the retreat well in advance finds at the last minute that he or she cannot make it? We use what we call the Tahiti Rule. If the reason someone gives for skipping the retreat wouldn't cause that person to return early from a long-planned vacation to Tahiti, it isn't a valid reason.

But sometimes people who have agreed to participate really can't make it. Someone gets sick, family emergencies arise, unanticipated snowstorms strand people in faraway cities. If a participant suddenly has to cancel, the retreat can usually proceed as planned without serious consequences. If, however, the participant who must cancel is a key decision maker or has special skills or information critical to the success of the retreat, you have a dilemma.

How you deal with the situation depends on the circumstances. Will the retreat facility let you postpone? Can the other busy people who have planned to attend change their plans? Will the facilitator be available when you want to reschedule?

If not, consider whether it's worthwhile to proceed as planned even if a critical person cannot attend. There's no definitive answer because each situation is unique, but we offer these observations:

The Tahiti Rule

"Why are you thinking about missing the retreat? Would that reason cause you to return early from your vacation in Tahiti? If not, it's not a reason to miss the retreat either."

- The absence of a key player or several of the invited participants can ruin the retreat.
- It's important not to allow individuals to be casual about their commitments to take part in the retreat. Hold their feet to the fire if their stated reasons for missing the retreat don't justify their absence.
- If the reason given is work-related ("I have a big project to complete"), try to help the person overcome the problem. You might, for instance, ask his or her boss to extend the deadline or arrange for someone else who won't be at the retreat to take it over.
- If key players really cannot participate, try to obtain their commitment to support the outcomes even though they won't have contributed to them. Make sure that the facilitator takes the key players' absence into account in the design and facilitation of the offsite.
- Make a special effort after the retreat to inform absentees—especially any key figures who couldn't attend—what happened and why, what recommendations and decisions were made, and what the thinking behind them was.

Where Should You Hold Your Retreat?

Retreats work best in flexible, casual environments. The setting doesn't have to be fancy. In fact, if you hold a retreat in a posh resort, some participants will be more interested in finding time for a set of tennis or a round of golf than in the business at hand. Instead, look for a place that encourages quiet reflection.

Many conference centers have sprung up around the United States and elsewhere in recent years. These large facilities are usually located outside the city center, often in a park-like setting. They are specifically set up for handling group meetings, so they have flexible space and advanced audiovisual capabilities onsite. Their meeting rooms generally have fixed, soundproof walls, easily moveable tables, and executive-type rolling chairs.

Most conference centers include meeting space, lodging, meals, continuous snacks, and a broad array of AV equipment for flat per-person prices. Because conference centers specialize in group events, their staffs are typically well-trained, responsive to convenors' and facilitators' needs, and adept at making the unanticipated changes that offsites often require.

If a hotel is the only possibility for your retreat, we suggest avoiding their usual meeting rooms and ballrooms, which are often noisy and nearly always lack natural light from windows. Try instead to schedule a small group in a large hospitality suite, where participants can relax in living room style chairs and have access to a kitchen area where snacks and drinks are available all day. Also, keep in mind how much privacy from other groups you need. Meeting in a rented house or condo at a resort, for instance, will give your group more privacy than meeting in a hotel or a large conference center that lacks private dining rooms and has a common area for snacks.

Some organizations hold retreats in religious retreat houses. While such facilities can be attractive and inexpensive, we recommend against this option unless yours is a religious organization. Not everyone feels at ease in a religious retreat house, even if its meeting facilities appear as secular as those in a hotel, and people might feel uncomfortable raising their objections.

Resorts in their off-seasons are perfect for retreats: a beach house in winter, a ski resort in summer. They have beautiful natural settings; they aren't crowded; they're much less expensive in low season; and the participants will be less tempted to play instead of work. An inexpensive alternative can be rustic lodges and cabins offered by many state, county, and municipal park systems. You might even consider holding the retreat in the living room of someone's house, if it's large enough. Although you'll have to bring in everything you need—flip charts and markers, coffee urns, meals, and snacks—the casual atmosphere is often just right to spark good dialogue.

No matter where you schedule the retreat, we suggest you look for a site that offers as many of the following amenities as possible:

- Soundproof rooms, so you won't have to compete with a speaker on a microphone on the other side of a thin wall
- Hard-surfaced, easy-to-move tables that don't have to be covered by tablecloths
- Comfortable chairs—either padded, rolling executive style or comfy sofas and upholstered chairs
- Enough room in the main meeting space to allow participants to pull the chairs into a circle and work away from the tables when required
- Space to use for breakout groups, either a main room with moveable chairs,

Have you heard of a great place to hold a retreat? We'd love to know about it. Please share the information at www.retreatsthatwork.com.

large enough for groups to move away from each other, or smaller rooms adjacent to the main space or very close by

- Ample supplies of flip charts on easels, flip chart paper, and markers
- Space where people can congregate informally to talk or grounds where they can take walks
- Snacks and drinks available all day, rather than just at scheduled breaks

Sleeping Rooms and Meals

For overnight retreats, one question that will come up immediately is: "Will we have to share sleeping rooms?" Budget restraints often make that answer, "Yes, you will."

We prefer that roommates be assigned, rather than allowing people to choose whom they would like to share with, especially if the offsite will last for only one night. When close friends share rooms, they naturally compare notes on what's going on and what they think of other people. That kind of discussion does not help advance the teamwork that you need for a successful retreat.

To create an environment that is conducive to open and equal communication, avoid setting up a double standard by giving senior executives single rooms while everyone else doubles up. If the retreat location is within fifty miles of home, some participants may want to return home in the evenings. We discourage allowing people to go home unless remaining at the retreat site overnight would be a substantial hardship. People who return home will miss some of the "downtime" discussions that add to the richness of the retreat dialogue, and they often arrive late for the morning sessions.

It's a good idea for all participants (including you and other top executives) to take their meals together during the retreat. Mealtimes provide opportunities for people to talk over ideas informally.

Here are some points to keep in mind about meals:

- Lunch should be light (you don't want people falling asleep in the early afternoon) and reasonably quick.
- To make the most of your time in a one-day retreat, the facilitator might want to assign topics for lunchtime discussion.

It's sometimes fun for the participants themselves to prepare dinner if the retreat facility has a kitchen you can use. Working together to plan, cook, and clean up can give people a great opportunity to practice their teamwork skills. At some retreats, meal preparation is actually part of the content. A facilitator observes how the group works together and gives them feedback later.

- Find out in advance if people have food allergies or special requirements. Many retreat facilities have buffets, which is perhaps the easiest way to handle meals and allows people to select what they eat. You can also provide participants with a menu to choose from in advance of the retreat.
- If participants order in advance, the administrator should keep a list of everyone's food orders, because people will forget what they requested. It's a good idea to order a couple of extra meals just in case there's a problem—a meal doesn't arrive, someone is given someone else's food, and so on.
- It's much better for meals to be served in a separate room from the work sessions. People need a visual break, and it will be distracting to the group if servers come in to set up while you're in session.

Sports and Recreation

Sometimes the retreat site will be so attractive that participants will ask if they may bring their families, whom they'll expect to see at mealtimes and in the evenings. With rare exceptions, family members are a distraction from the work of the retreat.

Retreats are intense experiences. If your retreat will run two days or longer, at some point the facilitator should give participants a break long enough for them to visit the gym, get a massage, take a nap, or stroll around the grounds.

Once you announce the retreat location, many participants will look it up on the Web. If the facility offers tennis, golf, skiing, or other sports, or if there are shopping opportunities nearby, be sure to specify in your retreat invitation whether there will be time to participate in these activities.

Notifying Participants

In addition to the initial memo you send notifying participants where and when the retreat will be held (see Chapter 2, p. 38), they'll need logistical information closer to the date. Make sure to include directions and route maps to the site, amenities people can expect, and how their families can contact them in an

Logistics Checklist

☐ After selecting the facilitator, consult with him or her on the appropriate length for the retreat.

☐ Determine when the facilitator is available for your retreat.

☐ Check available dates with senior managers whose participation in the retreat is critical to its success.

☐ Select a retreat facility and determine dates when it is available. (Your facilitator may have suggestions for appropriate facilities.)

☐ Announce the retreat and give participants two or three options for dates. They should tell you which dates, if any, *do not* work.

☐ Contract with the retreat facility for the dates you choose.

☐ Make arrangements for transportation, meals, lodging, and audiovisual support required.

☐ Announce the dates of the retreat and provide participants with the information they need, including lodging arrangements, directions to the site, recreational options, if any, the dress code, and how family members can get messages to them during the retreat.

☐ Ask invitees to confirm their participation, indicate any food preferences or limitations, and supply emergency contact information.

emergency. This is a good time to collect emergency contact information from the participants in case of illness or accident at the retreat.

Be clear about what to wear. "Jeans and sweats" is a lot easier to decode than "casual attire." Let people know whether there's a gym or swimming pool they'll be able to use so they can bring appropriate clothing. (This is the time to inform participants whether they'll have time for a game of tennis or golf.)

Provide a list of what people need to bring with them to the retreat sessions. If they will need pens and the retreat facility doesn't provide them, say so. (It's surprising how many people show up at a retreat without something to write with or on.)

At large retreats for companies spread across the country, and at offsites for boards of directors, you may have to arrange to pick people up at the airport and transport them to the site. But most retreats take place within one to three hours' driving distance of the office. Since participants won't need cars once they've arrived, you might want to encourage carpooling. Carpools have the added benefit of reducing the number of stragglers who arrive late.

Provide each driver with very clear directions and maps. For drives of over an hour, you might give each carload an easy assignment to work on, for example: "Think of one thing you'd like to be different after the retreat."

In this chapter, we've looked at what it takes to set the stage for a successful retreat: determining how long your retreat will last, where and when it will take place, what sort of accommodations to arrange, and what to tell participants in advance.

The next chapter discusses your role as convenor of the retreat. It's a very important role because your actions are key to the success of the offsite.

Chapter 4

The Role of Leaders
at the Retreat

D uring an interview we conducted prior to a retreat for a mid-size
association, an employee expressed concern that the executive
director would dominate the discussion and inhibit the open exchange of ideas.
"Cliff isn't always right," she said, "but he's the boss."

This employee had put her finger on arguably the most single important
factor in determining whether a retreat will succeed or fail: the role that the leaders play.

How you and other organization leaders behave before, during, and after
the retreat is critical to its success.

Reaching an Understanding
About Participants' Authority

An organization's leaders can undermine retreat participants' efforts either by
ignoring or changing their recommendations or by denying them the resources
required to carry them out. They can delay the change process or punish people

for their outspokenness. They can use their positions and status to dominate, thwart, or hijack the discussions.

This is why it's important for you and the facilitator to reach a clear understanding prior to the retreat about the limits of participants' authority and to enforce those limits at the retreat itself.

For an offsite to be successful, participants must really believe that they can speak out honestly about their concerns without fear of retribution. They need an ironclad guarantee that there will be no repercussions if they express themselves candidly. If you, as the convenor, do not have the authority to make such a guarantee stick, it should come from the person who does.

One CEO we know, Dee, opened a retreat by issuing "Giraffe Awards" to recognize staff members who had "stuck their necks out" in the recent past. She praised them for taking risks and telling her things she might not have wanted to hear. This sent a clear signal to the other participants that Dee wanted them to be candid.

We encourage you and the other leaders present to assure participants that you are eager to listen and willing to consider the part you play both in moving your organization forward and in holding it back. And you must mean what you say.

The participants will take their cue about what's important—consciously or not—from the organization's leaders. Daniel Goleman, Richard Boyatzis, and Annie McKee (2001), in their article "Primal Leadership: Realizing the Power of Emotional Intelligence," cite research that shows that a "leader's mood and behaviors drive the moods and behaviors of everyone else." While this is an important principle of organizational life, it particularly holds true at an offsite. The leader isn't behind closed doors or off on a trip. She's right there, across the room or in the next chair.

What Goleman, Boyatzis, and McKee call the "premier task" of a leader is "emotional leadership." This fosters "information sharing, trust, healthy risk-taking, and learning"—ideal conditions for a retreat. A low level of emotional leadership, they say, produces "fear and anxiety"—precisely what will doom an offsite to failure. While a leader's emotional intelligence and its impact on an organization are rarely, if ever, discussed in the workplace, nothing could be more important to the success of a retreat.

We always assume that the convenor hopes the retreat will stimulate positive change. For this reason, when we first talk with a convenor we explore the role his or her behavior will play. If the convenor rejects a connection between his or her behavior and the success of the retreat, we are likely to recommend against holding an offsite, or we at least suggest considerably downscaling participants' expectations. But the vast majority of convenors we've worked with do recognize the important role they play, and they welcome coaching on how best to contribute to the retreat's success.

Leadership Behavior During the Retreat

As a general rule, we offer the following guidelines for convenors and others in leadership roles.

Be Aware of the Impact of Your Presence

Your opinions, expressions, body language—indeed, your very presence—carry a great deal of weight. If yours is a high-trust organization, you will have an easier time because you start out in an open and positive environment.

How Leaders Can Help Ensure a Successful Retreat

- Be aware of the impact of your presence on participants' willingness to speak out.
- Don't dominate the discussions.
- Tell people what you think without quashing their ability to think differently.
- Work with the entire group, not just a favored few.
- Provide realistic guidelines on the limits to participants' authority.
- Know when to hold back so ideas can emerge from the group.
- Be open with participants about what you've learned about yourself and what you're willing to change.
- Minimize the differences between you and the other participants.
- Be present, on time, and focused on the work of the retreat.
- Manage your emotions.
- Let the facilitator lead the retreat.
- Be open to trying new things.

If yours is a relatively low-trust organization, however, you will have to make a serious effort to convince participants that it is safe to speak candidly. This can be a real challenge, because you may have played a role, however unintentionally, in fostering the environment of distrust. One of the facilitator's jobs is to coach you in how best to encourage open participation. Take advantage of that assistance; it will be invaluable.

Don't Dominate the Discussions

Don't take over the proceedings, even if others defer to you (which they probably will, at least at first). Holding back may go against your nature, but if you are an "air hog," serious discussion will be inhibited and differing viewpoints will be suppressed. Also, let participants know why you're holding back, so they won't attribute false motives to your actions.

Because most people find it difficult to change habitual behavior, it's helpful to agree in advance with the facilitator that he or she can tell you immediately if you cross the line from participating to dominating.

Tell People What You Think—Carefully

On the other hand, don't clam up and fail to express your opinions. You're not, as the saying goes, a potted plant. If you don't participate in the discussions, you will become a silent force in the room, and other participants will try to guess what your silence implies. Approval? Disapproval? Lack of interest? In any case, you certainly shouldn't hold back until, like a sleeping dragon, you suddenly awake and breathe fire on everyone in the room.

Rather, you should feel as free as any other participant to express your opinion, although in most cases you should not be the first to do so. Be particularly sensitive to the words and body language you use when you speak. (This is true even during breaks and "hanging out" time; your voice carries weight no matter when you use it.)

There are exceptions to the don't-speak-first rule. At a retreat we led for senior managers of a manufacturing company, we gave feedback to the group from the interviews we had conducted while planning the retreat. The feedback indicated that managers were afraid to express their views freely because they were concerned that Lonnie, the CEO, would criticize or punish them.

When we asked whether the feedback accurately reflected the group's perspective, there was a profound silence in the room. After a while, it was Lonnie himself who broke the silence. "That sounds right to me," he said, "and I want to change it." His comments made it safe for others to speak out and helped establish a tone of openness that encouraged participants to recommend workable strategies for improving the company's operations.

Work with the Entire Group

Don't raise your concerns privately with select participants. If there is an issue you need to raise, do it in front of the whole group. Retreats provide rare opportunities for everyone to speak candidly and openly. When you decline to raise issues publicly, you lose the opportunity to build the trust a retreat can foster. When you raise them openly, on the other hand, you model ideal behavior.

Provide Realistic Guidelines About What Can Be Changed

There will be times when it is more productive for you to participate not as an "equal" but as the leader—when, for example, you have information people need to make realistic decisions and develop workable action plans. If participants are recommending an action that you know the board has already voted against, for example, tell them so. If you know that the company doesn't have the resources to pursue the particular course of action the group is recommending, say so and save everyone a lot of time. Such information will allow participants to alter their course. It's very frustrating for the group when a leader waits until the discussion is over and then says, "Sorry, but that won't fly."

Know When to Hold Back

On rare occasions you should refrain from participating at all in a discussion, especially if your involvement would inhibit participants from bringing a particularly thorny issue to the surface. You and the facilitator should put your heads together to decide what your participation in the various activities will be. Sometimes, your role might be to listen intently but not to join in the conversation. At another time, you might explain to participants why you are leaving the room temporarily.

Be Open About What You've Learned About Yourself

For more information on feedback, see Chapter 6, "Giving Feedback to the Group," pp. 97–98.

If the facilitator gives you feedback on the impact of your behavior on others, tell the participants what you've learned about yourself. If there are things you can do differently, say so. Also tell participants what they can do to help you make changes they and you would like to see. It's useful as well to tell people what you aren't willing or able to change and why. Understanding why certain things are the way they are can help minimize grousing and wishful thinking. Your willingness to address the feedback you receive is critical for setting the tone of the retreat by showing participants that you value their candor.

Minimize the Differences

We asked Marc, the commanding officer of a civilian-military unit, not to wear his uniform to the retreat, but to come in casual civilian clothes. Marc also made a point of inviting participants to address him by his first name instead of by his rank. While that did not make his subordinates forget his rank, it did help narrow the gap between them.

During the retreat, eliminate unnecessary symbols of your status that remind participants that you are the boss. If the whole group is supposed to eat lunch together, don't make an exception for yourself. If participants are expected to share rooms, make sure that you also have a roommate. If the dress code is casual, don't turn up in a business suit. If everyone else is on a first-name basis, you should be too.

Be Present

Woody Allen once famously observed that 80 percent of success is simply showing up. It's critical to the success of a retreat that the leaders be there—physically and mentally. A retreat shouldn't be an event for *others* to attend. If you and your peers don't make the commitment of time and energy to be present and engaged, the participants won't take the work seriously. As a result, the retreat, at best, will yield no significant benefit; at worst it could do a great deal of harm.

And you should not only be present, but you should be *present*. Show up on time for retreat sessions and activities. Turn off your cell phone and pager (you might even want to make a public show of doing so) and make it clear that you are not to be interrupted for any reason short of a real emergency. Pay attention; don't read documents or make notes of things to do when you get back to the office.

The Importance of Being There

There's nothing deadlier than twenty people sitting around waiting for the convenor to turn up. They won't want to start without you, and they're likely to interpret your absence or tardiness to mean that you don't consider the business of the retreat all that important.

Here's an example of what can happen when a leader does not make the retreat his first priority. We led a year-long series of offsites for a large media company, aimed at rethinking the way the company did business. As the culmination of the middle managers' work, the executive committee had committed to come to the last afternoon of the final retreat to hear the managers' recommendations. As all the vice presidents were arriving, Rob, the CEO, called to say that he was held up in an important client meeting, but that the managers should give their report without him.

It was extremely disheartening for the group. After they finished their presentation, we asked the managers to write down their reactions to what happened and post them anonymously on a wall. Several people wrote versions of, "If this is such important work, where's Rob?" With the group's permission, when Rob made it to the retreat site, we asked him to read the comments that had been posted on the wall.

It was a tense moment as everyone watched Rob walk the length of the wall and read how people felt about his not showing up. He took a few moments to gather his thoughts, then said, "I'm so embarrassed. I've let you down, and that was never my intention. What can I do to make this right?" What ensued was possibly the first open conversation between the CEO and middle management that had ever taken place.

Manage Your Emotions

Be careful not to let your emotions get the best of you during a retreat. No matter what you are feeling, you must control your behavior. It's very unsettling for participants to have the convenor start shouting in anger or break into tears of defensiveness or frustration. That doesn't mean you should hide what you are feeling. If you are upset, angry, dissatisfied, or disappointed, say so. Don't be afraid to speak your mind, but do so in a way that isn't accusatory or threatening. If the issue is too "hot" for you to talk about calmly, ask the facilitator to call a break and get coaching from him or her on how to raise your concern.

Let the Facilitator Lead the Retreat

You've done your homework and chosen a facilitator you trust. Now let that person do the job. You may not understand why a facilitator is or isn't doing something at a given moment, but it's the facilitator's responsibility—not yours—to get you to your agreed-on destination.

That doesn't mean you should abdicate all responsibility for the retreat's success to the facilitator. On the contrary, you must communicate any concerns that arise so they can be dealt with on the spot. The most straightforward way to do that is to raise your concern in front of the group, just as any other participant should do. A skilled facilitator will know how to handle the interruption and will also be able to incorporate the group's perspective into deciding how to address your concern. For example, if you think the discussions have gone off track, the facilitator can solicit the group's input and help everyone decide what to do about the new issues being raised.

If you think that your concern is too sensitive to raise publicly (if, for example, you are concerned that an employee with whom you have had difficulty is trying to sabotage the retreat), then discuss the problem privately with the facilitator during a break. Avoid expressing your concerns covertly (through someone else, for instance, or by passing a note that everyone can see to the facilitator) or in an angry manner. Find a way to discuss differences that respect the facilitator's professionalism.

Be Open to Change

You should know that what happens at retreats is often hardest on the organization's leadership—you and your peers. When you hear feedback from the facilitator at the retreat, you may be surprised—perhaps unpleasantly—by how people have perceived your actions and how things are going in the organization. It takes self-discipline to listen intently and not become defensive.

When a client tells us that what he wants to get out of a retreat is a change in staff behavior or attitudes, we ask, "Are you prepared to do the most changing? Because that's probably what will be called for."

A Common Post-Retreat Concern

In our many years of attending and leading offsites, we've observed an interesting and potentially unsettling phenomenon. Very often—so often that we warn our clients about it—within a month or so after a retreat, one or more of the participants quits or seeks a transfer to another department.

As part of a retreat we were conducting for the public relations department of a large broadcasting company, for instance, we asked participants to think about the direction they'd like to take in their careers and in their lives in general. Then we asked them to think about how the company could help them achieve their goals.

One of the participants, Allison, told the group that what she really wanted was to get married and have a child and that the long hours she put into her work were never going to permit her to do this. Over the course of the retreat, as the participants laid out more and more ambitious plans for the department, Allison grew quieter and quieter. Three weeks after the retreat, Allison called Mary Margaret, the department head, to say she was leaving. She had decided that she needed a less stressful and time-consuming job so that she could find what she really wanted from life. While Mary Margaret was dismayed that Allison had decided to leave, she was not surprised, and she was also relieved. Allison had obviously been increasingly unhappy, and her dissatisfaction was contributing to a tense environment in the office.

A well-run retreat can do a great deal to clarify an organization's values, priorities, and future direction. Once those have been clarified, employees who were pulling in other directions may shift their efforts, or they may realize that their jobs (and perhaps the organization itself) do not match well with their values or aspirations. Discovering that their goals are fundamentally incompatible with those of the organization, they decide to look for other jobs. When this happens, it's usually healthier for everyone concerned, and for the organization itself.

Having examined the critical role the convenor and other leaders play in the success or failure of the retreat, we now move on to explore the role of the facilitator, starting with a look at the design process.

Note for the convenor: While we wrote Section Three, Chapters 7 through 9 for the facilitator, we strongly recommend that you look over these chapters as well. The more prepared you are for what might go on at the retreat and how the facilitator might respond, the better able you will be to participate effectively and thus help ensure a successful outcome. And of course, don't skip the Epilogue, which is written to help you take what was accomplished at the retreat back to the office.

SECTION TWO

The Facilitator's Guide to Designing and Planning the Retreat

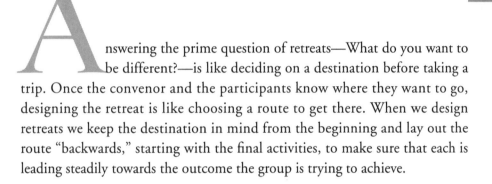

Chapter 5

Retreat Design Issues

Answering the prime question of retreats—What do you want to be different?—is like deciding on a destination before taking a trip. Once the convenor and the participants know where they want to go, designing the retreat is like choosing a route to get there. When we design retreats we keep the destination in mind from the beginning and lay out the route "backwards," starting with the final activities, to make sure that each is leading steadily towards the outcome the group is trying to achieve.

Aligning Yourself with the Convenor

Although it is your responsibility to design the retreat, you must be fully aligned with the convenor—the person who has called for the retreat to take place. Otherwise, you may end up with an elegant but inappropriate design. No matter how well you design retreats, you cannot afford to plunge ahead with your vision at the expense of your client's. Keep in mind that you have never designed this particular retreat before. No matter what successes you've enjoyed in the past, each retreat is an adventure into uncharted territory.

A Cautionary Tale

In one of the most famous cases of a designer and client not seeing eye-to-eye, artist James McNeill Whistler was hired by an English millionaire, Frederick Leyland, to decorate his dining room so it would accent his collection of Japanese porcelain. Then Leyland went off on a trip and left Whistler to his work.

The artist decided that the best way to showcase the porcelain would be to paint over Leyland's priceless hand-crafted leather walls. Even though the result was stunning (one of the most famous rooms in history, it's now in the Freer Gallery, part of the Smithsonian Institution, in Washington, DC), Leyland was furious; it was certainly not the result he had in mind.

For more discussion on this point, see Chapter 1, "Ten Reasons Not to Hold a Retreat," pp. 9–11.

But what if the convenor isn't sure what outcome he wants? Beware of trying to design a retreat with no explicit change goal. People assume that when they're invited to a retreat their opinions will be heard and decisions will be made as a result. If the convenor is unfocused, heavily invested in the *status quo,* or has already decided not only what will change but how the change should be accomplished, you need to be sure he understands that the retreat participants will probably try to derail his plans.

In some situations, the convenor will be your primary contact; in others, he will delegate that responsibility to someone else, such as the human resources director. Even if the convenor wants you to work closely with another person during the design stage, you must have ample access to him throughout the process so you can be sure that you're working to meet his expectations. It's equally important that you and the convenor agree that the retreat will be designed with all participants' interests in mind. Ask the convenor to inform the participants that, as facilitator, you are working on everyone's behalf. The off-site will fail if it is seen merely as a tool to advance the convenor's agenda.

You and the convenor must be clear about what you expect of one another. The convenor, for instance, has the right to expect that the design of the retreat will:

- Be suitable for the participants, taking into consideration their level of experience and expertise and their comfort level with certain types of activities
- Focus sharply on delivering the expected outcomes
- Engage the participants so they are strongly committed to the decisions they make

- Use participants' time wisely
- Be flexible enough to allow changes to the plan if something unexpected happens, but still move the group toward the desired outcomes
- Include time to discuss how decisions reached at the retreat will be implemented and integrated into the organization's work

You also need commitments from the convenor, particularly that:

- He has no hidden agenda
- You will have access to him and other retreat participants in advance to solicit their input
- He will make available to you all relevant documents (such as staffing patterns, organization charts, previous studies, internal and external surveys, reports from other retreats, and the like) that you might need
- He intends to implement the action plans agreed to
- Participants will not be punished (by him or anyone else in the organization) for expressing their opinions
- You will have the freedom to "design in the moment" to ensure that the retreat stays on track toward meeting its goals
- You will not be asked to violate participants' confidentiality or make an assessment of any individual's behavior

In your conversations with the convenor, you must understand his specific desired outcomes for the retreat. Urge him to express these outcomes in observable terms so you will both be able to tell whether you have achieved them.

You may need to ask him some pointed questions to make sure you'll be helping the group address core issues, not merely symptoms of the problems they're experiencing. Facilitators are often presented with issues that appear to be process problems ("We don't get along with each other.") when what is underneath may be a much more basic problem ("We don't agree on the priorities for our business.")

Make sure the convenor knows how you plan to lead the retreat. Discuss with him the extent of your participation. For instance, we conduct many creative thinking retreats. As a result, we have become skilled at generating innovative, even off-the-wall, ideas that in turn often spark even better ideas from the participants.

We know of no better resource to guide you in contracting discussions with your client than Peter Block's classic book, *Flawless Consulting*.

In planning such a retreat, we ask whether the client would like us to contribute ideas or just facilitate the participants' idea-generating process. When we take an active part, the organization often ends up with more diverse ideas, but sometimes the convenor (or the group) doesn't want the facilitator involved with the issues. If we think we have content expertise to offer in a given situation, we discuss in advance with the convenor and, if possible, the group what role they want us to play, instead of simply jumping in and offering our expertise.

Finally, you will need an explicit understanding from the convenor about the kinds of decisions that can be made at the retreat. Participants often are asked to come up with new ideas without being given the authority to make final decisions about what will be implemented. If this is the case, you will have to make the boundaries clear to the participants up front: "At this retreat we're going to explore issues and come up with alternatives to resolve them, but we won't make any hard decisions about how to proceed. Our recommendations will go to the management team for final consideration."

Pre-Retreat Interviews with Participants

Never—repeat, never—agree to design or lead a retreat without having conducted some preliminary interviews to assess what's on participants' minds. Many years ago, when we first started doing this work, the president of a small Canadian company—let's call them Maple Leaf, Inc.—asked us to design a staff retreat. To save money, the president, Jane, suggested that we talk with her alone about the company's issues and work climate. Foolishly, we agreed.

Jane painted a picture of a happy, harmonious work environment. (Okay, we should have seen through this right away, but we didn't.) Teamwork was great, she reported, morale high, and turnover low.

On the second day of the retreat, we broke the staff into small groups and asked them to come up with a creative way to illustrate what was positive about the company's culture. All went well until the last group made its presentation. In an amazing show of bravado, this group announced, "The truth must be told." And then each person in turn recounted a story about how the staff felt abused by management. Everyone in the room sat in stunned silence.

Had we interviewed staff members in advance, we would have picked up signals that the company's leaders were out of touch with the staff's perceptions. We could then have designed a retreat that addressed the real problems. Unfortunately, by the time the issue surfaced, it was too late for the group to explore it in any constructive way.

We learned a very important lesson from this horrifying experience. The convenor does not have all the information you need. There are many viewpoints represented in every organization, and you need to hear lots of them. It's critical to talk with at least a healthy sample of the retreat participants before designing the retreat. Besides keeping you from being blindsided, interviewing participants will foster greater commitment to the success of the retreat. When participants have had some say about the retreat's focus, they are less likely to view the experience as being manipulated by management.

If the retreat has ten or fewer participants, you will probably be able to talk with everyone who will attend before you begin designing. If the group is too large for that, you might interview between a third and half of the participants. You might also speak with some people who will be affected by the outcome but who won't be at the retreat, such as participants' subordinates, people in other departments, or customers.

The interviews can be conducted in person or over the phone. We have found telephone interviews to be a highly effective and efficient means of eliciting information prior to a retreat. Surprisingly, prospective participants are often more comfortable speaking candidly over the phone than in person. Another advantage of telephone interviews is that participants can speak from a location other than the office if cubicles provide little privacy. Although focus groups are popular, they don't usually result in the same degree of candor or wealth of information as one-on-one interviews. If you use focus groups, you'll want to supplement them with individual interviews.

Written surveys can also be helpful in collecting information from a large group, but they don't permit the follow-up questions that a skilled interviewer can ask in the moment to clarify or expand on an interesting point. In some situations, you might do interviews with a cross section of participants and supplement these with surveys of all participants.

Here are some suggestions for conducting effective pre-retreat interviews:

- Establish with the convenor in advance that you will not reveal to him or anyone else who said what. Then stand your ground if pressed.
- To foster the necessary candor, assure everyone you interview that you will be reporting broad themes only and will not disclose what any individual tells you.
- In preparing your interview questions, keep in mind that you are not conducting a scientific survey. Different people have different areas of expertise and interest, so you don't need to ask each person identical questions. If everyone in the first half of your interviews provides much the same information, use your time in subsequent interviews to explore new ground.
- Don't be afraid to abandon your carefully prepared list of questions if you hear something intriguing. See whether following that new thread opens up new perspectives.
- Listen for common themes. Pay attention to the ideas and concerns that come up repeatedly.
- Don't express your own opinions during the interviews. Don't agree or disagree with what you hear, and don't talk about what you've learned from others, even if you don't reveal identities. Any of these actions could affect what people tell you and thus skew your conclusions.

Particularly in telephone interviews—perhaps because people feel more anonymous—they often will talk openly about their relationships with other people in the organization. They may express sharp opinions of the abilities of the company's leaders, for instance. Don't try to steer people away from these personal comments. Listen, but don't comment on, confirm, or dissent from any negative allegations. Your goal is simply to get a sense of what people think and how they feel.

Some people may see the interview as an opportunity to send a message to management by telling you something they expect you to repeat. Don't allow yourself to be used as a conduit for covert messages. A senior manager once told us in an interview, "If I don't get promoted to vice president by the end of the year, I'm leaving. I already have two job offers for more money than I'm making now." That comment had nothing to do with the retreat, and it wasn't our role to report it. If he wanted management to know he was thinking about leaving, it was his responsibility to tell them—not ours.

It's a good idea to interview the convenor last so that you won't be overly influenced by his comments when you speak with others. Interviewing the convenor last allows you to probe him about issues—without disclosing specifics—that emerged in your interviews with other participants. This will give you important information about the extent to which the convenor's point of view corresponds with the perspectives of others who will participate in the retreat.

In Chapter 6, "Giving Feedback to the Group," pp. 97–100, we help you organize what you have learned in your interviews to present the information at the retreat.

Sample Interview Questions

These are some of the interview questions we often ask. This list is far from exhaustive. We encourage you to adapt the questions or substitute others that best suit the needs of the organization and are most likely to advance the retreat's purpose. But don't ask too many questions; a mountain of data is difficult to mine, and you'll quickly reach the point of diminishing returns. Asking ten to fifteen questions is usually sufficient. Finally, order your questions in a logical progression so your interviews will flow more naturally like conversations.

- What do you think is most important to accomplish at this retreat?

- What might impede our ability to achieve that outcome?

- [If this group has held retreats before] What did you find most helpful at the last retreat? Did you find anything troubling or frustrating about the last retreat and the actions that resulted from it?

- What words would you use to describe your experience at [your organization]?

- What do you think is going well at [your organization]? What do you like most about it?

- How would you describe relationships among the staff? Between staff and management? [Or between the staff and the board?]

- In every organization there is some conflict, disagreement, or difference of opinion. How is conflict or disagreement handled at [your organization]?

- If you had the power to change anything at [your organization], what would you change?

- Of the changes you said you'd like to see, are there any that you think would not be possible? Why not?

- How do you feel about taking part in this retreat?

- Do you have any concerns about what might take place?

- Is there anything else you think I should know, anything I haven't thought of asking, or anything you'd like to add to something you've said before?

Identifying the Scope of Issues and Creating the Retreat Plan

A retreat is limited in time, so it must also be limited in scope. The more tightly focused, the more likely the retreat is to be productive.

Many issues will have arisen during the interview process. Understanding them will help you guide the group through its decision-making processes and bolster participants' ability to identify and tackle potential obstacles to their action plans. But you will not be able to address all—or even most—of these issues at the retreat itself.

> Chapter 6 describes each segment you will need to consider when creating your retreat plan.

We find it most effective to talk with the convenor in our initial meeting (and throughout the process as we have a better grasp of the issues) about what might be accomplished at the retreat. "Will you consider the time well spent," we might ask a convenor for a church retreat, "if at the end we have clarified the roles of each committee, agreed on a new reporting structure, and laid out an action plan for putting the new structure into place?"

> Allow at least as much time to design the retreat as the duration of the retreat itself.

Once you have identified the issues the retreat will address, you can begin to create your design. The design spells out exactly what you are planning to do (emphasis on *planning to do*) at the retreat, hour-by-hour, including start and stop times for each activity and the methods by which you will assign people to each breakout session. The finished design will include lists of what you will need, such as supplies, flip charts, an overhead projector and transparencies, and so forth, and the room setup requirements for each segment.

> One useful method for looking at the whole retreat in the planning stage is to lay out the design elements on a wall or flip chart using Post-it® Notes. This will give you maximum flexibility to add, remove, and rearrange exercises before committing the design to paper.

We strongly recommend that you not show your retreat plan to the convenor, nor provide him with anything more than an overview of what you intend to do. It's best if everyone (including the convenor) experiences the activities without advance preparation.

Capturing the Work Product

You'll also need to plan how you will record what was decided at the retreat. This is not something you can leave to the last minute to work out.

Before you walk into the room, you should know who will be responsible for converting voluminous flip chart pages into usable notes and whether the group will need a retreat report that is more formal than simply capturing the data on the flip charts.

There are four possible answers to "Who will type the charts?"—you, the facilitator; one of the retreat participants; an administrative assistant (AA) back at the office; or an AA who attends the retreat solely for the purpose of recording its proceedings.

Read more about preparing the retreat report in Chapter 14, "Writing the Follow-Up Report," p. 301.

Although we often encourage an organization to choose a participant to take responsibility for typing the notes, sometimes it's just easier for the facilitator to produce the report. At least you can read your own handwriting. A facilitator-written report is likely to be a straightforward account of the retreat and its results, with little personal interpretation.

The advantage of a participant writing the notes is that he or she understands the organization's operations and can clarify items in a way the facilitator might miss.

The third option—having someone who did not attend type up the notes—isn't particularly desirable. Retreat flip charts are notoriously messy. They're full of acronyms (some of which have been invented on the spot), abbreviations, arrows to link things that are out of sequence, diagrams, colored dots, and sticky notes—and just plain sloppy handwriting. Anyone who types from those charts is going to have a hard time deciphering them, and they're bound to make some misinterpretations. Often, however, you may have no choice but to have someone who wasn't there get the basics into a computer. Then a participant can edit those notes.

The Grove Consultants International offers a training program in "graphic facilitation." The course teaches consultants how to use graphics to produce an engaging and well-organized system of work charts that can be copied directly as a record of the session. You can find out more about this technique at www.grove.com.

We don't believe it's a good idea to have someone attend the retreat only to take notes. That person's presence, no matter how unobtrusive, may cause people to self-censor their contributions to the group's discussions.

No matter who will actually handle the flip chart sheets, there is much you can do to make that job easier as you progress through the retreat. Number and title every flip chart page as it is produced, including those from breakout groups. They may not all make it into the final document, but you'll have an easier time locating the information you need later if you have at least this chronological numbering.

At every long break, and at the end of the day, organize the flip charts produced so far. Note on each whether it contains decisions and action points or is merely a record of the thinking process that went into decision making. Take any charts the group no longer needs off the wall, label them, make any necessary numbering corrections needed, and set them aside in a safe place where they won't accidentally be thrown out.

Finally, at the end, take down all the remaining charts (those at the end are likely to be the most important) and sort them. Although there are usually willing hands to help you in this process, we suggest you take the charts down yourself so that you can organize them as you go.

For flip chart paper covered in Post-it® Notes, it's most convenient to remove the notes and stack them into folders. (Just be sure to carefully label each folder!) The notes are much less likely to be lost than if you leave them on the flip chart sheets. If the sticky notes are arranged on the paper in a specific way— for instance, in columns under headings—then tape the notes down in place and fold the chart with them inside.

If much of the work of the retreat is done in breakout sessions, you might want to have laptop computers and printers available for session leaders to record and distribute their notes on the spot. That way, participants in each separate session get a sense of progress in real time. In addition, having these notes already in the computer speeds up the report-writing process.

Using Behavioral Assessments

We occasionally use behavioral assessments during a retreat to spark discussions about individual thinking styles and habits that may be affecting people's ability to work together effectively. Often called "instruments" (and, frequently but inaccurately, "tests"), they can help the group identify and resolve communication or conflict issues. For example, you might use an assessment to help the group discuss the level of trust, degree of cooperation, leadership styles, or patterns of communication within their organization.

In designing the retreat, keep in mind that the best and most reliable assessments usually take time to administer and debrief. Factor that into your planning, and include assessments only if they are the best means to accomplish the objectives.

These are some of the assessments that we have used successfully in retreats.

Myers–Briggs

The *Myers-Briggs Type Indicator*® (MBTI®), based on concepts developed by the Swiss psychiatrist Carl Jung (1875–1961), is the most widely used personality type inventory. It is often administered as part of team-building retreats because it helps people who work together understand one another's perspectives.

According to Isabel Briggs Myers, one of the instrument's creators along with her mother, Katharine Cook Briggs, the MBTI's results describe "valuable differences between normal, healthy people." The MBTI assesses an individual's preferred and habitual behavior on four scales (the meanings of which are *not* self-evident):

- Extraversion—Introversion (E-I)
- Sensing—Intuition (S-N)
- Thinking—Feeling (T-F)
- Judging—Perceiving (J-P)

If you decide to include the MBTI in your retreat plan, we recommend that you devote at least one full day to debriefing it. This will give you enough time to dispel the notion that an individual's Myers-Briggs "type" limits that person's range of behaviors and focus participants instead on the MBTI's capacities to give participants a freer and fuller choice of behaviors.

The MBTI can be administered only by persons who have received appropriate training and certification.*

> There are MBTI lookalikes available for free on the Internet. In fact, the Internet has become a rich source of assessment instruments, some of them useful and some of them, frankly, very poor. *Caveat emptor;* buyer beware.

*If you are a qualified user, you can obtain the MBTI assessment at www.mbti.com. For information on organizations that are authorized to conduct workshops to train facilitators to use the MBTI, go to www.mbti.com/qual/worklist.asp#mbti.

Thomas–Kilmann Conflict Mode Instrument (TKI)

The Thomas-Kilmann Conflict Mode Instrument® is a self-scoring instrument developed by Kenneth W. Thomas and Ralph H. Kilmann. It assesses an individual's preferred and habitual behavior vis a vis five modes for managing conflict:

- Competing
- Avoiding
- Compromising
- Collaborating
- Accommodating

See the Chapter 12 activity "How Conflict Affects Us," p. 260.

We often use the TKI in combination with activities that help the participants assess how they personally deal with conflict and how conflict is generally handled in their organization or work group. The TKI gives the group a framework for exploring individual as well as organizational behavior.

The TKI takes a minimum of two hours to debrief in an interactive way that allows participants to explore the benefits and pitfalls of their various conflict-management preferences. If you include the TKI as part of a fuller exploration of conflict in the organization, you should allow at least half a day.

The TKI is available through www.mbti.com for use without any special training or credentials.

Kirton Adaption Innovation Index (KAI)

The KAI was developed in response to a phenomenon its developer, Dr. Michael Kirton, observed in organizations: Some people are very effective in persuading others to accept their ideas, while others are not. And the difference does not seem to lie in the quality of the ideas. Kirton developed the KAI to measure the root causes of this phenomenon.

The KAI is often used to help people understand their styles of creativity, as well as how their patterns of communication may help or hinder understanding and acceptance of their ideas. It can be used both for individual feedback and as a group assessment. It usually takes about three hours to get full value from using the KAI in a retreat.

The KAI is licensed only to certified users and must be completed in advance by the participants and scored by the facilitator.*

KEYS: *Assessing the Climate for Creativity*

Created by Theresa Amabile for the Center for Creative Leadership (CCL), KEYS assesses an organization's climate for creativity. It measures characteristics that have been identified in extensive research as prime determinants of creativity in the workplace, such as the amount of autonomy people have and how supportive their supervisors and work groups are. In our experience, KEYS also provides an outstanding framework for discussing such issues as morale, productivity, and effective work practices. In addition, because KEYS is an organizational rather than an individual assessment, it allows a comparison of how various departments and hierarchical levels perceive the work environment.

KEYS is available to users who have been qualified by the Center for Creative Leadership.** The instrument must be completed in advance of the retreat in time for it to be scored by CCL. A full debriefing generally takes at least half a day.

Using Assessments Skillfully

Because assessments collect and assess data in what appears to be an objective manner, participants often view such instruments as highly credible or even definitive. While you'll only want to use instruments whose validity and reliability have been thoroughly tested, it's important to emphasize the fundamentally subjective nature of the results.

Make it clear to participants that assessments are nearly always descriptive, not prescriptive. Depending on how accurately the participants answer the

*For information on KAI Certification Course, go to http://ai.indstate.edu/uscertcourse.htm and www.theinnovationagency.com/events/welcome.html.

**For more information on the Center for Creative Leadership and KEYS", go to www.ccl.org.

questions, the results might describe how things are in the present, but they don't necessarily project or limit how things might be in the future. Point out that, while the conclusions drawn from assessments may provide helpful data about the organization or group, they aren't "proof" of anything.

Focus the conversation on helping people understand how their preferred and habitual styles of behavior—based on their choices, conscious and unconscious—may help or hinder them at work. Then encourage participants to develop strategies to respond in a more flexible and thoughtful way to the circumstances they typically encounter.

Don't let participants use an assessment to categorize one another's behavior as a stereotype defined by their "type." Emphasize that assessments are designed for self-understanding and individual growth, not as tools to analyze, evaluate, assign, promote or demote, manipulate, or justify attempts to change others.

If the instrument you are using can be completed and self-scored relatively quickly, we recommend administering it during the retreat. If you hand out assessments in advance for participants to fill out and bring with them, there will inevitably be one or two people who haven't completed them. This means you will have to decide whether to proceed without that person's results, send the person out of the room to complete the instrument (and thus miss part of the retreat), or delay the debriefing exercise so the person can complete the form. None of these alternatives is particularly attractive.

If the instrument you use must be scored in advance, ask the convenor to distribute it well before the retreat with a cover letter explaining its purpose and the importance of completing the assessment and turning it back to you on time. Allow several extra days to accommodate stragglers who don't meet the initial deadline.

> Take care in choosing assessments; many instruments are copyrighted and licensed for use only by people who have been trained and certified by their developers.

Pre-Work for Retreat Participants

Occasionally you or the convenor will want to give the participants reading or work assignments to complete before the retreat. For a strategic planning retreat, for example, participants may need to review progress against last year's plan and year-to-date budget figures. Department heads might be asked to bring preliminary descriptions of any new projects they are contemplating for the next year or an evaluation of this year's initiatives.

Pre-work assignments should be distributed by the convenor in plenty of time for people to finish the work. But don't overdo it; discuss pre-work requirements with the convenor to make sure that any work you assign is absolutely necessary. Assigning pre-work can save time during the retreat, but expect uneven compliance. Some people will eagerly do all that the convenor asks; others will not. In a two-day retreat, we often schedule the activities that rely on pre-work for the second day, giving the participants who didn't finish the pre-work time to pull something together.

If technical or detailed information will be discussed at the retreat, it can be helpful for the convenor and administrator to assemble a briefing book to be handed out in advance. Even though some people won't have read it, they will have the book with them to refer to during the offsite. Asking individuals to contribute material for the briefing book may also inspire them to complete their assignments rather than leaving an empty section in the book where their contribution should be.

Inevitably, some participants will forget their briefing books. It's a good idea to have one or two extras on hand.

Using "White Space"

Throughout the retreat, there will be times when the group is formally in session and other times when it is out of session. The time between organized discussions or activities, when there's no program and the facilitator isn't managing events, is known as "white space."

Some of the most meaningful work of the retreat can occur during the white space—in particular in the evenings after dinner—while people are engaged in purely social interaction or physical activities. And you, the facilitator, might not be there to observe it.

At a retreat for a publishing company held in the north woods of Minnesota, for instance, the executive committee spent much of one afternoon discussing how to reorganize two departments. That night, long after most of us had gone to bed, Tom, the CEO, and Mike, one of the two department heads, had a few beers out on the dock. The next morning at breakfast, we heard people asking,

"Did you hear Tom and Mike yelling last night? What was that all about?" It turned out that Mike was strongly opposed to most of what he'd agreed to during the afternoon session. He hadn't said anything at the time, feeling it would make him appear defensive. But late at night, out on the dock (and with a couple of beers under his belt), he told Tom the truth about how he felt, and Tom reacted angrily. Awkward as the incident was, it brought forward Mike's true feelings so the group could address them.

People often feel compelled (or relaxed enough) to call things as they see them outside the formal sessions. Offering unstructured space for such candid conversations to take place is one reason (although not the only reason) we nearly always prefer that a retreat include an overnight stay.

A challenge for you as the facilitator is to discover what has happened in the white space and bring it back into the formal process. The easiest way is simply to begin the next morning's session by asking, "Did anybody have any new ideas or second thoughts that we should hear about?"

Thinking About Logistics

See Chapter 3, "Where Should You Hold Your Retreat?" pp. 45–47, for a discussion of key retreat facility concerns.

Make sure the facility sets up a large table near the front of the room for your notes, supplies, and materials.

Although the convenor will decide where to hold the retreat, you and she should discuss your needs and preferences as early in the process as possible. The convenor will need to know how large a space would be ideal, whether you'll need smaller rooms for breakout sessions, what kind of room setup would be most conducive for the desired outcome, and what audiovisual equipment is necessary. It's also a good idea to discuss the timing of meals, so you won't be in the middle of an important discussion while participants' food is growing cold in the dining room.

Years of leading retreats have led us to observe that there's something about sitting around a big table that inhibits free-flowing communication. When people talk across tables, they perceive the conversation as "official" and are more cautious in offering opinions. The most effective setup is often chairs arranged in a circle or—for small groups—living room-like settings where participants sit in comfortable sofas and chairs. It's all right if participants don't feel quite comfortable without a table in front of them. Retreats should push participants at least a little beyond their comfort zones.

When a particular activity demands that people be seated around tables, the most conversation-friendly arrangement is to have six or eight people at small round or rectangular tables. Then you can move people around to different tables for various segments of the work. Avoid long board-style tables or U-shaped table arrangements. Those setups encourage formality, and people tend to settle into "their" places and may be reluctant to change seats.

Virtually all retreats have some small group breakout sessions. Although the facility may be able to provide rooms for such sessions, we suggest you keep all the action in one large room if possible, so you can monitor what's going on. A very large room will accommodate people pulling their chairs together to work in different groupings without interfering with one another. They may be able to spill into a wide hall or sitting area if the main room is too small to accommodate breakout groups, or even go outdoors (weather permitting).

It's helpful for each breakout area to have its own flip chart and markers, although many facilities charge for each easel and flip chart pad, so the convenor may prefer to request as few as possible. In that case, give each group a pad or just a few loose sheets of flip chart paper to write on.

Here are some points to keep in mind about flip charts:

- No matter how much flip chart paper you think you will use, ask the convenor to order two or even three times as much. It is easy to return if

> A retreat is not a place for *Robert's Rules of Order*. The group's own ground rules will be enough.

> Tables that aren't covered with tablecloths (called "hard surface tables" by conference centers) are more easily rearranged and provide a nicer surface for writing and drawing.

Using Nametags

We recommend using nametags, even if the participants know each other (and sometimes you can't be sure of this anyway). Tags foster the use of first names and will help you keep participants' identities straight. (You should wear one as well.) The type of tag doesn't matter all that much, but keep in mind that stick-on tags are hard to reuse after lunch or on the second day.

you don't use it, but nothing stops a retreat faster than running out of paper.

- Use non-adhesive flip chart paper and old-fashioned masking tape. While the sticky-backed 3M flip chart pages are convenient to put up on the walls, they stick to each other very inconveniently when you take them down to prepare the retreat report.
- Make sure easels have a solid back. Easels made for displaying artwork are very difficult to write on.
- Do not depend on the retreat facility to supply flip chart markers. Facilities rarely supply enough markers, and inevitably, some of those few will have little life left in them. Purchase new markers; a good rule of thumb is to bring one new marker for every participant.

Sins of Omission: The Top Ten Retreat Design Mistakes

If you design and lead many retreats, you'll quickly find your own style—that unique quality you bring to the work that makes you valuable to your clients. The more creative you are in trying out new ideas, the better results you'll get.

While we're always interested in fresh approaches to retreat design, we believe that there are a few principles that should never be ignored. (We've made or observed all these mistakes, and by listing them here we hope to shorten your learning curve.)

1. Not Coming to Clear Agreement with the Convenor About Expectations

See the section earlier in this chapter titled "Aligning Yourself with the Convenor," pp. 63–66.

Unforeseen events occur at almost every retreat. You and the convenor must be clearly aligned on your respective roles and expectations so that when something you couldn't foresee takes place, you won't struggle over how to handle it.

2. *Not Interviewing Participants in Advance*

A retreat is for everyone in the room, not only the person who convened it. Participants will cooperate far more enthusiastically when they have had input beforehand. Conducting even a few interviews can help prepare you for possible hidden agendas and covert attacks.

See "Pre-Retreat Interviews with Participants" earlier in this chapter.

3. *Not Providing Enough Variety*

Using the same techniques over and over simply bores people. It's hard to keep people's attention through a two-day offsite. Use all your creativity to keep people fully engaged.

See Chapter 6, "Content Segments," pp. 100–110.

4. *Not Making Opportunities for People to Think Before They Speak*

Before an important discussion, give participants a few minutes to silently collect their thoughts before they speak. You might even have them write their ideas down. (You may have to "force" extroverts to refrain from speaking up immediately.) This brief pause in the discussions will encourage more thoughtful responses from all.

See Chapter 6, "Content Segments," pp. 100–110.

5. *Not Allowing for Spontaneous Changes to the Retreat Plan*

Sticking to your carefully developed sequence of activities and precise timetable can blind you to the dynamics of what's happening in the room. You must be ready to stay with a point that participants become really engaged in or to abandon an activity that isn't contributing to the outcome you anticipated. You may have to insert an activity you hadn't planned on to take advantage of an unexpected opportunity or eliminate an exercise you intended to include because you don't have time for it or it's no longer appropriate.

See Chapter 6, "Introduction," pp. 92–93 and Chapter 7, "Changing the Plan," pp. 134–136.

6. *Not Being Transparent When Changes Occur*

See Chapter 9, How to Recover When Things Go Awry.

There is no such thing as a perfect retreat. You'll forget something. Participants won't follow instructions correctly. Managers will speak out inappropriately. The biggest mistake you can make when something unexpected occurs is to pretend that nothing happened. Acknowledge that something has gone wrong and ask the group for help in setting it right. We're all human, and participants will appreciate seeing your humanity too.

7. *Not Letting Go of Control During the Unstructured Time*

See Using the "White Space" earlier in this chapter, pp. 77–78.

Sometimes the best work in a retreat occurs when the facilitator isn't managing the discussions. Be sure to build some out of session time into your design to let those moments occur naturally. Remember that sometimes your presence can inhibit this sort of "white space" spontaneity among participants, so be strategic about your place and behavior in such activities. (We tend to leave participants to themselves out of session.)

8. *Not Forcing Hard Choices*

See Chapter 8, "The Nub: Action Planning," pp. 146–153.

Participants will perceive that the retreat was a waste of time if the action plan is really a plan to think more about actions. You may be uncomfortable pressing people to make difficult choices throughout the retreat, but that work is critical for the participants to be able to create an action plan that will lead to meaningful change.

9. *Not Leaving Adequate Time for Action Planning*

Facilitators too often leave insufficient time at the end of the retreat for participants to review their decisions and put them into a plan that assigns responsibilities, fixes target dates, and defines ways to measure progress. The time required will depend on the length of the retreat and the complexity of the challenges, but since the action plan is the end product of the offsite, it should not be hurried.

10. *Not Providing an Appropriate Close*

Retreats are emotionally intense experiences for many participants. People need some time to reflect on what they have achieved together, appreciate one another's contributions, and plan for their re-entry back in the workplace. A rushed closing can undermine some of the good work the group did over the course of the retreat.

See Chapter 14, Closing the Retreat, pp. 289–302.

Special Design Considerations for Board Retreats

Boards of directors are like snowflakes: They form intricate patterns, and no two are exactly alike. At the same time, they have much in common, and we've seen some recurring patterns.

Nonprofit Boards

Boards of nonprofit organizations typically are comprised of unpaid volunteers who donate their time and expertise because they care about the organization's work. Some know a great deal about the substance of the organization's mission (for example, nurses on the board of a public health clinic) and less about management and business issues. Other board members (such as corporate executives on the board of a museum) may be knowledgeable about business, but have little expertise in the substance of the organization's mission. For this reason, board members may use different "languages" and speak past each other.

Bringing this diversity of interests and experience to bear on the challenges many nonprofits face can be a daunting task. While retreats don't guarantee more effective boards, they can foster significant changes in how boards contribute to their organizations' success.

This is what we often observe in nonprofit boards:

- A small fraction of the members (usually the executive committee and maybe a few others) do the lion's share of the work. As a consequence, those individuals may be headed for burnout and often grow resentful of others who don't pull their weight.

- From the staff's perspective, the board typically either meddles and micro-manages, or does too little to help the organization.
- The board doesn't seem to "get" that raising funds is one of its central responsibilities. Precious time is taken up figuring out how to move the organization beyond short-term crises precipitated by insufficient operating funds.
- There is a perception that there are "in" groups who can influence the direction of the organization and "out" groups who resent just being asked for money without having much input into what the organization does with that money.
- There are signs of dissension: griping after meetings, whispering or raised eyebrows when certain issues are discussed, or a general lack of interest in the board's discussions.
- It's a struggle to get people to attend meetings or participate constructively when they do.

When designing a retreat for the board of a nonprofit organization, focus on what the board and staff jointly agree are the key strategic issues and on how the board can help the organization achieve its mission. These can include:

- Clarifying the organization's purpose and goals, identifying strategic issues, jump-starting a strategic planning process, and measuring progress against goals
- Orienting new board members to the issues facing the organization and what they can do to address them, as well as to the ways in which nonprofit boards differ from corporate boards with which new members might be more familiar (This has the added benefit of engaging more senior board members in the process of mentoring new members, thus reinforcing their own commitment)
- Increasing the board's involvement in choices and tradeoffs necessary to decide which programs and services the organization should offer
- Engaging in creative thinking about programs, services, processes, or constituents
- Defining board and staff roles and responsibilities
- Improving how board members work together and with the staff by addressing

For more about strategic planning, making tradeoffs, and making choices about programs and services, see Chapter 10, "Leading a Strategic Planning Retreat," pages 173–211.

To read more about creative thinking, see Chapter 13, "Leading a Creativity and Innovation Retreat," pp. 269–287.

such issues as communication, conflict management, and decision making

- Dealing with a significant issue such as a public affairs crisis or the need to change the organization's leadership
- Evaluating the board's effectiveness and agreeing on standards of performance for the future
- Exploring and modifying the board's policies and structure, if necessary
- Enhancing the board's operations by exploring such issues as how members use their time at meetings and how the board's committee system functions

Chapter 11, "Leading a Culture Change Retreat" and Chapter 12, "Leading a Relationship-Building and Teamwork Retreat" include activities to clarify roles and improve internal communications.

But here's the rub: You'll have to be aware as you design this sort of retreat that sometimes (maybe often) executive directors don't want a strong board that will challenge their thinking or demand extensive documentation of the organization's expenditures and activities.

Many executive directors believe they know how to run their programs and would prefer that their boards concentrate exclusively on raising money. But it's not realistic to expect board members to care enough to accept the responsibility for fiscal, legal, and policy oversight and fundraising, while at the same time not wanting to be involved to some extent in program and service decisions. After all, their interest in what the organization does is probably what inspired them to become board members in the first place.

In essence, then, you may have two clients, the board and the staff, each with different outcomes in mind. When you're designing a nonprofit board retreat, you'll want to include activities that help the staff and board members bring these issues to the surface and deal with their differences while still focusing on what they have in common: their passion for the mission.

A well-designed retreat offers an outstanding opportunity for board members to learn the staff's thinking about program and service offerings and to communicate to the staff their own interests and concerns. Most importantly, perhaps, it can help board members see how their efforts affect the organization's operations and what they can do individually and collectively to contribute even more to its success.

Corporate Boards

Corporate boards differ from nonprofit boards in significant ways. Members tend to come to such boards with executive experience in industry or government, and they may be paid handsomely for their time and expertise. Even members of boards of small companies are likely to have experience in business or finance. Corporate boards don't often hold retreats, but usually conduct their business at regular meetings, to which some members may travel from great distances.

Facilitator's Pre-Retreat Checklist

You will want to get into the retreat room the night before the retreat begins, if possible, or at least two hours before the group arrives on the first day. Like a pilot checking out the aircraft before takeoff, you need to be sure that everything is arranged as you specified and in proper working order.

This is the checklist we use:

☐ *Room Arrangement.* Are the chairs and tables set up exactly as you planned? If not, move them now.

☐ *Your Materials.* Is there a table for your notes and supplies? Has the facility provided the supplies you requested, such as pads of flip chart paper and masking tape?

☐ *Wall Space.* Where will you post flip chart pages as they are filled? Is access to the walls blocked by tables, chairs, or lamps? Will you have to post flip chart pages on windows? Where will you put charts as the walls fill up?

☐ *Equipment Supplied by the Facility.* Do you have the right number of flip charts and pads of flip chart paper? Are the pads full, or do some only have a few sheets left? Is all the AV equipment you ordered in the room and set up properly? Does it work?

☐ *Flip Chart Markers.* If you haven't brought boxes of new markers, have you tested every marker supplied by the facility and discarded those that are dried out?

☐ *Facilities.* Do you know where the bathrooms are? Where the snacks will be set up? Where lunch and dinner will be served?

☐ *Participant Place Setups.* Are the supplies—markers, writing pads, pens or pencils, and handouts that participants need—in place? Do you have extras in case they're required?

Always check the overhead projector in advance, and ask the AV people to leave an extra bulb.

Yet increasing public and government scrutiny of how these boards direct the fortunes of their companies and protect the interests of their stockholders has led many companies to search for better ways to harness the members' collective expertise. This has prompted a deepening interest in corporate board retreats.

Such retreats can be effective in improving communication among board members, increasing their understanding of significant business issues and problems, and—perhaps most important—fostering disclosure of and honest discussion about concerns that lie beneath the surface, waiting to snare the unwary executive or uninformed investor.

Many of the issues we outlined for nonprofit boards also apply to the board and staff dynamic of corporate boards. Senior executives may look on their boards as potentially interfering with and challenging the way they run their companies. Some boards are comprised of members who serve at the pleasure of major stockholders and whose points of view therefore might be skewed in one direction or another.

In contrast to the formal nature of corporate board meetings, the more informal atmosphere of a retreat can encourage greater sharing of information, freer and more candid discussion, and deeper inquiry into important issues.

As with nonprofit boards, retreats are not a cure-all, but a well-designed offsite can play a significant role in helping corporate boards become more effective in carrying out the increasingly important and public role they play.

Design Issues for a Series of Retreats

A complex change initiative, such as a major restructuring, often requires several retreats held over a period of months. Rather than think of these as discrete events, it is best to consider them as part of one multi-session retreat. That way, you can build on what has come before while at the same time remaining alert to the need to bring new participants up to speed.

A series of retreats allows participants time between sessions to reflect on what has taken place, test new ideas, solicit input from colleagues who weren't present, gather new perspectives, and think about how they can best contribute to the next session.

To design a series of retreats, you must be prepared to deal with changes in the landscape that will take place over time. New leadership, promotions, transfers, turnover, downsizing, growth, new economic realities, shifts in focus and priorities, and personal concerns can all affect successive retreats. In the time between retreats, new people will become involved in the process and others will drop out. People may change their minds about certain issues, and concerns might crop up at one session that could have been explored more fruitfully at an earlier stage. Issues that you thought had been resolved may re-emerge. "Retreat fatigue" can set in, and participants who were eager to participate at one retreat might be reluctant at another.

The longer the process, the more important it is for participants to communicate between sessions among themselves and with colleagues who weren't at the retreats to prevent potential misinformation and misunderstandings from undermining the process.

The Facilitator's Toolkit

Certain basics belong in every facilitator's stock of supplies. No matter how dependable the retreat facility seems, we always bring these things with us:

- [ ] Several sets of fresh markers, in black, blue, green, and red

- [ ] Two sizes of Post-it® Notes, in multiple colors, one pad of each size for every participant, plus about 20 percent extra

- [ ] Nametags

- [ ] Several rolls of masking tape

- [ ] Colored labeling dots (for "voting" on choices; see Chapter 8, "Types of Retreat Decisions," pp. 142–146.)

- [ ] Pocketknife or case cutter for opening boxes of supplies, if you ship them ahead. (Note: You'll have to put the knife or cutter in your checked baggage if you are flying to the retreat site.)

- [ ] Bell, chime, whistle, or whatever you like to use to indicate the beginning and ending of timed exercises

- [ ] A clock or timer (so you won't have to keep looking at your watch during timed exercises)

You'll want to stay in regular and frequent contact with the convenor between retreats to observe events as they unfold, provide advice and coaching, and gather up-to-date information to consider in designing the next retreat. You may need to conduct additional interviews with some of the continuing participants or interview new participants. It almost never happens that what was valid at the beginning of the process remains valid throughout.

In this chapter we've looked at the elements and steps involved in designing a retreat that will meet the needs of the organization and of the participants.

We've explored why you and the convenor must be aligned with one another and stressed the importance of doing a pre-retreat assessment of your own. We've emphasized the necessity of limiting the scope—and thus reducing the likelihood of unrealistically ambitious expectations—before the retreat.

We've discussed how to build the retreat plan and explored how to incorporate behavioral assessments and pre-work into your design.

We've underscored the importance of out-of-session time at retreats, listed our top ten retreat design mistakes, and taken a close look at logistics issues that the facilitator needs to be aware of. We've also examined a couple of special cases—board retreats and a series of retreats that build on each other over time. And finally, we included a pre-retreat checklist and a list of the items we recommend for your retreat toolkit.

In the next chapter, we'll delve more deeply into design issues, helping you plan a retreat step by step.

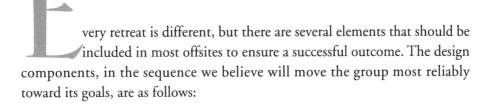

Chapter 6

Retreat Design Components

Every retreat is different, but there are several elements that should be included in most offsites to ensure a successful outcome. The design components, in the sequence we believe will move the group most reliably toward its goals, are as follows:

- Introduction
- Ground Rules
- Individual Check-In
- Group Feedback
- Content Segments
- Decision Making
- Action Planning
- Closing

Introduction

Every retreat should start with a brief welcoming statement. We emphasize "brief"; five minutes should be more than long enough. The convenor or another high-ranking person in the organization greets the participants and calls the session to order. The purpose of this introduction is to reinforce participants' understanding of the goals of the retreat, set the tone for the work that will follow, and confirm senior management's commitment to following up on the recommendations and decisions that come out of the offsite.

In the welcoming statement, the convenor should reiterate his or her desire for an open and candid dialogue and emphasize that there will be no repercussions for speaking out within the parameters of the ground rules the group agrees on. The convenor should also thank participants for the sacrifices they are making by taking time away from work and home.

People will take their cues about the retreat from the words and tone of the introduction. Encourage the convenor to make the introduction friendly and informal. We encourage convenors not to use charts or PowerPoint® presentations. People won't remember a long list of bulleted items. They will, however, remember a compelling personal story from a senior manager or a sincere explanation of what the convenor hopes will be different after the retreat. Then the convenor should introduce you.

You can then explain your role as facilitator, give the participants an overview of what's going to happen, and describe briefly and in general terms what kinds of activities you have planned. We recommend against handing out or posting a detailed agenda specifying the schedule for each exercise, as you might do for a meeting agenda.

While you will have prepared a detailed agenda for yourself, think of your design as a game plan, not a script to be followed no matter what. The timing never goes exactly as you think it will, and, more important, you'll have to be ready to add elements and abandon others to take advantage of opportunities that will present themselves at the retreat.

If you hand out or post a point-by-point agenda, some participants will invariably worry about sticking to it, even when you know the outcome will best be achieved by taking a detour from your planned route. We typically show retreat participants a flip chart with a very general agenda that covers the major

For further discussion on creating a retreat plan, see Chapter 5, "Identifying the Scope of Issues and Creating the Retreat Plan," p. 70.

topics, without listing times other than the start and finish of each day. We stress that the agenda is just a guide, and that we will add or subtract activities as necessary to help the group move forward.

It's also a good idea at this point for you to make your role and responsibilities clear to the group. We typically explain that as facilitators we will:

- Focus the participants on accomplishing their goals
- Keep the sessions on track and moving along
- Encourage participants to bring difficult issues or "undiscussables" to the surface and devise strategies to deal with them
- Use our outsider status to push, challenge, and guide participants

> The "Expectations and Outcomes" activity in Chapter 14, p. 298, collects participants' expectations of the retreat at the beginning and then allows them to compare the final outcomes with their original expectations.

We also frequently outline what organization dynamics expert Robert Marshak calls the "Introvert's Protection Act." Some people need time to gather their thoughts before they speak, so we let participants know that we've designed activities to allow for that. For example, we intentionally include time for quiet reflection, and we often ask people to write down their thoughts before they speak.

Participants will also have questions about logistics, for example, Will there be scheduled morning and afternoon breaks? Will breaks be long enough for them to call the office? What time will they have lunch? When will the session end for the day? Answering these questions up-front allows participants to relax and concentrate on the substance of the retreat.

Ground Rules

After the introductory remarks, help the participants establish ground rules—the behavioral norms they will follow during the retreat. Ground rules help keep discussions focused on the task and ensure that participants treat one another with respect. They provide a framework for the group in determining what behavior is acceptable and what is not.

Some facilitators like to guide participants in establishing their own ground rules from scratch. Unless you have the luxury of a lot of time, however, we recommend that you suggest a set of ground rules and then invite participants to propose additions, deletions, and language changes that will make those ground rules more relevant.

Here's a list of ground rules that we often suggest as a starting point for discussion:

- Speak openly and honestly—and only for yourself.
- Participate fully.
- Let one person speak at a time. Don't interrupt or engage in side conversations.
- Listen to understand others, not to judge them.
- Assume that other people have positive intentions.
- Turn off cell phones and pagers during sessions.
- Safeguard other participants' confidentiality.
- Be on time.

Some participants, especially those who are new to retreats, may need reminding that, despite the casual style of the discussions, they must be as responsible for their comments at the offsite as they are back at work. They must understand that they cannot humiliate someone else or engage in behaviors that could threaten another person's well-being. They also need to think about the potential consequences of launching an aggressive attack on someone else, suggesting that certain colleagues are incompetent, or recommending that someone else's core program be eliminated. The call for candor—which is crucial—is not a license for rude or tactless behavior.

Consider, too, whether the composition of the group indicates the need for special ground rules. If people come from different parts of the organization, for instance, help the participants discuss whether individuals are expected to represent their departments (for example, marketing) or functions (for example, engineers or administrative assistants), or just themselves during the sessions. (Whichever the case, all participants should be encouraged to work for the good of the whole organization.)

Individual Check-In

The introduction and discussion about ground rules should not take much more than twenty minutes. Then it's time to hear from the retreat participants. If participants invest time in discussing their expectations and concerns with each other at the start, that investment will pay off later in freer expression and greater engagement. If, on the other hand, people sit silently for too long at the beginning, they're likely to settle into a pattern of passive listening rather than active participation.

If any of the participants don't know each other, ask people to state their names and jobs as part of the check-in. Questions such as those that follow often elicit powerful responses that help establish an open and supportive atmosphere:

- What do you hope we will achieve in this retreat?
- What can you contribute to the success of this retreat?
- What concerns do you have about this retreat?
- What might you need help with during this retreat?

Notice that the emphasis in these questions is on behavior *during this retreat*—not behavior back at the workplace. You or the convenor might start by giving an example—both to show participants the kind of information that is helpful and to model openness. If the convenor will check in first, coach her in advance on what kinds of opening comments are most likely to foster a positive environment for the rest of the offsite.

Marianne, the CEO of a marketing consulting firm, for instance, started her management retreat with this personal check-in:

"What I hope to achieve by the end of the day tomorrow is a new strategic direction for our company that will set us apart from our competitors. I hope we'll have some fresh ideas about how we work with our clients—ideas that no one else in our industry has come up with.

"What I can contribute to the success of this retreat is my deep appreciation of the talents of each person in this room. I believe that together we are an incredibly creative set of minds. I want to encourage all of us to contribute our unique viewpoints and talents.

"But I have to admit that while I'm calling for big new ideas, I'm afraid of change. I'm very comfortable with the company right now, even though I know intellectually that we must change if we want to grow. So I'd like to ask you all to help me accept the new ideas we're going to come up with, and to challenge me if I get stuck in resisting the unfamiliar."

Everyone in the room knew that Marianne was resistant to change, but they were surprised that she recognized that tendency in herself. This honest check-in encouraged people to believe that the ideas they generated might actually come to fruition. And it inspired other participants to be equally candid in their check-ins. A check-in can help people appreciate others' abilities and can promote an atmosphere of trust.

Rather than calling on participants or having the check-in proceed in order around the room, it's best for people to speak up when they are ready. Be aware of who hasn't spoken, however, and, if necessary, call on those people at the end. Remind participants to speak to the group, not to you or to the convenor, during their check-ins. When we facilitate a check-in, we often sit out of the obvious line of sight—perhaps at the back of the room or outside of the circle of chairs—to avoid people's natural inclination to address their comments to the facilitators.

Unless something comes up that would affect the group's ability to proceed, don't allow the check-ins to spark conversation or debate. When you give the instructions, be sure to tell the group that the check-ins should move from one person to the next without commentary from others.

If your group is so large that individual check-ins would take an inordinate amount of time, have participants break into subgroups; every participant should be heard by others in the room. When you have a day or less for the retreat, you might want to use a shorter process. We call this a 30-Second Check-In:

Caution: Tennis balls and other semi-hard objects can cause injury when thrown from one person to another in a small space. That's why we recommend Koosh™ balls, which are soft, light, and easy to catch. They are available in most toy stores.

Toss someone a Koosh™ ball. Ask that person to quickly say her name and give her hopes and concerns for the retreat, then toss the ball—underhand and gently—to another person. Watching for the ball to come their way gives people a little shot of adrenaline, and you can hear from many people in a short time.

Other 30-Second Check-In questions include:

- Give us a metaphor—a visual symbol—for how you feel about being here today.
- Tell us one thing you'd like to see come out of this retreat.

Be careful to ask only one or two questions; otherwise, your 30-Second Check-In will become a marathon.

We are sometimes asked for our favorite retreat "ice-breakers." We don't have any. Icebreakers tend to be games that are unrelated to the work ahead. They can send the wrong signal right at the start of the retreat—that participants are here only to have fun and games. While a good retreat is often enjoyable, retreats that have long-term impact are not about playing games.

Giving Feedback to the Group

At some point during the retreat, you will need to give the group feedback from the interviews you conducted. While there are sometimes reasons to present this information later in the retreat—if it relates to a specific issue, for instance—we prefer to give the feedback as early as possible on the first day of the retreat.

Remember that retreat interviews do not provide statistically valid data. Collectively, they will have given you a sense of the major issues and concerns, but until you hear from the participants themselves how accurate they believe the feedback is, you won't know whether you have captured the whole picture.

We often introduce the feedback with a statement such as, "I'd like to describe the impressions I've formed from the interviews I conducted with a number of you. I'll tell you what I believe I heard, and then you can let me know if you think I've drawn an accurate picture of how things are around here." We suggest that participants take notes of anything that strikes them as surprising, puzzling, inaccurate, or especially interesting or significant, so that when it's time to respond they can recall what they heard.

There are several reasons to give participants feedback from your interviews:

- The people who gave you information are entitled to hear what was said. The information belongs to them, not to you.

- Participants who were interviewed often talk with one another about the issues they raised. If concerns that they know several people expressed are not included in the feedback, participants may be reluctant to raise these issues at the retreat. The group loses the opportunity to discuss their concerns and may also lose their trust in the interview process and thus in you.
- Participants who raised an issue in the interviews learn that they are not crazy or alone when they hear that others feel the same way.
- Once something has been said out loud, even if only by the facilitator providing feedback, it becomes less of a taboo subject and is easier to talk about openly.
- The feedback will stimulate conversation about what really matters to the participants.

Once we have given the feedback, we take time to debrief it. We typically ask the participants to discuss, in small groups or as a whole group, their reactions to what they've heard. We often suggest such discussion questions as these:

- What themes emerged from the feedback?
- What are the implications for [your organization]?
- What surprises you about the feedback?
- What is missing from the feedback?

The discussion that ensues is often the richest part of the retreat, as participants learn how much common ground they share in terms of the issues they identified.

Should You Give Feedback to the Convenor in Advance?

Sharing the feedback with the convenor in advance, rather than having him hear it along with the other participants, has advantages and disadvantages. If you provide a preview of the feedback to the convenor:

- He will have time to think about the issues before being called on to react to them, rather than having to react in the moment at the retreat.

- You will be able to give him some perspective on the issues that were raised.
- You will have an opportunity to coach him on how to address the issues that were raised without appearing defensive.

On the other hand:

- Interviewees might be less frank with you if they know that top management will hear the interview results before they do.
- The convenor might show up at the retreat prepared to refute the points he doesn't agree with.
- The convenor might ask you to delete some information or otherwise edit your presentation, even though you both agreed prior to the interviews that you would report the feedback comprehensively and accurately.

Knowing your own client, choose your strategy accordingly.

How to Present the Feedback

You will gather much more data than you can possibly report to the participants. So you'll have to limit your feedback to the themes and trends that several people raised.

After you finish the interviews, sift through the data to find common elements that are affecting how the organization does business, not just a few individuals' pet peeves. Anything you report back at the retreat will be seen as significant, so use your judgment about what to include. Although this responsibility may make you feel anxious, don't worry. If you get something wrong (such as not including something important or highlighting something that doesn't make sense to the participants), the group will let you know.

When deciding what to include, you may be tempted to leave out particularly thorny issues. The convenor might even encourage you to do so. But if you censor the feedback to make things more comfortable for you or more palatable to the convenor, you deprive the organization of an opportunity to face up to and address important concerns. Rather than protecting participants from difficult issues, you want to help them create a climate in which they can discuss such issues openly.

For more on the power of building on the positive, see the material in Chapter 2 on Appreciative Inquiry, p. 34.

Don't become so focused on the things that people told you are going wrong that you forget to mention what's going right. A focus only on the negative can be devastating to the group's morale and lead participants to believe that it's futile to try to change anything. Use the feedback as an opportunity to help people recognize what's going well and to look for ways to build on past successes.

A word about language: Even if the people you interviewed used highly personal or judgmental language (such as "idiot," "not a team player," "incompetent," or "unfeeling") to describe their colleagues, find ways to express these concerns that allow the points to be made clearly without provoking defensiveness.

There are several ways to organize the data to help participants understand the feedback. Whatever method you choose, remember that the goal is to focus on a few key issues that the group needs to address, not on a whole laundry list of complaints.

Possibilities for organizing the feedback include:

- By broad themes (see the following sidebar, "What We Told 'Lassiter & Tompkins'")
- According to organizational strengths and weaknesses and external opportunities and threats
- By key strategic issues, with an analysis of the likely consequences of not addressing them
- By turning the feedback into a story or a narrative (which itself could be organized along any of the lines described above)

Content Segments

A good retreat is an exploration into new territory. As with a challenging trek in mountainous terrain, it takes time to reach your destination. The trip can be an exhilarating experience or a tedious one. Content segments must provide enough variety and flexibility to maintain participants' interest.

Because a retreat takes so much more time than a typical meeting, it would be deadly to have everyone sitting around a table, working their way through a rigid agenda. Instead, the content of the retreat—the actual work—should be organized into segments that take people through different processes

What We Told "Lassiter & Tompkins"

These are some of the themes that emerged from our interviews with the managers of a mid-size advertising agency prior to a strategic planning retreat:

Management Group Dynamics

- While you individually have respect for each other, you are not a cohesive team.

- The people in this room have different goals and priorities for the agency.

- Critical decisions are made by the CEO, not by this group.

- You tend to agree with each other in meetings, but then leave and do whatever you want.

- Some women executives feel that there is a strain of male chauvinism among the people who are here today.

Strategic Direction

- Your internal slogan, "Let's do great work, have fun, and make money" doesn't help you determine the strategic direction of the agency. The three ideas conflict in many people's minds.

- Your greatest threat is that one huge account dominates your client list. Everyone is afraid of what would happen if the agency lost that client.

- You're generating lots of new business contacts but not winning a lot of new business.

Organizational Issues

- The creative department is an enclave unto itself, different in spirit and intent from the rest of the agency. The rest of the agency feels shut out of a special club.

- Finance is seen as the "schoolmarm" of the agency, scolding people but not necessarily helping them do their jobs.

- The agency is reluctant to fire marginal performers because, "We are too nice."

- The people who will have to guide this agency in the future don't fully understand the succession plan.

for thinking, communicating, and planning. Each exercise or activity should be appropriate for the specific topic and should flow sequentially into the next.

Keep in mind that people process information in many different ways and have different preferred learning styles. To keep participants engaged, include a variety of experiences in your retreat design, some very active and some more reflective, some aural and some visual. Some of the experiential elements you might use include:

- Whole group conversation
- Breakout group discussions
- Listening
- Asking and answering questions
- Observing other people's actions or discussions
- Reflecting back on experiences
- Participating in improvisation, role play, or storytelling
- Making up and presenting skits
- Applying theories to real situations
- Learning about what has happened elsewhere
- Using metaphor to express thoughts and feelings
- Envisioning possibilities and generating new ideas
- Drawing, writing verse, performing songs, making collages
- Physical activities

Whole Group Conversation

Virtually every retreat begins and ends with the whole group in the room participating in one facilitated conversation. If the retreat group is small (twenty or fewer) you can spend more of the total retreat time in whole group conversation. But even with small numbers of people, you will need to introduce other experiential modes as well to keep up the group's interest.

No matter what the group's size, it will take skillful facilitation to make sure that everyone is heard and that some participants don't dominate the discussions. You may have to institute a temporary rule, for instance, that no one will speak twice before everyone has spoken once.

Breakout Group Discussions

Breaking the whole group into subgroups for simultaneous discussions is a classic retreat technique. Breakout groups, typically consisting of fewer than ten people each, discuss the question at hand and then report their ideas to the entire assembly. Breakout groups may move into smaller rooms or simply pull chairs together in different corners of the main room. We suggest you vary the composition of these subgroups throughout the course of the retreat so the same people aren't always working together.

See Chapter 5, "Thinking About Logistics," pp. 78–80.

Using subgroups helps ensure that many different voices are heard. Even so, it happens that different groups discussing the same question come to similar conclusions. If there is duplication of opinion on a topic, breakout group reports can be—let's be honest—boring. One way to avoid repetition is to give each small group a slightly different assignment. In that way, each group's report provides a different perspective on the issue. Another method is to ask each breakout group to report only those elements that are different from what other subgroups have already reported. (A third method—which we recommend against—is having one group report one thing, then another group, and then another group and so on in a round robin until it's the first group's turn again. This can be a time-consuming process, and it's not really necessary.)

Consider how you will assign people to breakout groups for each activity. Some exercises will yield better results if participants work in certain pre-determined groups. Depending on the activity, you might want to group people in some of the following ways:

If there will be multiple reports on different issues from the same subgroups, be sure to vary the order in which the groups present their information, so that one group doesn't always go first.

Forming Subgroups

Having a limit of ten people in a subgroup isn't a hard-and-fast rule. Circumstances may dictate that subgroups be larger. If you have more than ten people, however, participants will have the same problem that the whole group has: It may be difficult for everyone to be heard. And sometimes breakout groups can be as small as a pair or a trio.

- All managers in one group with subordinates in other groups
- Intact work groups
- People from different organizational levels
- People from different disciplines
- Random cross sections of participants

Assigning people to breakout groups in advance saves time at the retreat. One simple method is to put various stickers on people's nametags that indicate their groups for each activity. (This method requires that you acquire the nametags in advance from the convenor or administrator or that you make the nametags yourself. It adds to your workload before the retreat, but it can make things much easier onsite.)

As an alternative, you can count off to assign people into groups. You might also pass around various objects to the participants, such as multi-colored Post-it® pads and then have everyone with the same color pads work together in a group. Or you can simply prepare rosters of different groupings and read one off each time you have a breakout session.

No matter how you assign people to groups, the decision of who should work in which groups should never be left to the convenor, because she probably won't be able to distance herself from what she knows about the personalities involved. When you put people into groups yourself, you're much more likely to get a true representational makeup—including, of course, some people who don't especially care for each other. Often a side benefit of retreats is that they give people a positive experience working with others with whom they have had previous difficulties or little prior contact.

A Technique for Dividing Participants into Groups

When you use stickers to specify which groups participants are assigned to for different exercises, you can move people into subgroups quickly. You can say, for instance, "All the blue fish go to room A, all the yellow fish to room B," and so on. While you might think retreat participants would find such stickers childish, people seem to enjoy them. Stickers with various versions of the same symbol—different colored animals, fish, birds, objects—can be found in office supply stores.

For certain exercises, the best way to get people into breakout groups is to allow them to choose from among several topics the one they'd most like to talk about. We often post flip chart pages—each with a different topic—around the room. Every chart has space for a specific number of people to sign up; participants select their own breakout groups by signing their names to topics. This method is particularly effective when the topics under discussion require specialized knowledge, experience, or interest.

While using breakouts can help a group deal more quickly with large or complex topics, be careful not to overuse them. A day should not simply be a repeated series of breakouts, followed by small group reports, followed by whole group conversation.

Listening

Often when people need to be brought up to date on an issue, someone is asked to prepare a report before the retreat. If possible, ask the convenor to send the report to participants ahead of time so you won't have to take time conveying basic information to them.

If it's necessary to have oral reports, ask the presenters to keep them short and simple—ideally, no more than ten minutes—and leave those PowerPoint presentations back at the office. It's hard for most people to listen intently and absorb information for very long. If there are several such reports, intersperse them with other activities.

> There will always be someone in the room who didn't do the assigned reading. Bring extra copies of any reports and distribute them early in the retreat to participants who haven't brought their own copies.

Asking and Answering Questions

Participants may have questions they are reluctant to ask, particularly if the retreat includes senior executives with whom they do not have daily contact. They may not want to appear misinformed or ignorant, or come across as challenging a more senior official. Or they might simply be shy.

You can create a safer environment for asking questions by having people write them down on index cards. Collect the cards and read the questions aloud, addressing each one to the appropriate individual or group, or you can toss them into a paper bag and ask various participants to draw them at random and read them out loud. Both of these methods allow participants to maintain their anonymity while still getting their questions asked. Retreat participants usually appreciate top management's willingness to answer questions in this manner, and they often acquire important new information and perspectives.

But senior managers must be prepared to handle the unexpected. In a retreat we conducted for a federal agency field office, for example, Jeffrey, the widely admired leader, was asked, "Is it true you're leaving us to go to headquarters in Washington?"

It was indeed true. Jeffrey hadn't realized that anyone on the staff knew about his upcoming promotion and consequent transfer, and he had to decide on the spot how to handle the issue. Jeffrey dealt with this potentially awkward situation effectively by confirming that he would indeed be leaving, but that the final paperwork hadn't come through and he had felt it was premature to announce something that wasn't 100 percent final.

If executives invite questions at the retreat, they must be prepared to answer them truthfully or at least explain forthrightly why they cannot. A retreat is not a place to evade or mislead.

Observing Other People's Actions or Discussions

When participants need to understand others' viewpoints, you can use a technique in which part of the group silently observes other people speaking about an issue or working on a problem. The well-known "fishbowl" is typical of this kind of experience. Chairs are set up in inner and outer circles. People sitting in the inner ring discuss a topic, while those in the outer ring simply observe and listen.

In a longer retreat, you can structure more innovative observational opportunities. For a marketing retreat, for instance, you might take the group on an excursion to watch customer behavior in stores and then, back at the retreat, apply what they've learned to their merchandising strategies.

Another possibility is to give a group a task to complete under a time constraint, and then ask other participants to observe patterns in how members of the group work together. For example, in a retreat for an arts organization, half the participants were asked to come up with a creative closing for the offsite, while the other half made notes about how the group worked as a team. This sparked a rich dialogue about how the group's work reflected relationships and teamwork back in the office.

Reflecting Back on Experiences

The need to be in conversation hour after hour can be exhausting. It's a good idea to provide some time for individual reflection, so people can gather their thoughts outside the flurry of activity. You might provide time for participants to take a walk outside or make notes in a personal journal.

Writing down their thoughts often helps people clarify their ideas, even to themselves. As you'll see in the exercises in the later chapters of this book, we often ask participants to write their thoughts on Post-it® Notes before sharing them with the group. Writing makes extroverts reflect before they speak, allows introverts to be heard, and helps ensure that participants don't just agree with the first two or three suggestions. The group will gain a much greater diversity of options to choose from if people have some focused time to think before they can influence (or be influenced by) others.

Participating in Improvisation, Role Play, or Storytelling

Increasingly, organizations are using improvisation to help people try out new experiences and express their feelings in fun and relatively nonthreatening ways. As a facilitator, you might find it useful to take an improvisation course to become familiar with the principles and techniques. Role plays offer another means for people to try out new behaviors and responses to what are often familiar situations.

These techniques, which engage participants' emotions and bodies as well as their intellect, tend to be highly memorable. When these activities are skillfully led, even the shyest participants may raise important issues using these forms of "adult play." These techniques can, however, leave people feeling awkward if the facilitator doesn't have a mastery of them. You must assess your own ability to create an engaging and meaningful exercise with these techniques.

Making Up and Presenting Skits

You might invite small groups to create short skits that demonstrate some significant points—"Illustrate how we work together," for instance, or "Create a TV spot, complete with jingle, to promote our new product line." Skits are almost always funny and memorable, especially if people are given hats, toys, or artifacts from their offices to work with.

A group can generally work up a skit in twenty minutes or less. But beware of participants becoming so wrapped up in the humor of their performance that the central point is lost. If your retreat includes an overnight stay, after-dinner skits can be an excellent way to get people working together and having fun at the same time.

Applying Theories to Real Situations

Before participants can fully engage in certain activities, they may need some theoretical background. In a strategic planning retreat, for example, they may need to understand different planning models.

If the theoretical framework is new to people, they frequently need time to try the ideas out before they can fully understand them. Don't assume that just because people have *heard* something that they *know* it—or even will remember it. We believe that theory should be presented in as experiential a manner as possible. It's better to give people small pieces of information, have them use the information in some way, and then move on to the next learning point.

Learning About What Has Happened Elsewhere

Hearing what is possible in another organization confronting similar issues can give participants a new lens through which to view old problems. As part of a series of planning retreats that we facilitated for an art museum, for example, members of the staff conducted a benchmarking study. First they identified organizations—not just museums, but amusement parks and department stores as well—that were renowned in areas the museum wanted to improve, such as customer service.

Museum staff interviewed people from the selected organizations and brought that information into the retreats. The group then adapted ideas from the benchmarking study to suggest more innovative ways for the museum to improve the experience of its visitors.

Using Metaphor to Express Thoughts and Feelings

Participants may need a way to express their feelings about sensitive issues in an indirect way. We frequently ask people to use metaphors (visual symbols) to describe how they feel. Metaphors can free people up to be more creative and more candid about issues they're reluctant to discuss.

At a retreat for a rather formal group of investment fund executives, for instance, we scattered Beanie Babies® around the room. When the executives began talking about how they worked together, we asked each person to choose an animal that represented how they saw their roles in the group.

These executives told us later that it proved easier for them, as high-powered and serious as they were, to grab a couple of toys to illustrate, "Everybody thinks I'm a shark, but inside I'm really a lamb," than it would have been to say, "Hey, you guys think I'm so tough, but I get my feelings hurt around here." This activity was memorable, fun, and helped loosen people up.

Envisioning Possibilities and Generating New Ideas

We all tend to fall back on what's familiar. It's hard sometimes to imagine what we've never seen. To create positive change in the workplace, however, people must be able to imagine how things could be. As a retreat designer, you'll need to boost participants' envisioning powers by structuring activities that help them reflect on what's possible. You might bring such materials as photographs and magazines to provide visual symbols that could trigger participants' imaginations.

Drawing, Writing Verse, Performing Songs, Making Collages

Using their aesthetic abilities often helps people think differently about issues. Drawing or making collages can be individual or group activities that help participants express what's on their minds. For instance, you could ask people to make a collage at the start of a long retreat that illustrates how they see the organization and then create a second collage at the end, to focus on the future they're aiming to create. You'd be surprised how many top executives enjoy rolling up their sleeves and really getting into this kind of activity.

Physical Activities

Most of us aren't accustomed to sitting in one place all day. Even in desk jobs, we wander down the halls, climb stairs, visit other offices, go out for lunch, walk to meetings. Retreat participants need similar opportunities to move around. On a nice day, you can send breakout groups outdoors and ask them to conduct their discussions while walking. (You'll definitely get a different result than from a seated discussion.) Ask people to move around to illustrate what they think. For instance, draw an imaginary line from one end of the room to the other and designate each end an opposite position: "The front of the room represents throwing out our budgeting process and inventing something completely new. The back of the room represents leaving our budgeting process exactly as it is. Arrange yourselves along a continuum. Where do you stand?" It's a great way to see what people are thinking, and it gets participants' blood circulating. (This sort of exercise is even more energizing when conducted in silence.)

The Importance of Timing

The check-in that launches the retreat and the exercises that start each day should engage participants fully; if they don't, people are likely to stay indifferent. And the activity that takes place after lunch should be lively. Get people out of their chairs, if possible. Otherwise, participants may fall into the post-lunch doldrums.

You'll also need to pay particular attention to the final activities of the retreat. They should be highly engaging and even inspiring, because the impression made in the final hours is likely to be the one they will remember. Just as the first exercise helps set people's expectations, the final activity colors their memory and judgment of the whole offsite.

Decision Making

Because decisions made at a retreat are often complex and involve a change in direction, it is critical that those decisions have the support of the participants and represent their best thinking.

There are several methods for making decisions, each with its advantages and disadvantages. Typically the group will need to use different methods at different times. But before you help the participants, determine what decision-making method they will use. You and they must be clear on the group's mandate: Do participants have the authority to make decisions on their own? Will their decisions have to be reviewed and endorsed by a higher authority? Are the participants charged with making recommendations only? It will be dispiriting to people if they learn after the fact that the decisions they thought they were authorized to make have been denied, amended beyond recognition, or ignored by top executives.

At each step of the process, participants need to know, "Are we deciding, or are we just recommending?" If the end product of the retreat is a set of recommendations, the group will need to spend some time assembling the rationale for their ideas and discussing how the recommendations will be presented to senior management.

Participants also need to know whether the recommendations they are making must fit within the organization's current resources of time, money, and people or if additional resources are available. If it's the former (and it often is), we ask the group to think how current resources can be used more effectively and to assume that these resources won't increase.

> For more information about decision making, see Chapter 8.

While such a limitation might seem inhibiting to people's creativity, it's far worse to encourage participants to generate a host of terrific ideas only to have senior management respond, "Sorry, we don't have the resources to do that." It's better for people to know in advance the constraints they're working within.

In addition to making final choices about goals and actions, the group will have to make other choices, and you will need a plan for guiding them through each type of decision.

Action Planning

For a thorough discussion of this topic, see Chapter 8, "The Nub: Action Planning," p. 146.

Planning how retreat participants will involve others in implementing (and perhaps modifying) recommendations is an important part of action planning—so important, in fact, that we have devoted Chapter 15 to that topic.

Well before the last few hours of the retreat, you will need to guide the group in making commitments to a specific plan of action. Even if the participants reached agreement on action items as they went along, you will have to put everything together and look at it in totality. (Sometimes a decision made on Day One will conflict with a decision made on Day Two.) That process will take several hours—possibly an entire morning or afternoon.

At this point, you're getting near the end of the retreat, when people's energy may be flagging, but there's still difficult work to be done. If the retreat lasts longer than a day, we suggest you review the notes at the end of the first day and consolidate key points on a few flip charts that will need to be included in the action plan. The group's work in action planning will be much more streamlined if people aren't trying to pick action points out of a blizzard of flip chart pages covered with abbreviations, arrows, and notes in a more or less legible handwriting.

A key part of action planning must focus on how the group will let people back at the office know what happened at the retreat and its likely effect on them. You'll need to discuss both the immediate questions that will come up on participants' first day back ("Well, how did it go? What did you all decide?") and the longer-term question of how to introduce, build support for, and implement proposed initiatives and changes. Responding effectively to the concerns of people who weren't at the retreat is critical to the success of any proposed changes.

Closing

At the end of the retreat, allow forty-five minutes to an hour for a closing exercise (we suggest several in Chapter 14). An effective closing exercise allows participants to reflect on the work they've done together, appreciate others' contributions, and prepare themselves to integrate what they've learned when they return to the office.

In this chapter, we examined the several elements of retreat design. We will move on to discuss what happens next, when it's show time—how the facilitator applies the design and leads the retreat.

SECTION THREE

The Facilitator's Guide to Leading the Retreat

Chapter 7

Leading the Retreat

Your primary job as facilitator is to lead the retreat. When you do your job well, you make it easier for the participants to achieve their objectives by creating an environment in which the hard things can be discussed.

In his book *Masterful Facilitation,* A. Glenn Kiser (1998) defines facilitation as "a purposeful, systematic intervention into the actions of an individual or group that results in an enhanced, ongoing capability to meet desired objectives."

We like that definition because to be an effective facilitator, you have to be purposeful. You must know what you are doing and why you are doing it at all times. You must be willing to intervene to help the group become aware of how they work together and to explore more productive ways of interacting.

A key element of Kiser's definition is "to meet desired objectives." The point of facilitation is not to foster change for its own sake, but to help the group reach its goals. For this reason, you must understand these goals and ensure that participants agree on what they are.

> The word "facilitation" comes from the Latin root "facilis," which means "easy."

Your Effect on the Group

By your very presence—even if you do nothing—you are intervening in the group. Anthropologist Margaret Mead noted that simply by observing another culture you affect and subtly alter it. Similarly, merely by shining a light on participants' typical behavior when they're working together, you help foster changes in their behavior.

You need to monitor what is going on in the room at all times and be able to guide participants through difficult discussions, both by knowing when to prod them forward and when to encourage them to change course.

A facilitator is like a traffic cop—keeping the conversation flowing, noticing when the stoplights are broken, and reacting quickly to prevent nasty accidents. This means you must be very alert to what is happening and anticipate what is about to happen. You must respond skillfully, so participants feel they are being guided to a destination they want to reach.

The key to effective facilitation is self-awareness. You should be keenly aware of what you are experiencing at any given moment and be able to elicit responses from the participants about how your experience matches theirs. In addition, you will have to make conscious choices about how you behave when interacting with the group, since they will look to you as a model.

As a facilitator, you'll want to help participants accomplish several things:

- Create a positive, collaborative environment in which they can explore common interests and goals
- Participate actively
- Stay on task and complete their work
- Establish a framework for addressing issues
- Create a safe space for surfacing, exploring, and addressing difficult issues
- Distinguish between concerns about content (such as finding a solution to a certain problem) and those about process (such as people feeling pressured to come to agreement)
- Manage conflict effectively
- Ensure that everyone who has something to say is heard
- Examine and modify behavior that is hampering the group's effectiveness

- Stimulate the widest range of thinking
- Identify and solve problems
- Make intelligent decisions
- Summarize agreements
- Determine appropriate action steps

In their classic book *Theory in Practice: Increasing Professional Effectiveness,* Chris Argyris and Don Schön (1974) talk about three values that we believe are the underpinnings of effective retreat facilitation:

- *Valid Information.* Participants share all relevant information in a way that others can understand it and, if necessary, verify it independently. This means that you as the facilitator have no hidden agenda and will encourage everyone in the room to be straightforward about what they want and don't want.
- *Free and Informed Choice.* Participants define their own goals (within larger organizational goals) and determine the methods for achieving them. They are not coerced or manipulated into making choices against their will.
- *Internal Commitment to the Choice.* Participants take responsibility for their own choices and make those choices because they find them intrinsically rewarding.

We suggest you abide by these values and encourage the group to commit to them as well.

There must be an explicit agreement with the group about what your role is and what it isn't. While you may deal most directly with the convenor, it must be clear to the convenor and the participants that you're working for the good of the whole group. Although this message should be communicated to the participants in advance, we encourage you to reinforce it at the beginning of the retreat.

Process or Content Facilitator?

Every facilitator has a different approach to leading retreats, and you'll want to make sure yours is compatible with the organization's culture and consistent with the convenor's expectations.

The convenor may want you to be a *process facilitator* or a *content expert,* or possibly to play some of both roles.

As a Process Facilitator

If you will be acting as a process facilitator, your focus will be on helping the participants understand how they are working together to accomplish their tasks. You will observe who speaks up and who does not and how participants interact and collaborate with one another. (Do they interrupt each other or listen respectfully? Are ideas considered or are they rejected out of hand? Is communication generally supportive or competitive? Who makes decisions and how are they made?) You will help participants set ground rules at the beginning of the retreat and call attention to those rules as needed. You will keep the discussions focused and ensure that everyone can be heard.

At appropriate times, you may question the participants about the way they are working together. In doing so, you'll help them see and correct dysfunctional communication patterns.

Even if you are doing pure process facilitation, you should be knowledgeable about the organization and the issues participants are concerned about. If you don't have personal experience in an industry, do some research—reading internal reports provided by the convenor, checking out websites, reviewing industry trend reports, even conducting some outside interviews—to make sure you understand the business and can speak its language. Knowledge of the full range of an organization's concerns will pay off in countless ways. No client will be pleased about a retreat—no matter how flawless the process—that led to decisions that the organization couldn't support. Unless you are knowledgeable enough about the organization and the issues it faces, you might inadvertently lead a retreat that wastes the whole group's time.

As a Content Facilitator

If you have content knowledge, you can draw on your experience with other organizations in the same industry as well as your expertise in areas such as strategy or teamwork to help participants make more informed decisions. By paying attention to the content of the work and not just the processes, you will be able to challenge participants to examine their assumptions, help them make thoughtful decisions, and ask the group tough questions about actions they are proposing to take. In *Organization Consulting: A Gestalt Approach,* author Ed Nevis (1987) describes this as the difference between "evocative" and "provocative" modes of influence.

When working in the *evocative* mode, the facilitator helps the group gain "fresh awareness" of its behavior with the aim of fostering action. A facilitator might observe, "You seem to be reluctant to address this issue openly. You're talking around it, and you're stuck. To break through, you'll have to confront the issue head on." The facilitator would then help ensure that the group dealt with the issue forthrightly and didn't wander off into a thicket of euphemisms and tangents.

In the *provocative* mode, the facilitator intervenes to sharpen the group's focus and press the participants toward a specific goal or narrow range of possible outcomes. A facilitator might say, "You keep talking about several options for dealing with the problem, yet from what I've heard you say and what I know of your organization, three of the options clearly are beyond the range of what's doable, and two of the others are practically identical. I think you're more likely to come up with a practical action plan if you focus only on X and Y, decide which of the two you prefer, and move on from there."

While a facilitator typically acts to increase awareness so that participants can find their own way, sometimes provoking them is the only way to help them reach a viable goal. You might, for example, want to press participants to explain, "What makes you so sure your idea will work? Have you considered. . .?" The point is not to pass judgment on the participants' proposals or decisions, but to urge them to explore every aspect of an issue so they can come up with the most thoughtful and feasible conclusions.

Content knowledge allows you to play this provocative role. Sometimes asking "naïve" or incredulous questions can stimulate participants to see things more clearly. "Are you saying that if you take this action, you're likely to get this result?" a facilitator might ask. "Hmm," a participant might respond, "I guess that doesn't make much sense, does it?"

You and the convenor should decide in advance of the retreat whether you will focus strictly on process or whether you will become involved with content as well.

When Should the Facilitator Intervene?

You need to help participants recognize behaviors that are fostering or hampering their effectiveness by calling attention to them yourself and by continually making decisions about whether it is helpful or not to intervene when confronted with specific dysfunctional behaviors.

Our advice is to intervene only when it is truly necessary and only when you are reasonably sure that your intervention will advance the discussion. Before jumping in to "help" participants, ask yourself these questions. If your answer is yes to any of them, *do not* intervene.

- Does the dysfunctional behavior seem like a one-time occurrence that participants will move beyond easily?
- Is the behavior bothering only you, not the group?
- Will a member of the group likely intervene if you do not?
- Will the intervention distract the group from tackling a tough issue?
- Would intervening later, if necessary, be as useful as intervening now?
- Are you so staked in the outcome that it will upset you if the group rejects your intervention?
- Might the intervention take more time than the group has available to process it?

On the other hand, you don't want to adopt a hands-off style that invites participants to waste time on fruitless discussions. If you decide it is appropriate to intervene, you must determine which of three levels of intervention—personal, interpersonal, or group—is most likely to elicit the best response.

Let's say you have noticed that the participants keep wandering off task, largely because Lisa keeps bringing up extraneous matters and Silvio is arguing with her.

A *personal intervention* might be simply to encourage Lisa to remain focused on the agenda. Or it might be to remind Silvio of the ground rule: Listen to understand, not to judge.

An *interpersonal intervention* might be to have Silvio and Lisa practice giving and receiving feedback effectively.

But in this case, the best course of action would probably be a *group intervention*. After all, the whole group is allowing Silvio and Lisa to derail the conversation. Reminding the group about the ground rules and stressing the need to stick to the agenda (or to decide explicitly that another topic is more important) would probably be the most beneficial intervention.

Or let's say that the group is getting off track because every time Chris raises a question, Ron rolls his eyes and tells Chris that the question is irrelevant to the discussion at hand. Other group members try to defend Chris, whom they think was attacked, but Ron's behavior does not change. In this case, the best intervention would likely be personal—calling Ron's attention to the ground rules, for example.

Facilitators, particularly inexperienced ones, are often tempted to intervene any time there is a strong emotional reaction in the room, especially if someone becomes angry or bursts into tears. This is treacherous terrain. We urge you to curb your natural instincts to "make everything all right." It's perfectly okay to remain silent when someone becomes emotional.

Emotional responses might occur when participants are:

- Dealing with an issue that has been frustrating them for a long time and just discussing it is releasing pent-up feelings
- Feeling threatened in some way
- Feeling embarrassed or exposed
- Passionate about a particular course of action and are concerned that the organization is moving in the "wrong" direction
- Feeling left out, unheard, ignored, or not valued
- Feeling pressured to support the growing consensus in the room, with which they disagree
- Preoccupied with something else that is unrelated to the subject under discussion (Someone may be worried about a family problem or be very tired)

Allowing an airing of these emotions will often reveal the passions in the room and save the group from making costly mistakes. Such mistakes occur when groups rush discussions along on a wave of emotion or in a misguided effort to defuse that emotion.

It's common for emotions to rise to the surface at retreats, and we think this is generally a positive development because emotions are a sign that participants care about the issues. Emotions *per se* shouldn't be of concern; intervene only if they lead to dysfunctional behavior such as name calling, negative stereotyping, or the threat of physical violence.

It's a different story, though, when a participant becomes emotional with you. Then you must respond, not to the emotions but to what triggered them.

First, ask yourself whether the person's emotional response may have been prompted by something inappropriate that you did or said. If so, don't be defensive. Acknowledge the person's point of view, explain your intention, and express regret for the impact. This has the added benefit of modeling the kind of behavior that will help the participants themselves work together most productively.

If you are convinced that the emotional reaction is really an attempt (conscious or not) to distract the group from a difficult issue, it is worth drawing out not only that participant but others as well. Asking the group what you might do to make it easier to discuss a particular issue will often lower the emotional temperature by focusing people on something practical.

Giving Feedback to Retreat Participants

As a facilitator, you have a great deal of power. You can interrupt the proceedings. You can make a participant look good in the eyes of her co-workers or embarrass another.

By the mere act of standing up in the front of the room, you are having an impact on the participants. It may or may not be the impact you intend. Most facilitators have good intentions; they want to help the participants work together better. The key is for you to match your impact with your intent.

This is especially true if you decide it's absolutely necessary for the work of the group to give feedback to individual participants. If Ed has been interrupting Carolina every time she speaks, for instance, and if subtle reminders of the ground rules haven't made an impact on Ed's behavior, you might want to raise the issue with him privately at the next break (or even call a break if Ed's behavior is disruptive enough that it cannot be allowed to continue). You're not trying to embarrass him, only to call his attention to his behavior and the impact it is having on the group. So don't confront him in public. If you do, everyone else in the room will take note of your action.

Ask permission first ("May I talk with you about something, Ed?") and be sensitive about your timing. Don't give feedback to a participant who is in the throes of an intense emotional reaction. He won't be able to hear it. Then take care to describe specific, observable behavior, not your opinions or judgments. ("I couldn't help noticing that you keep interrupting Carolina, and this is making it very difficult for Carolina to be heard.") Finally, ask Ed for the behavior that would be more helpful instead. ("You'll have a chance to express yourself, but it would help your colleagues if you'd let Carolina have her say without interrupting her.")

If all else fails, ask the convenor what she wants you to do. She might then have to tell Ed that if he wants to participate in the retreat, he must abide by the ground rules.

Working with Co-Facilitators

There are advantages and disadvantages to having more than one facilitator in the room.

We like having co-facilitators at retreats and believe that when two facilitators work together well, clients benefit from the equation that one plus one equals more than two. It's exhausting for one facilitator to be monitoring too many things at once and, over the course of a multi-day retreat, even the most seasoned facilitator is likely to become fatigued and may miss something important.

When two facilitators collaborate effectively, they trade off responsibilities seamlessly. While one is setting up an activity, for example, the other may be scanning the room to make sure everyone understands the directions. Or they can watch for different behaviors that might be interfering with the group's effectiveness.

Facilitators are human beings. We all have our blind spots and emotional triggers. Working with a colleague can help us see the whole picture and respond appropriately. And co-facilitators can give us feedback that will help us improve how we interact with the group.

It's disastrous to the group's effectiveness, however, if facilitators start jockeying for power. To avoid such messiness, co-facilitators must take the time to negotiate how they will work together *before* they agree to lead a retreat. If they find they have values differences or don't think they can work collaboratively, they should *not* lead a retreat together.

Even with the best intentions and extensive pre-planning, co-facilitators will sometimes disagree about the best course of action to take at a given moment. Here's how we handle it:

- We never contradict or correct one another in front of the group.
- We check in and consult with one another frequently. (During breaks, we ask each other how effectively we handled a particular intervention, for example, or if we should change course based on something that happened in the room.)
- We ask for help from one another publicly when we need it. We might say, for instance, "Did I cover everything I was supposed to?" This creates an opening for the other person to chime in.
- We debrief one another at the end of each session and each day, as well as after the whole retreat to explore what worked well and what we might do differently next time.

Every facilitator team will have to establish its own norms for working together, but the important thing is to have these discussions in advance. Here are some of the things we recommend discussing with any potential co-facilitator:

- How open are you to changing the agenda in response to what is happening in the room?
- When do you believe it's important to intervene and when do you like to leave things up to the group?

- How do you want to handle our differences if they occur in front of the group?
- What are some of the things you do particularly well as a facilitator? Are there areas of your facilitation skills you would like to develop? Can I help you in some way to sharpen those areas?
- When one of us is presenting in front of the room, what do you think the other should be doing?

For Internal Facilitators: Partnering with Another Facilitator

If you are an employee of the organization that is convening the retreat, there are occasions when you might want to work with an external facilitator. Perhaps you are interested in strengthening your own facilitation skills by collaborating with someone more experienced, or you might want to enhance your credibility with the group so you can lead post-retreat sessions successfully. Or the size or complexity of the group might require two facilitators.

Internal consultants often opt for partnerships with external consultants because internal consultants may be perceived (often unfairly) as more biased about outcomes than external consultants. In addition, when an internal facilitator challenges something the boss says, she runs the risk—which an external facilitator does not—of appearing insubordinate or disloyal. By the same token, if an internal consultant agrees with or goes along with something the boss says, she may be seen as currying the boss's favor.

Experienced external consultants can more easily negotiate how they will work with the convenor and senior management, both behind the scenes and in front of the group. For instance, we use our role as objective outsiders to coach executives on what behaviors might foster or hinder the success of the retreat. If the behavior of a senior manager seems counterproductive to the work of the retreat, we are able to take that person aside during a break and discuss our concern, something that might be difficult for an internal facilitator to do.

The internal facilitator in such an arrangement can contribute a deeper knowledge of the organization and its culture and a greater acquaintance with the people in the room. The external facilitator contributes expertise in designing and leading retreats as well as a more independent status.

Often the reasons for two internal facilitators to partner with one another are similar to those for working with an external facilitator. For example, the retreat might require two facilitators but the organization cannot afford to hire outside expertise. While two internal facilitators can work effectively together, they should discuss how they'll collaborate in advance to overcome this arrangement's potential liabilities. These include the perception that one or both facilitators are biased, that they are not free to stand up to an overbearing executive, or that they may compete against one another for top management's attention.

Diversity Issues at the Retreat

Your job requires that you be aware of and sensitive to the role that diversity plays at a retreat. It's a delicate balancing act to remain attuned to possible cultural differences while at the same time not categorizing participants' responses as the products of their cultural identity. Some of the diversity variables that you'll have to consider are related to the organization itself (what part of the organization individuals work in, their position in the hierarchy, the length of their tenure, the breadth of their experience), and some have to do with individual backgrounds (age, gender, race, ethnicity, national origin, religion, and even personality preferences).

Cultural disconnects occur when behavior that is the norm in one cultural group (ethnic, racial, religious, and so forth) is inappropriate in another, creating a kind of "We're okay, you're not okay" mentality. Such clashes can be destructive when the individuals involved are unaware that the different behavior stems from different cultural values and norms and instead judge the behavior in absolute, right-wrong terms.

Cultural differences can come up in many ways at a retreat. Let's say Heather expresses frustration with Sam because Sam "won't stand up for what he believes." Heather sees Sam's reticence and reluctance to take issue with others' opinions as evidence of his lack of intellect, paucity of ideas, and shameless fawning. But Sam is merely acting in a way that he considers respectful; according to his cultural norms, you simply don't challenge others in public.

As the facilitator, you must be mindful of how adherence to different cultural norms might affect interactions among participants, not only at the retreat itself but back at the office as well. Reactions to such interactions could run the gamut from simple misunderstandings to unexpressed resentment to open and angry confrontation. You'll have to help the group manage possible cultural clashes before they hamper its effectiveness. At the same time, you have to engage everyone in the work of the retreat and foster behavior in keeping with the ground rules the participants agreed to—a balance that is sometimes difficult to maintain.

More Resources on Diversity

Diversity is a vast, complex, and important topic, which we cannot possibly fully address in this book. For facilitators who want to learn more, we recommend the following:

- *Redefining Diversity*, by R. Roosevelt Thomas (1996)

- *Intercultural Communication in the Global Workplace*, by Iris Varner and Linda Beamer (1995)

- *The Promise of Diversity*, edited by Elsie Y. Cross, Judith H. Katz, Frederick A. Miller, and Edith W. Seashore (1994)

- *Workplace Diversity*, by Katharine Esty, Richard Griffin, and Marcie Schorr-Hirsch (1995)

Some—but by no means all—of the cultural dimensions that might affect how participants interact during the retreat include:

- How direct and candid individuals are willing to be in a group setting
- What level of formality and respect participants believe is proper
- Participants' perspectives on time
- Participants' orientation toward the individual or toward the group
- Participants' comfort showing emotion
- Participants' comfort with physical closeness
- Language differences
- The meaning of body language

How Direct and Candid Individuals Are Willing to Be in a Group Setting

See Chapter 6, "Content Segments," pp. 100–102, for ideas on how to vary the exercises to help all participants feel free to contribute.

Certain cultures rely more on context and subtle non-verbal cues to express meaning, while others value "putting all the cards on the table." Since the retreat format favors the latter, we recommend that you structure exercises that will encourage more reticent participants to contribute.

What Level of Formality and Respect Participants Believe Is Proper

Some cultures are very hierarchical and formal. Titles are important. People typically address strangers, their elders, and social and organizational superiors by titles or last names and may consider the practice of using first names even with strangers—which is increasingly common in business settings in the United States—to be disrespectful. People in such cultures rarely express disagreement with their seniors (in age and rank), particularly in public settings. Contrast that with a culture that is more informal and where leaders value dissenting views. Since the retreat format favors the latter (at least nominally), it's important to take this potential cultural difference into account when structuring and leading the various exercises.

Participants' Perspectives on Time

In his book *The Dance of Life: The Other Dimension of Time*, cultural anthropologist Edward Hall (1983) contrasts cultures that value punctuality, adherence to schedules, and accomplishing tasks with those that give interpersonal relations precedence over precise schedules and specific accomplishments. In a retreat setting, you'll have to manage the push and pull between the two orientations, as participants struggle with task and process issues.

Participants' Orientation Toward the Individual or the Group

Some cultures encourage individuals to look after themselves and their immediate families primarily (broadly speaking, majority American culture is an example), while other cultures stress the primary importance of looking after the welfare of larger groups to which individuals belong. In the former it is perfectly appropriate to recognize the work of an individual. In the latter, it might not be. You'll have to keep these differences in mind when structuring activities where the work of individuals might be recognized. This might also come up if you ask participants to express their personal views and not represent their teams, departments, or divisions.

Participants' Comfort Showing Emotion

Some cultures value emotional expression, and others value keeping emotions in check (although there are obviously individual variations and personal preferences within both traditions). You have to be cognizant of these differences throughout the retreat, as emotional responses often come out during discussions. This will help you guide the group's discussions, balancing sensitivity to differences with the need to avoid (and help the group avoid) stereotyping participants' reactions.

Participants' Comfort with Physical Closeness

The concept of personal space differs from culture to culture and within cultures. What feels intuitively appropriate in one culture might seem like a violation of personal space in another. Since certain retreat exercises may have participants working in closer proximity than some in the group might feel comfortable with, be sensitive to this possibility when designing and leading retreat activities.

Language Differences

Words in the same language can have different meanings from one culture to the next, depending on the context. We were doing some work in Africa with a mixed group of Africans and Americans. During the course of a retreat, an American participant expressed some frustration that when he was told that something would happen "any time from now," nothing transpired while he waited. The American thought that phrase meant "right away." One of his African colleagues explained that it meant literally "*any* time from now," and probably later rather than sooner. Moreover, people who are communicating in a second or foreign language are likely to miss some of the nuances associated with word choice—meanings that most native speakers would recognize immediately, usually without even thinking about it.

As a facilitator, it's important to be aware of the potential snares associated with language, to define terms that might be unclear or have different meanings to different people, and to notice when people are talking past each other or reacting to incorrect meanings they attach to something someone else said.

While the potential for misunderstanding may be fairly obvious when the participants are an international group, there will also inevitably be differences among those who ostensibly speak the same language, such as, for instance, operations and marketing staff, or program directors and administrative personnel. You'll have to be mindful of those as well.

The Meaning of Body Language

In some cultures, it's what you say that's important; in others, it's how you act. If someone quietly says she's upset about something that happened, members of cultures that emphasize the importance of body language might ignore the comment or not take it seriously because it was not accompanied by congruent behavior such as raising her voice, for example. They may not understand that the words alone are expressing a serious concern for the speaker. And identical behavior doesn't necessarily convey the same meaning from culture to culture. For example, in one culture, giggling might mean that someone is terribly embarrassed; in another, it might mean that someone finds what's being said amusing.

How can you tell for sure? You can't; so to ensure that people understand what others are saying and are not misinterpreting one another's words or body language, you'll sometimes have to play the role of cultural anthropologist and ask questions that help shed light on possible misunderstandings.

Managing Differences

Sometimes it's hard to distinguish between cultural norms and personality differences. No behavior is common to all members of a culture, so resist the temptation to stereotype.

While cultural differences may be real and are not in any way trivial, they do not have to tie you or the group in knots. Just as you might help participants navigate the communication differences between extroverts and introverts, so might you have to help them bridge cultural differences, which, although more subtle, can still be brought to the surface and managed.

It's important not to ignore these differences or favor one cultural tradition over another. That would be like a Peruvian telling a Belgian that Spanish is better than French. Rather, you'll need to design and lead the retreat in such a way that participants from various cultural backgrounds can contribute in equal measure to its success.

There is no absolute rule for dealing with cultural differences, but this general guideline may be helpful: Participants should respect the same behavioral norms they do in the workplace in addition to adhering to the ground rules they established for the retreat. Thus, for example, if the organization wouldn't tolerate someone arriving late for an important meeting back at the office, neither should such behavior be allowed at the retreat, even if it might be more acceptable in one culture than in another.

Similarly, if the ground rules call for everyone to participate actively in discussions and activities, those who are inclined toward reticence (whether as a cultural imperative or as a personality trait) should be encouraged to speak up at the retreat, just as those who tend to be outspoken, for whatever reason, should be urged to hold back and make space for others to express themselves. While you'll want to help participants be sensitive to cultural differences, they may all have to get out of their comfort zones at some points during the retreat if anything meaningful is to be accomplished.

Encouraging Participation

The success of the retreat will depend in large measure on your ability to elicit broad participation. The following examples provide guidelines to help you keep participants involved in the discussion.

Encourage Participants to Engage the Issue. It's natural for people to be reticent when they're dealing with issues that are difficult, even scary. You can help participants overcome this by urging them to say what's on their minds. Ask such questions as, "Rayna, do you have thoughts about this?" or "Do you have anything to add, Tojo?" When you ask the group, "Does anyone have anything to add?" wait, wait, wait for someone to respond. A moment of silence (even an uncomfortably long moment of silence) can stimulate someone to speak up who might otherwise remain silent. Some people tend to be quieter than others and may actually be fully engaged even if they are not saying much—and often you can't tell unless you ask.

Ask Clarifying Questions. When you don't understand something completely, ask the person to provide more details: "Bill, could you tell us a bit more about how this new procedure would change your job?" If you aren't sure (or think participants aren't sure) what someone is proposing, check for understanding by asking a question like: "I'm not certain I understand exactly what you mean, Paula. Are you proposing that we follow Chip's recommendation?"

Ask for Suggestions. As a facilitator, you don't have to have all the answers. Sometimes it's helpful to ask a participant: "Philomena, how would you suggest that we proceed on this?"

Paraphrase. Restate what a participant has said to confirm whether you understood him or her. ("Andi, let me see if I understand your perspective on this issue. Are you saying that. . . ?") If so, other participants will hear a concise summary of the speaker's point to confirm their own understanding. If you've missed the point, chances are that others have too, and your question will give the participant a chance to clarify.

Be careful, however, when you are capturing peoples' comments on a flip chart. You won't be able to write everything in its entirety, so you'll have to summarize. Even though you'll have to edit for space, however, try to use as many of the person's exact words as possible and check with the person you're quoting. ("Does this reflect what you said, Larry?") Interpreting someone else's meaning can make it appear that you don't understand, don't approve of, or disagree with what the person said.

Suggest a Process. Have some procedures handy for those times when the group gets stuck. You might ask the group if they need to revisit the ground rules, suggest that participants take on another person's point of view, or conduct a quick vote to see if the group is ready to move on.

Ask for Options. When the group seems to be concluding a discussion too quickly, you can encourage them to explore other options with questions such as: "Are there other ways to approach this problem, Jon?" "Marlene, is there anything else you think we should consider?" "Briana, do you see another way we can do this?" Don't beat a dead horse, though. If the group is done, it's done.

Ask Participants to Pair Up or Conduct a "Round Robin." When it is very important to give everyone a chance to discuss a key issue, you can ask participants to pair up and report their conclusions back to the group. Or on rare occasions you might conduct a "round robin," asking each participant to speak in turn. We recommend reserving this technique for when you absolutely must hear from everyone in the room. It will quickly grow tedious if participants who have little to add to what others have said feel compelled to say something anyway. And if someone doesn't want to comment, allow him or her to pass. The point here is to give everyone a chance to speak up, not force people to say something.

Reflect What You Read in Someone's Body Language. Body language can be a more powerful form of communication than words, but don't assume that you know what someone else is thinking just by observing them. Ask such questions as, "Jeremy, I sense that you don't agree with Sharon's proposal. Is that right?" or "Roshana, you seem to be uncomfortable with David's response. Am I right about that?"

Pull Ideas Together. Help participants see how their ideas relate to one another and encourage them to build on each other's suggestions. An observation such as, "From what we've heard from Ahmed and Alicia, it seems that you have the resources and commitment to expand sales in the eastern region," can help participants see common ground.

Ask for a Summary or Provide One Yourself. At key points in the conversation, it is very important to have a summary of what has been proposed or agreed to. You should periodically ask questions such as, "Can someone summarize what we've agreed to do?" Do not ask a question like, "Does everyone understand what you've agreed to so far?" because people might think they do, even if they don't. Or they all might be afraid to admit that they don't.

It's helpful to have participants themselves summarize agreements or action steps. It encourages the group to take responsibility for the commitments being made. If no one else can summarize, however, don't belabor the point. Just summarize and move on.

Changing the Plan

What's important is not that you follow your retreat plan but that you achieve the outcome. At the end of each segment, ask yourself, "Have we gotten to where we need to be at this point?" If the group has reached agreement on an issue sooner than you expected, you may be able to skip the next planned activity. Or if things haven't gone as smoothly as you had hoped, you may have to decide on the spot to lead an activity you hadn't planned on.

What comes up spontaneously during a retreat is often at the core of what can propel a change initiative forward or stop it in its tracks. For example, several people we interviewed in preparing a retreat for the international division of a telecommunications company expressed concern that the division was not dealing with diversity issues with enough sensitivity. They told us how people of different nationalities were offending one another without necessarily intending to. We designed activities we thought would help participants get to the root of some of these issues.

In the middle of one of the activities, Dennis said testily, "This is stupid! Nobody would respond in real life in the polite ways we are in this exercise."

Had we been wedded to our agenda, we might have simply thanked Dennis for his observation and continued the exercise. Instead, we engaged him in a conversation about how he saw the communication issues. Dennis talked about how hurt he felt when he was blamed for offending someone and how much he disliked being thought of as insensitive.

His candor and passion sparked an intense discussion in the group about the causes of conflict in the division and how they might be addressed. As a result, participants got to the source of something that was irritating many of them and agreed on a framework for how they wanted to manage the differences that would certainly occur among a multi-ethnic staff.

The discussion went on much longer than we had planned, but had we ignored what was going on in the room, the participants would not have made such a dramatic breakthrough on this important concern. After all, the point of any activity is to engage participants and get at real issues, not merely to complete the activity and move on.

This is not to suggest that you can get away with developing only a sketchy idea of what you are going to do and then improvise from moment to moment. On the contrary, we typically prepare much more than we'll have time for because we can't be certain what will come up, and we want to be able to take advantage of real-time opportunities that arise. And no matter what we plan for, we'll almost always be surprised by what happens in the room and find ourselves designing something on the spot to move the group forward.

In this chapter, we covered several key aspects of facilitating the retreat you've designed. We discussed the differences between a process facilitator and a content expert, when the facilitator should intervene at the retreat, and how and when to give feedback to participants. We explored the issue of co-facilitation, for independent consultants and their internal counterparts, as well as the topic of diversity. Finally, we focused on how to encourage active participation and on the importance of flexibility—the willingness and ability to alter your design to take advantage of something significant that might be happening in the room.

In Chapter 8, we explore various decision-making techniques, look at how different kinds of decisions might play out at the retreat, and discuss how to help the group make decisions throughout the retreat that will lead to concrete action planning.

Chapter 8

Helping Participants Make Decisions and Plan for Action

Retreats are all about making decisions. Participants must decide what their priorities are, what to change, what actions to take after the retreat is over, and how to implement those actions. How participants make these decisions and how careful they are in planning for action are likely to determine the ultimate success or failure of the retreat. A key role for you as facilitator is to help participants make sound decisions and create action plans they will be willing and able to implement.

Just as there are many delicious dishes you can order at a fine restaurant, there are many effective ways to make decisions. Each has advantages and disadvantages, and any of them might be the best, depending on the circumstances and on what the group is trying to accomplish.

Methods of Decision Making

One of the most important things participants must decide is how they are going to make decisions. You'll have to be prepared in advance to help them decide which decision-making methods they will employ. If participants apply the appropriate decision-making techniques at the right times, it's more likely that the decisions will stick and gain widespread support.

Here's the menu:

- *Executive Authority*—the leader decides
- *Consultative Executive Authority*—the leader decides after seeking the group's perspective
- *Majority Rule*—the majority decides by voting
- *Decision by Default*—someone suggests a course of action and no one raises objections, even though some group members harbor doubts
- *Moving Right Along*—an idea is never considered because the group has moved on too quickly to the next idea
- *Minority Activism*—a few people use their influence to make the decision for the group
- *Compromise*—everyone gives up something in order to get something they can all live with
- *Consensus*—everyone agrees to support the decision
- *Unanimous Consent*—everyone is enthusiastic about the decision

Executive Authority

The most senior person makes the final decision on his or her own, involving few, if any, others in the process. This is a highly efficient way to make decisions,

Defining Moments

It's important that participants have a common understanding of what often-misused words mean. Many people think "consensus," for example, is the same as "majority." You may hear, "We've achieved an overwhelming consensus." Actually, as with pregnancy, there aren't degrees of consensus; you either have it or you don't.

There is also a common misunderstanding about the difference between consensus and unanimous consent, because in both instances everyone is in agreement. But there is a clear difference. In a consensus, everyone agrees to support the decision *even if it isn't their first choice.* (The approval of the U.S. Declaration of Independence is a good example, because there were many disagreements but all states agreed to the final document.) In the case of unanimous consent, there is no disagreement; everyone supports the decision without reservation.

but we don't recommend using this method at a retreat, as the whole purpose of convening an offsite is to involve the participants in decision making. If the executive *does* intend to make the final decision, however, that fact should be made clear at the outset.

Consultative Executive Authority

The top executive makes the final decision, but only after seeking input. Sometimes the executive might ask for the advice in the form of options to choose from.

This method is better than deciding by executive authority alone, because it takes multiple perspectives into consideration. (In fact, most decisions made by executive authority are really consultative to some extent, because the senior person is likely to have been listening to others all along.) Still, we recommend avoiding this method in a retreat setting, except in cases where the executive has relevant information other participants lack and that for some reason cannot be shared.

Majority Rule

The participants decide by a simple majority (or a pre-determined higher majority such as two-thirds or three-quarters). Although counting hands is a relatively quick and easy way to make a decision—and it is the method most groups choose most of the time—it has a serious disadvantage. Voting can create a win/lose situation. Participants who are in the majority win all the marbles, and those who voted with the minority may feel resentful. As a result, the "losers" may continue to raise the issue long after others in the group think it has already been decided, or may even work to undermine the implementation.

This "winners take all" situation can be mitigated if participants negotiate compromises (see "Compromise," below), but even compromise doesn't entirely overcome the disadvantages of using majority rule. So while voting can be useful to give you a quick survey of how the participants are feeling (and perhaps help avoid lots of fruitless discussion only to find out that everyone is in agreement), we recommend using this method only when the stakes for the decision are low.

Decision by Default

Someone suggests a course of action, and no one raises questions or objections. It is assumed that everyone is in agreement, and the suggestion becomes the decision—even if some participants silently harbor doubts or are actually hostile to the idea. Decisions by default are made most often when an executive who does not like to be challenged is the one who offered the suggestion. They also occur in low-trust or risk-averse groups, when people are exhausted and simply want to end the discussion, or when participants don't really care about the outcome.

Ideally, decisions are never made by default. If this phenomenon occurs, make it a point to seek positive confirmation that everyone is in agreement, or ask whether anyone has an observation or objection.

Moving Right Along

This is perhaps the most common and least effective method of group decision making. Someone suggests an idea and, before the participants even discuss it, someone else makes another proposal, and the first idea is lost. Moving right along gives the illusion of progress, but it creates an environment in which potentially excellent ideas may be left unexplored.

Not only are ideas lost, but participants whose contributions get dismissed are likely to become disgruntled. Bring it to the group's attention when you notice decisions being made this way. Slow down the process before some participants, whose ideas are not heard, become disengaged.

Minority Activism

A small group (often senior managers or people with particularly strong personalities) employs tactics that push the rest of the participants into going along with a particular decision. This method can be useful when time is of the essence, but it often results in friction, resentment, and a desire to revisit the issue. ("I went along against my better judgment. Let's look at that again.")

If you sense this is happening, poll the group to see if there truly is agreement. If you believe that participants might be feeling intimidated by the activists, you can create an anonymous mechanism, such as passing the written votes to you.

Compromise

This is the classic horse trading that occurs in many group situations: "I'll give in on this if you give in on that." Sometimes people do have to give up something they want to get something else they want. In a retreat, where people often develop empathy for one another's concerns, the sacrifices may not seem so great. Compromise can also be a good tool for coming up with temporary solutions for complex issues that will have to be decided later, outside the retreat setting. The problem is that participants might end up with a decision that none of them is really satisfied with, and such decisions rarely are implemented back at work. If you see the participants making compromises on important issues, encourage them to discuss whether they are making decisions everyone is lukewarm about or even opposed to, and, if so, suggest an alternative technique.

Consensus

Consensus is reached when all participants in the discussion understand and are prepared to support the decision, even if it isn't their first choice. When people have reached a true consensus, all of them feel that they have had a fair chance to influence the decision and are willing to work to implement it, even if some would prefer another course of action.

Consensus is a valuable tool for making key decisions that require the widest possible support (such as core strategies the organization will pursue or whether it makes sense to eliminate a signature product or service). It offers the advantage that everyone can support the decision. But it also has the disadvantage of requiring a great deal of time and effort. That's why it is important not to use this method to make decisions about inconsequential matters, as doing so may create frustration and disillusionment with consensus building in general.

Participants should come to agreement, with your help if necessary, on how much time they want to devote to consensus discussions. Then if the group cannot achieve consensus in the agreed-on time, participants can opt for another decision-making process, such as majority vote, compromise, or executive authority, or put off reaching a decision until a later time.

Overuse of consensus is often a sign of a low level of trust. You can help the group see that not every decision requires support from everyone—only those who will be most affected need to decide. You might also explore with the participants the issue of trust if you sense that it is important to do so.

Unanimous Consent

Unanimous consent looks a lot like consensus, but there are key differences. You only have unanimous consent when everyone truly agrees on and enthusiastically supports the course of action to be taken. You can achieve consensus with only a willingness on everyone's part to support a certain decision. Moreover, unanimous consent is most often achieved quickly and with little dissent, in contrast to consensus, which typically takes a good deal of time and discussion to build.

Be cautious, however, about accepting unanimous consent at face value. If the participants are simply climbing on the bandwagon, the result can be similar to that of decision by default, and the enthusiasm might fade as reality sets in.

Types of Retreat Decisions

Typically, participants make a variety of decisions, both individual and collective, throughout the course of a retreat. They make decisions to set priorities, for example, or to determine what's core to their organization and what's peripheral. The kinds of decisions retreat participants have to make include:

- Ranking importance
- Rating quality
- Categorizing
- Limiting issues
- Prioritizing actions
- Sequencing actions

Ranking Importance

The group may have to rank in order of relative importance such things as specific customers, products, services, and training needs. A simple ranking exercise can have a dramatic impact on what the retreat accomplishes.

A paint manufacturer and retailer, for example, had to choose between emphasizing its contractor base, which accounted for 70 percent of sales but yielded very low margins, and its homeowner customers, who were fewer in number but whose purchases yielded a much higher profit. If the company ranked homeowners higher in importance than contractors, virtually everything about its marketing and service strategies would have to change (as would relationships with contractors that had been built over the years).

When the relative ranking isn't immediately clear to a group, a quick way to get a snapshot of participants' inclinations is to list the various elements on a flip chart and give each participant three large colored self-sticking dots to post next to their three highest priorities. When everyone has finished posting their dots, the group will easily be able to see from the number of dots next to each item which are the highest ranked. While this is a simple method, it can be misused. We don't recommend counting dots and using a difference of one or two to definitively rank one item over another. Use this method as a basis for discussions only, *not* as the final determinant of priorities. And in the case of close numbers, invite people to give reasons for how they voted.

> Self-sticking dots, available in office supply stores and elsewhere, may be called color-coding labels or garage sale stickers. We refer to them as voting dots.

Rating Quality

Sometimes the group may need to rate certain items for quality. Participants often want an overall picture of how well the organization is performing in various areas. Although empirical data are best for understanding how well the company is doing, sometimes that information isn't available.

At a retreat for the sales division of a telecommunications firm, for example, it was important to rate the company on questions such as: "How good are the materials we use to promote ourselves?" and "How good are the presentation skills of our new hires?" These are difficult answers to obtain from research, so the executive group had to rate the issues themselves.

The most efficient way to handle ratings of such issues is simply to ask everyone to write a number from 1 (lowest) to 10 (highest) for each item to be rated on a slip of paper, fold it, and pass it to the facilitator to be tallied and averaged. (Anonymity usually evokes honest responses, so be prepared for the ratings to be lower than the organization's leaders had expected.) Just as with ranking, however, the participants shouldn't treat the numbers as empirical data. Encourage them to discuss the initial ratings to see if any adjustments ought to be made.

Categorization

If you're facilitating a large retreat with lots of breakout groups, you'll quickly fill up multiple flip chart pages with information, much of it redundant. Before you can move on after an important exercise, the participants will often need to collapse a wide range of points and ideas into a smaller number of categories.

Sorting usually seems like a relatively easy task, and facilitators are often tempted to do it for the group to save time. But it's good practice for the participants to figure out how to do it themselves. In addition, you'll learn a lot about how decisions are made in the group by observing how they approach this effort.

At other times, the group may need to sort items into types to be able to see them differently. You might want to structure an exercise that helps a company that typically looks at its clients by geographic regions to assess them according to profitability or the variety of services they buy. Or you might guide the group through a more subjective sorting exercise: "Which of your departments are under-performing, and which deserve more recognition and rewards?" The more subjective the topic, the more dissension you can expect—and the longer it may take to reach agreement.

Limiting Issues

If the organization you're working with does not have an effective process for addressing problems, a retreat can easily unearth many more issues than can be dealt with effectively in the time available. When that happens, help the participants make choices about which issues must be dealt with at the retreat and which will have to be left to another forum.

Prioritizing Actions

Prioritizing actions is similar to ranking, except that it relates to specific action steps the group is considering. A lively retreat often generates many more ideas than the organization can possibly act on. Choosing the few action steps that will make the most difference isn't merely a matter of selecting the actions that people are most interested in or that can be accomplished most easily.

The factors that the participants need to consider in deciding their priorities include:

- Potential impact on their goals
- Resources needed to implement this action
- Time required
- Interest in or enthusiasm for the action (The enthusiasm issue is, by the way, an important one, because even if an action makes sense, someone has to be willing to undertake it.)

If there are several factors, it might be helpful to create a matrix on a flip chart that lists down the left side each action to be considered and across the top the issues that will factor into making a choice. For each potential action, ask the group to agree on how important each factor is, on a scale, say, from 1 (least) to 5 (most). The numbers in each cell will give the group a visual summary of how the factors might affect their priorities.

On the other hand, if the actions under consideration are not too complicated, "energy voting" can be a fast and effective way to make choices. List the options on a flip chart, hand out markers, and tell participants to put a check next to any item they have energy for—as many as they like. This is not one person-one vote democracy. You're trying to identify the ideas people are truly enthusiastic about.

One characteristic of energy voting is that people see how others vote. When the vote isn't particularly sensitive, this can be an advantage: Participants may find that their colleagues' energy is a positive reinforcement for their own feelings. But we do not use energy voting for a contentious issue, where individuals might be reluctant to reveal their interest or lack of interest in a particular option.

Sequencing Actions

Part of the action-planning process may involve putting items in a time sequence. Certain actions may be prerequisites for others; some actions may lead to decision points; or limited resources may dictate hard choices about what to do next.

Time-sequencing decisions, unlike most other retreat decisions, are usually best made not by the entire group but by the people who will have to perform the tasks. We recommend that you structure time-sequencing discussions to give first consideration to the opinions of those who will do the work.

The Nub: Action Planning

Although it is the fashion in planning these days to write long, detailed lists of actions, numbered software style (1.1.1) and intensely cross-referenced, that's not what we recommend for your retreat action plan.

Retreats are much more suited to identifying strategic initiatives—broad blueprints for change aimed at a few specific goals—than to drawing up detailed plans. The more goals and initiatives you have, the less likely they are to be achieved. It's far better to leave the retreat with a few well-thought-out initiatives and an agreement on how the group will achieve them than with a long list of action steps that no one will be able to remember.

Keep the action plan format simple. Even very bright people get stuck on the definitions of terms like *goal, objective, strategy, tactic,* and *action step.* You can capture the essence of the results that participants are aiming to achieve by asking them these questions, in the following order:

1. What results do we want to achieve?
2. How will we know we have achieved a result?
3. What do we have to do to achieve each result?
4. Who will do which of these things?
5. Do we have the resources to do these things? If not, how will we get the resources?
6. When will these actions be completed?
7. What obstacles will we have to overcome to complete these actions?

1. *What Results Do We Want to Achieve?*

The answer to this question outlines the goals the group is committed to. Be careful in framing the answers so that they reflect a *result,* not an *action.* For instance, "Let's reorganize into cross-discipline teams" is an action, not a strategic result. In this example, the result that the group wants to achieve (the goal) might be, "We want to improve the quality and speed of our response to members' requests." Organizing into cross-discipline teams might be an action step to help the group achieve that goal.

Sometimes it's easier to ask an even more basic question than, "What do we want to achieve?" such as, "What do we want to happen as a result of these actions?"

We strongly recommend that the group not leave the retreat with more than three goals. Most people can remember two or three ideas, but very few can recite a list of six or seven. Unless people can remember what they're trying to achieve on a day-to-day, moment-to-moment basis, it's not likely that the goals they set will be reflected in their everyday priorities.

If the participants come up with more than three goals, see if you can help them combine several into strategic initiatives that relate to each other.

2. *How Will We Know We Have Achieved a Result?*

"What gets measured gets done" is an old adage, but an accurate one, at least in organizations. For each goal, the group will need to devise a means of indicating progress and noting when that goal has been achieved.

The Five Whys

If the group has trouble differentiating desired results from actions, you might use a variation of the "Five Whys" exercise recommended by Senge, Roberts, Ross, Smith, and Kleiner (1994) in the *Fifth Discipline Fieldbook.* If you're not sure whether something is a core result or an action, ask, "Why is that important?" If the answer doesn't help you find what seems core, keep asking, "And why is *that* important?" to each subsequent answer. By the time you've asked five times or so, you should have the core result people are trying to achieve. (If not, keep asking.)

The most effective measures are quantifiable or directly observable. For instance, if the goal for a hands-on science center is to increase visitation by 15 percent, the participants would need to know the current visitor counts and that the center will continue to measure the number of visitors.

Often, though, the issues aren't that easy to quantify. If the center had the goal of increasing diversity among its visitors, retreat participants would have to be specific about what kind of diversity the institution is seeking—racial, economic, gender, age, and so forth—and it might well have no empirical mechanism for collecting that information. So part of the work of the group would be inventing—and finding the funding for—a quantitative measure. Even harder to measure might be "visitor satisfaction," and the group would have to be particularly creative in devising a means to measure that.

It's tempting for people to say, "We'll know if we've been successful" or to rely on anecdotal information. Unfortunately, that kind of thinking sets the stage for later debates based on opinion, not on fact. It's far better to take the necessary time at the retreat to work out measurement criteria.

3. *What Do We Have to Do to Achieve Each Result?*

To specify the actions that will move the organization toward each strategic initiative or broad goal, the group will need to create a list of specific tactical activities that will be the heart of the action plan.

As facilitator, you'll want to help participants ensure that the proposed actions reflect what people or groups will *do,* rather than what they will think or feel. It's useful to keep asking, "Is this an observable action? Will you be able to see from the results if it happens or not?"

When participants recommend changing how people work together, for example, they often want to list a change of attitude instead of a specific action. "We'll all be more understanding of other people's mistakes" is a nice thought, but it's not likely to survive more than two days back in the real world, nor is it observable or measurable. Instead, the group might plan to hold a monthly meeting to celebrate what they've learned from their mistakes, with an award for the best new ideas that grew out of those mistakes.

You'll also want to make sure the group is not devising actions that are all for *other people* to take. "Let's get the accounting department to start tallying the customer service evaluation forms" is easy to say when no one from accounting is there to protest. Action plans are much more likely to be implemented when they are created by the people who will be taking the actions or by the managers of the ultimate actors. If action plans do require the active assistance of people who aren't in the room, ask, for example, "And what do you think the accounting department will say about that? How can you get them involved and committed?"

While it's important to keep the number of goals small, each goal may have five to ten action steps. If an action is likely to take months to complete, you might consider breaking it into several shorter pieces. Shorter time frames allow the organization to monitor progress more effectively. (No one wants to get to the six-month mark and find out that essentially nothing's been done.) And having smaller chunks to work on gives people a sense of achievement as they finish each one.

When the participants complete their list of action steps, apply the "Necessary and Sufficient" test to see whether they have a coherent plan. You do that by asking two questions:

- *If You Do All Those Things, Will You Achieve the Goal?* In other words, are all these actions, taken together, *sufficient* for their plan to succeed? A long list of actions may sometimes obscure the point that, despite a burst of activity, the goal is still out of reach. A series of action steps that are insufficient to reach the goal may have the long-term effect of discouraging people from taking on new initiatives.
- *Do You Have to Do All the Things You've Listed to Achieve the Goal?* Could they eliminate some of the items and still reach their objective? Sometimes a popular project is built into an action plan when it doesn't actually relate to the goal. Or a group can be so enthusiastic about action ideas that the list becomes too long. In both cases, the action plan will use up resources that could be saved or applied to other needs.

4. Who Will Do Which of These Things?

Next to each action step should be a name or names of people *who have accepted responsibility* for ensuring it is implemented. Notice the emphasis on "who have accepted responsibility." If at all possible, you want people to volunteer or at least agree to take on responsibility for the implementation, whether they are going to do the work themselves, oversee the work of others whom they supervise, or work to build a coalition with others who aren't in the room. Assigning an action step to someone who doesn't want the responsibility or isn't present can be a recipe for disaster.

If there's something the group has agreed to but no one is willing to take on, it's not likely that it will be done well, if at all. If no one volunteers to assume responsibility for a certain action step, an executive may decide to assign it to someone in the room, but it would be prudent first to explore why no one is interested. Is it onerous work? If so, should it be shared by more people? Is it so high-risk that people are concerned that failure would put their careers on the line? How could the risk be minimized? Was the item put on the list because someone in power suggested it but no one else actually believes in it?

Reluctance to accept responsibility for action steps can signal many things, including a workforce that is already overtaxed, but it always means that more discussion is necessary before the group can conclude it has an action plan.

Other questions participants should consider in deciding who will be responsible for what include: How many people do you need for each action step? Can one person do this, or do you need a team? Should the team members all come from one department? Should the team include representatives from several parts of the organization or outside stakeholders?

Finally, the group must consider whether there are people who are not in the room who have a vital role to play in accomplishing these actions. How will the group involve them? For instance, if the company database needs to be reformatted or some market research is needed, those tasks will have to be done by people with the appropriate technical expertise, and they may not be taking part in the retreat. If so, the action plan should include a process for getting input from the people whose collaboration is essential before the final action steps are decided. They'll often have perspectives that the participants lack.

5. *Do We Have the Resources to Do These Things?*

In the excitement of coming up with new ideas, staying focused on reality can be a tough task. But if participants fail to recognize current reality, the final plan is unlikely to be implemented.

In the course of a board retreat for a nonprofit community-based organization, for example, the participants came up with an extensive list of action steps. There was no doubt that these actions would significantly raise the organization's profile—if they got done. But everyone on the board had other full-time obligations, and the staff was already working long days and coming in on weekends. "When do you plan to do all of this?" we asked. That question sent them back to the list, looking for the few actions that would give them the greatest leverage, taking into account their most limited commodity, time.

Another issue is that of information or knowledge. Do the people who will take certain actions have the information they need? They may have to enroll in training courses or do a benchmarking study, for instance, before they set off for unfamiliar territory. If this is the case, those prerequisite actions will have to be part of the plan.

If the required time, money, and information are not available, and the action is truly important, participants will have to explore how to come up with these resources. Are there others in the organization who have the necessary skills or information? Could some of the workload of people assigned to this project be transferred to others? Could funds that are already allocated to one budget item be redistributed?

Of all the reasons that a retreat might fail to meet expectations, one of the most common is that the participants fail to allocate resources to the activities they've agreed to undertake. The resources question is tempting to ignore, but don't let the group shortchange this all-important aspect of action planning.

Organizations, whether strategically or inadvertently, set priorities by budgeting. It's a safe bet that no one wants to see the budget for his or her project cut, much less eliminated. But too often realistic budget constraints are overlooked in retreats, resulting in unfunded action plans that go nowhere.

Are the budgets for the next year set in stone? If they are, you'll need to remind the group that the money for new initiatives will have to come from some existing program or programs. The participants will have to discuss which current budget items might be valid tradeoffs. The group often won't have authority to make budget changes, but the participants should face up to the budget implications of their action plan by making recommendations about how to handle funding constraints.

6. When Will These Actions Be Completed?

For every action step, the group should specify a deadline for finishing the task and—for multiple steps—interim target dates as well. Without targets and deadlines, the plans made so enthusiastically at the retreat can slowly decelerate into inaction. Deadlines are best when they are hard dates (April 25, for instance), rather than inexact estimates, such as "by early spring."

But just as important as setting realistic deadlines is coordinating them. If several tasks are due to be completed on the same date, there will be more impetus for a follow-up meeting to review progress if they are related, rather than if there are many deadlines that don't seem to relate to each other. And this coordination will help ensure that no one person or office is overloaded by a series of competing demands for immediate action.

The group should decide on a mechanism to monitor agreed-on deadlines. Will a senior executive volunteer to coordinate the whole project? (This is not a responsibility to be handed off to someone without clout or commitment to the initiative.) If there isn't one person who can monitor compliance, does the group need to set up a series of regular status meetings of the action plan's "champions," or perhaps of department heads, specifically to review progress? The action plan is not a set of unrelated items; people will need to cooperate and keep each other apprised of what's being accomplished and where they are encountering rough patches and roadblocks.

The group will also have to discuss what happens if deadlines aren't met. How will that situation be handled? Will other people share the workload if it looks like a deadline might be missed? Who has the authority to extend a deadline?

7. What Obstacles Will We Have to Overcome to Complete These Actions?

We discuss strategies for dealing with the resistance that might surface at the retreat in Chapter 9, "Participants Are Resisting New Ideas," pp. 165–168.

This last question isn't essential at all retreats, but if the organization has a history of holding retreats that don't result in meaningful change, it is useful to confront the reasons for previous failures. Similarly, if the plans call for significant change in the way people operate, you can expect some resistance and should be prepared to bring it to light so it can be managed.

Finally, be wary of action plans that are in effect "plans to plan." If there are a lot of steps that begin with phrases like, "Think about . . ." or "Meet to decide . . .," the group may have avoided making real commitments. The retreat is the time for people to think and consider. But it will only be useful if it leads to real action.

This chapter focused on helping participants make decisions and plan for action. We listed and defined several ways of making decisions (executive authority, consultative executive authority, majority rule, decision by default, moving right along, minority activism, compromise, consensus, and unanimous consent) and outlined advantages and disadvantages of each. We described several types of retreat decisions (ranking, rating, categorizing, limiting, prioritizing, and sequencing) along with suggested methods of reaching them. And we named the key questions participants should ask as they engage in action planning (What results do we want? How will we know when we've achieved them? What do we have to do to achieve them? Who will be responsible for what? Do we have the resources we need? When will things be done? What obstacles must we anticipate and overcome?).

These are all factors in making things go right. In Chapter 9, we'll take a look at what to do when things go wrong.

Chapter 9

How to Recover When Things Go Awry

Even in the best-planned retreat, things go wrong. One of the most important skills for you as a facilitator is the ability to think on your feet and change course when necessary. You'll have to recognize and respond in the moment to unanticipated developments such as participants engaging in emotional conflict, wandering off task, or resisting suggestions for dealing with a highly charged issue.

Here are some of the things that might go wrong in a retreat, followed by a discussion of strategies for dealing with each:

- A few participants dominate the discussions
- The group keeps wandering off task
- The group's energy is flagging
- A participant keeps plowing the same ground
- A participant repeatedly disrupts the conversations
- A senior manager violates the ground rules
- People are misusing humor

155

- A participant is overtly hostile or refuses to participate
- A participant walks out
- The boss gets furious or bursts into tears
- Participants are resisting new ideas
- An intense conflict breaks out
- A participant breaches another's confidence

This might seem like a long list, but take our word for it—it's not complete by any means.

A Few Participants Dominate the Discussions

Let's say Peter and Marusa are dominating the conversation, and you sense the group's mounting frustration.

You might first ask if people who haven't spoken yet have anything to say. Next, remind the group of the ground rules (which should include something about listening to others and encouraging everyone to participate). If necessary, politely interrupt Peter or Marusa by saying something such as, "That's an interesting point, Peter. Perhaps we can hear what others think?"

If Peter and Marusa still don't modify their behavior, have a private conversation with them during a break. Explain how their behavior is affecting the group, and ask them to be mindful of the need to allow many voices to be heard.

The Group Keeps Wandering Off Task

Off-task conversations happen for a variety of reasons. Some people may feel that another topic is more important than the one being discussed. A topic may elicit strong emotional responses that some in the group would rather avoid. Participants may feel cynical about the possibility of any real change coming out of the retreat.

Keeping the discussions on track is a delicate art, because you must continually assess (and help the group assess) what "on track" means at any given moment. Is a particular comment advancing the conversation or derailing it? Is it helping the group identify and deal with the real issues or permitting participants to avoid them?

One clue that things have gone off track is if you are feeling bored or ill at ease during the group's discussions. When this happens to us, we tell the group what we are feeling and ask the participants to consider whether they may have lost focus. But it's important not to get stuck on what *we* think the task should be. Ask the group to assess whether *they* think the current topic is the most appropriate one or if they want to move on to something else.

If the group keeps wandering off task, and there is a ground rule about sticking to the topic at hand, call participants' attention to that rule. If there is no such rule, encourage them to develop one.

If you sense that the group is wandering off track to avoid discussing a sensitive but important issue, consider creating an anonymous mechanism for them to communicate what is hampering the discussions and determine what, if anything, can be done to allow this issue to be aired safely. For example, you can ask everyone to write a note (which you will read aloud to the whole group without identifying the author) that outlines what would help them feel more comfortable discussing this issue. Or you might ask participants to work in small groups to explore why they're reluctant to discuss the issue, then report the gist of what they find to the whole group.

Sometimes the group gets sidetracked because someone contributes a valuable idea at the wrong time. The group is talking about fundraising ideas for next year, for instance, and, seemingly out of nowhere, someone suggests a new board member orientation program. That's an interesting topic, so the group takes it up then and there. To keep the participants from being diverted from the main task in such situations, you need to hold that thought for later discussion.

Write the topic, with the name of the person who brought it up, on a flip chart titled "Other Topics." Keep the Other Topics sheet on the wall where everyone can see it, adding ideas to it when they come up. And be sure to keep it in mind so you can reintroduce those ideas when there is time to address them.

The Group's Energy Is Flagging

Although you'll diminish participant fatigue if you have planned a varied schedule of activities, participants are still bound to get weary in almost any retreat that lasts longer than a day. People are working intensely, and they get tired. Immediately after lunch, participants are particularly prone to lassitude (which is why we always try to plan an invigorating exercise for the first afternoon session).

See Chapter 6, "Content Segments," p. 100, for ideas about how to vary the experiential elements in a retreat.

Our first response when we notice that participants seem to be running low on energy is to express our observation and ask what they want to do. Most often, all they need is a chance to stand up and stretch or take a short break.

Sometimes, however, they are communicating that they have exhausted (and are exhausted by) the topic. If that's the case, it's time to move on.

Fatigue also can be an indication that the group is avoiding an issue. In that case, follow the procedures we outlined above for when the group is wandering off task.

A Participant Keeps Plowing the Same Ground

People tend to repeat themselves if they don't feel they've been heard. So if someone keeps inserting the same point into the conversation, the first thing to do is acknowledge that you've heard what he or she said. Make a point of writing the participant's words down on a flip chart to demonstrate that you've understood and recorded his or her point of view. Then, if it's not the right time to deal with the issue, record it on the Other Topics chart and ask the group when might be a more appropriate time to discuss it.

If the topic cannot be addressed at the retreat at all, ask the participants whether they would be willing to discuss it back at the office. Once you get agreement from the group that the issue will be addressed, ask the participant if he or she is willing to move on. If you sense that this is an issue of concern to many participants but it can't be resolved at the retreat, ask the participants what they would like to do to move on from where they got stuck.

A Participant Repeatedly Disrupts the Conversations

If a participant interrupts once or twice, you can handle it just as you would deal with participants dominating the conversation (see above). If the interruptions continue, however, none of those techniques will work. Participants who consistently disrupt discussions by interrupting, interjecting inappropriate comments, or initiating side conversations that distract the group are often crying out for attention. As facilitators we may be especially inclined to try to meet their needs. But that's not always a good idea.

If you have brought the issue to a participant's attention and he or she remains disruptive, you will have to stop paying attention to that person. Look at other participants and talk to them, not to the person whose behavior is obstructing the group's progress. If nothing you do works, take the convenor aside at a break, give him your observations, and ask him how he wants to handle the situation. Sometimes a private conversation between the disruptive individual and the convenor will turn the behavior around. Ultimately, if that individual can't or won't stop being disruptive, he or she may have to be asked to leave. This is a drastic step, but sometimes (although rarely) it's necessary for the good of the whole group.

A Senior Manager Violates the Ground Rules

Rules on paper mean little unless they are observed in practice. For this reason, it's important that participants adhere to the ground rules they agreed to. While all participants should observe the rules, it's critical that the convenor and other senior managers be model citizens. If the rules don't seem to apply to the boss, the participants are less likely to observe them. You may have to take special care to keep senior managers in compliance and, if they break a rule, to remind them of their commitment. In fact, in our pre-retreat coaching to senior managers, we emphasize that—more than anything else—their behavior will determine the success of the retreat.

Before we conducted a retreat at a military installation, for example, we had a series of conversations with the commanding officer, Murray, about the need for him to assume a different role at the retreat than he was accustomed to in the command-and-control culture of the base. Murray agreed that he would acknowledge up-front that he was taking on an unusual role. As part of his welcoming words to his staff, he reiterated that he would not be taking the lead in discussions and that he would be listening more than talking. He would allow ideas that he didn't agree with to get a thorough airing without shooting them down.

But Murray quickly reverted to his typical behavior. He interrupted others frequently, told participants why their ideas wouldn't fly, and was invariably the person who reported out the work of any small group he was a member of.

We called a break and had a private conversation to remind Murray of his commitment to behave differently. We gave him detailed feedback on his behavior and the impact we saw it having on the group. During this conversation, we assured him of our positive intent, which was to help the whole group, not to criticize him. We also encouraged him to respond to our observations by asking him how he saw his own behavior.

Based on our feedback, Murray decided to tell the group that he realized he had lapsed back into his old habits. He encouraged his staff to remind him of the new behavior he was trying to practice if he acted differently than he intended.

While his acknowledgment did not radically change the underlying culture of the base, it did give participants permission to help the commanding officer see how his behavior affected his staff's ability to do their work. And it set a positive tone that paid off in lively discussions and innovative solutions to long-standing problems.

People Are Misusing Humor

During a retreat we led for a trade association, several participants started "teasing" their general counsel, Paul, by trading wisecracks about lawyers. When we called this behavior to the group's attention, they insisted that it was just innocent fun. We asked if they thought it bothered Paul, and they told us, "Of course not. He knows it's just 'good-natured teasing.'"

So we asked Paul if that was how he saw it. With his voice cracking, this tough-as-nails attorney responded, "I hate lawyer jokes. I hope I never have to hear another one. I can't tell you how bad they make me feel." Dead silence in the room, and no more "good-natured" ribbing of lawyers.

Remarkably, similar "good-natured teasing" still goes on at some offsites (just as in some workplaces) with respect to women and minorities as well.

It's important for you to recognize your own internal reaction to such humor. If something bothers you, chances are it's bothering some of the participants as well. Let the group know how you are reacting to the humor and why. Try to communicate your observations without judgment, and talk about your own discomfort, rather than the inappropriateness of the humor.

If someone seems to withdraw emotionally after being subjected to a "joke," ask the group (not just the person being targeted for the "humor") what they think the impact of such humor is and what would help them work together most productively. You might also encourage the group to point out when people aren't using humor appropriately. If you notice that the group uses such humor routinely, suggest adding a ground rule about the appropriate use of humor.

If none of the above works, have a private conversation with participants who insist on skewering others in the name of "good fun."

Don't misunderstand us. We're all for humor. It's the grease that lubricates progress. But it must be respectful and appropriate. Whatever the intentions of the persons teasing others or telling such jokes—and their intentions may well be perfectly "innocent"—having fun at someone else's expense isn't fun for the people being "teased" or for others present who don't like to see their colleagues embarrassed.

A Participant Is Overtly Hostile or Refuses to Participate

When a participant is displaying hostility or refusing to take part in an exercise or the business of the retreat in general, it may be because the particular exercise has touched a nerve, he is upset about something else, or he is rebelling against your perceived power. (Indeed, it's not uncommon for participants to express resentment or direct anger at you that they might be feeling toward the organization or the convenor. Or, judging that it's safe to do so in the context of the retreat, they might express their feelings overtly and directly, when they would be more circumspect back at work.)

The first rule here is: Don't take it personally. Facilitators get into trouble when they turn such incidents into power struggles. You decrease the likelihood of such an occurrence if you have designed a retreat that addresses participants' major concerns, but it will still happen. It's essential to remain empathetic to the participant's concerns and not become defensive or combative yourself.

See Chapter 5, "Pre-Retreat Interviews with Participants," p. 66, for more information on unearthing participants' concerns in advance.

Here's an example. In a retreat we led for a government agency that was rife with turf issues, we included a simulation early on the first day that would provide a framework for discussing these issues. The nature of the simulation required participants to follow certain precise instructions for which we could not provide reasons until later in the exercise. Alan, the mailroom supervisor, stood up and declared that there was no way we could make him follow those instructions. When a low-key effort to convince him to reconsider failed, we asked him if he could think of an alternative that might help him stay engaged in the exercise. He came up with conditions that he was willing to meet, and we moved on.

Alan turned out to be a very constructive participant, who at several times during the retreat helped people see when they were avoiding tough conversations. Later that day, we asked Alan if we might have done anything differently that would have persuaded him to comply with the original instructions. He said that we hadn't earned his trust at that point and that he gets pushed around too much at work for him to be pushed around at the retreat.

The next morning when participants were talking about what they had learned the previous day, several waxed enthusiastic about how useful the simulation had been in helping them identify and address their turf problems. Alan stood up abruptly. (We must confess we were a little nervous.) He told the group that he had learned something by our not having made an issue of his refusal to go along with our instructions, and that if we were doing the simulation today, he would have followed those instructions.

"I'm Outta Here": A Participant Walks Out

There are three likely scenarios in which a participant might actually walk out:

- A discussion becomes too emotionally intense for one of the participants. He gets up and leaves, visibly upset, without saying a word.
- A participant becomes increasingly frustrated with the direction in which the discussion is heading and her inability to affect it. She announces to the whole group, "I don't have time for this. I'm leaving."
- A participant doesn't show up for the next morning's session or doesn't return from lunch or from a break.

The first two are particularly difficult scenarios to deal with if there is only one facilitator. If there are two facilitators, we recommend that the one who is not leading the group at the moment quietly go after the participant who left to hear what he or she is concerned about.

Obviously, the person who can't stand being in the room any more is experiencing intense feelings, so it is crucial that you not fan the emotional flames. Your role should mostly be to listen to the nature of his or her concerns. You can reassure the person that he or she will be welcomed back to the group and ask if there is anything that would make it easier to discuss the difficult issue. If the participant is not ready to come back to the room, ask if there is anyone else he or she would feel comfortable talking to. If there is, ask that person to speak with the participant who is upset.

If the participant refuses to return, keep in mind that you are neither a therapist nor a disciplinarian. Talk privately with the convenor about how she wishes to address the issue. She might decide to speak with the participant directly and discuss options.

If you are the only facilitator and it's not an appropriate time to call a break, we recommend that you ask if there is anyone who would be willing to listen to the participant's concerns.

Although only one person may have actually left the room when a participant walks out, chances are others are also feeling intense emotion, both because of the nature of the previous discussion and because of their colleague's visible distress. That's why it's important to allow participants to talk about how they're feeling, not just plow forward. The worst thing you can do is pretend that nothing happened. Not only has something happened, but it has changed the climate in the room, and you must acknowledge that.

If someone doesn't return to a session following a break, the first thing to do is determine where the missing person is and whether he or she is alright. Perhaps somebody in the group knows what happened and can help head off any rumors that might start. "Does anyone know where Enrique is? Is he okay? Can someone go and check on him?" If the participants don't know what happened, ask the convenor how she wants to address the issue of the missing participant.

The Boss Gets Furious or Bursts into Tears

Sometimes something comes up in a retreat that is just too much for a participant to handle, and you will have to manage the results of an emotional outburst. This is particularly difficult when the person happens to be a senior executive. He or she might feel cornered, challenged, or blamed, overloaded, misunderstood, or disrespected. The discussion might strike a nerve that triggers an embarrassed or tearful response. If not managed skillfully, such an event can affect the course of the retreat, usually in a negative way.

As compassionate human beings, our first impulse might be to avoid an awkward situation by calling a break and—after emotions have cooled—resuming as if nothing happened. Or we might be inclined to rush in and "rescue" someone who is having trouble handling tough feedback. Neither of these approaches is the best way to respond.

You can't ignore what happened, and neither can the executive or the other participants. If you all implicitly conspire to do so, you will be hobbled from that point on by this bit of important unfinished business. But leaping into the fray isn't the best approach either. It is rarely effective to try to engage someone who's in a highly emotional state.

So you need to deal with the situation, but maybe not at precisely that moment.

Know When to Move On

As the facilitator, you can't judge what's going on in someone else's head. Only the person having the emotional reaction can decide if he or she can handle more information. If a participant is unwilling to discuss a subject any further, move on to something else, at least for the moment. Later, during a break, you can try to encourage the person to reintroduce the topic.

We suggest that you call a break: "I think maybe we should take ten minutes to stretch. Let's all be back in the room ready to resume at 11:30." Take the executive aside and ask if he is willing to continue the conversation that triggered the emotional response when the group reconvenes. If so, give the executive the floor to explain what prompted that response and to let the group know that he would like to take up where he left off.

If the executive is unwilling to discuss the subject any further, move on to something else, at least for the moment. Later, during another break, you can explain to the executive how important it is to address the contentious issue and encourage him to reintroduce the topic when he has had a chance to think about it and calm down further.

Participants Are Resisting New Ideas

"Resistance" is often used as a pejorative word. Actually, resistance is often a healthy reaction to change initiatives. It can serve as a brake for those who would embrace change for its own sake and as a reality check when new ideas are presented that, while perhaps bold and novel, aren't very good.

But sometimes resistance is reactive, not a rational response to the prospect of change, but simply a digging in of the heels. Such resistance, if you don't manage it well, can stop a change initiative in its tracks.

Fear of the unknown is often cited as the reason people resist new ideas, and certainly it plays a role. But a good deal of resistance stems from people's reluctance to give up things they are comfortable with and—more importantly—things that matter to them. People's concerns about change are valid and should

Holding On to the Familiar

It's natural for people to want to hold on to things. It is said that the hardest thing for a trapeze artist isn't grabbing hold of the new trapeze as it swings within reach but letting go of the one she's already gripping. So it is with change; it's hard to let go of the familiar and comfortable.

be addressed as soon as they surface. Before focusing on areas for change, we typically ask participants to turn their attention to things that already work, things they're proud of, and things they would particularly like to keep. This helps participants define the babies they don't want to throw out with the bath water, and often it's sufficient to resolve the human tendency to resist something new for the sake of resistance.

Often resistance emerges when the group starts making decisions. Just when you think people have reached agreement on a course of action, one or more participants start revisiting the arguments against it. Statements such as, "We tried this years ago and it didn't work," signal resistance.

Since resistance often stems from the anticipation of loss, whether real or imagined, having the convenor or other participants simply restate the wisdom of the proposed change is unlikely to build support. And dismissing such last-minute objections is likely only to increase resistance, if not at the retreat, then back in the office during the implementation effort. So you must help the group address that feeling of anticipatory loss.

The first step in dealing with resistance is to encourage it to emerge throughout the retreat. Early on in a discussion, invite dissenting views: "Does anyone have a different take on this issue?"

In *Beyond the Wall of Resistance*, Rick Maurer (1996) talks about the intensity of resistance. In what Maurer calls "Level 1 Resistance," *people are reacting to the idea itself.* When this occurs at a retreat, help ensure that participants are communicating clearly with one another and that everyone has a chance to influence the shape of the idea that is under discussion. You do this by:

- Asking the convenor and other senior leaders to re-emphasize that they want to hear and learn from different opinions and that candor will not be punished

- Encouraging the participants to listen carefully to one another's ideas and concerns without defending their own points of view
- Urging the group to consider what people's objections might be communicating about the feasibility of these new ideas

In what Maurer calls "Level 2 Resistance," which is almost always present when the group is contemplating major changes, *people are reacting to something deeper. Often it's the fear of loss.* When this happens, ask the whole group, not just those resisting the ideas, to identify things they *don't* want to lose. Focusing on what's important to them, what they want to retain, may help reassure resisters that not everything they care about (indeed, perhaps not anything) will disappear.

Encourage resisters to talk about what they want for the organization, not what they *don't* want. Ask them to be as specific as possible. Ask if anything would help resisters support the new idea. Often a minor adjustment would make an idea acceptable.

Sometimes you'll be confronted with what Maurer calls "Level 3 Resistance." At this greatest intensity of resistance, *people may have conflicting values or sharply contrasting visions* for the future of the organization, or they may have a history of sabotaging one another's successes.

Ideally, the experience of working together at the retreat and striving to find common ground will have diminished resistance of this third level of intensity, but that's not always going to be the case. Sometimes the differences among group members are so sharply delineated around a certain issue that they just cannot be resolved at the retreat. In this case, we suggest you encourage the group to table the discussion (see "Drop the Issue . . . for Now," below) and decide on another forum in which it can be addressed.

If resistance asserts itself just as the discussion seems to be winding down and decisions are near, don't dismiss it (or let participants dismiss it) as coming too late. It's important not to let momentum roll over people or impatience carry the day. And don't think of resistance as an attack on you and your well-thought-out retreat plan. Participants who are resisting something may be doing you and the others a favor, even at the eleventh hour.

It's far better to address the resistance openly than to force participants to deal with it later on back at the office, where it can derail the effort to implement what they worked so hard throughout the retreat to accomplish.

At the same time, you can't permit last-minute resistance to derail the retreat just as the train is approaching the station. Use your best judgment about how much discussion is necessary at this late stage, and balance that against the need to draw the retreat to a close.

An Intense Conflict Breaks Out

Sometimes progress is sidetracked because two or more participants get into an escalating disagreement and cannot listen to one another or back down from their own strongly held positions.

Here are some techniques we use to help prevent minor disagreements from getting out of hand:

- *Help participants hear and understand one another.* People involved in a disagreement are often thinking of their rebuttal rather than listening to what others are saying. When you hear something like, "Yeah, but . . .," stop the action and make sure each party in the disagreement has really heard and can state the other person's point of view.
- *Look for points of agreement.* Often there is substantial agreement with most points and disagreement on only one or two. If you can lead participants to discover areas on which they agree, you greatly enhance the climate for resolving the areas of disagreement.
- *Involve others in the discussion.* Getting others who have not expressed a strong point of view engaged can help clarify points of misunderstanding and identify areas of agreement. "Virginia and Amy seem to be having a problem understanding each other's points of view. Can anyone help out?"
- *Help participants understand why the issue matters.* Sometimes the people in a conflict are so bogged down in defending their own positions and in attacking others' positions that they are unable to express clearly why the issue really matters to them. You can ask participants on both sides of a conflict to restate their concerns in terms of what they're hoping to accomplish and why it is important to them. It's much easier for people to be empathetic about something that matters deeply to someone else. When the people who are engaged in the conflict understand what their "adver-

saries" want, they may be able to come up with mutually agreeable solutions that neither could think of when they were focused only on defending their positions.

For a fuller discussion on how to use breakout groups and silence at the retreat, see Chapter 6, "Content Segments," pp. 100–110.

- *Break participants into smaller groups.* Have participants discuss the issue for five to ten minutes in pairs or trios.
- *Have participants write down ideas.* Ask the participants to stop talking and write down their thoughts. This will often calm emotions and put participants in a more reflective mindset. It will also help quieter participants (who might have excellent suggestions for resolving the issue) collect their thoughts and express them.
- *Explore options.* Encourage group members who are not at either extreme of the conflict to help generate options that might satisfy the needs of all parties in the disagreement.
- *Establish a deadline.* Often, when you say, "Okay, let's give this just another five minutes," participants will focus more intensely not only on their arguments but on reaching an agreement. People who aren't part of the heated discussion are particularly likely to help find a solution so the group can move on.
- *Call a break.* A short break can give people a chance to cool off. Often an issue that seems impossible to resolve can yield to a solution after people have had a chance to stretch their legs or chat informally with someone else.
- *Change seats.* Ask participants to change their seats. This may seem silly, but it can literally give people a new vantage point. (This action can be combined with taking a break. Ask people to move to different seats upon returning to the room.)
- *Postpone the discussion.* In a multi-day retreat, it is often useful to delay the discussion of a particularly contentious issue when some time is needed to reflect or to lower the emotional temperature. People who have advocated for a position strongly usually find it difficult to change their minds on the spot. Postponing the discussion gives participants time to do some research, reflect on the issues, and find common ground without losing face.
- *Drop the issue . . . for now.* If you are convinced that the group is at an impasse, suggest tabling the discussion to another time and place. Essentially, this would mean agreeing to disagree on this topic so participants

can move on to other matters in the limited time available to them at the retreat. Emphasize, however, that the disagreement shouldn't be swept under the rug, but should be revisited back at the office or at another retreat scheduled specifically to address the issue.

A Participant Breaches Another's Confidence

A breach of confidence is a serious transgression that could threaten the environment of trust you've worked to establish, and you must deal with it immediately. In our experience, it doesn't happen often, but when it does, it's highly corrosive.

Here's how a breach of confidence might play out: Grace and Dianne are part of the same small breakout group. Dianne suggests to the group that their supervisor, Susan (who is working in another group), may be responsible for the delays in the production schedule. Others nod their assent, and they record specific recommendations for how Susan should modify her behavior, which they then report as a group to the other participants. At a break, Grace tells Susan that it was Dianne who raised the issue in the small group. Other participants hear this conversation and report it to you.

If this happened to us, we would tell the group that a breach of confidence had occurred. If the group had established a ground rule about confidentiality, we would remind them of that rule. If there were no such rule, we'd suggest that the group put one in place.

We would then ask participants how they would prefer to deal with sensitive topics and ask for their suggestions about what might be done to rebuild trust.

In this chapter we've acknowledged that "stuff happens." Things go wrong. And you, the facilitator, are responsible for making them right. (We never said this was easy.)

We've listed many of the situations that might arise to threaten the progress of the retreat and discussed strategies for dealing with them.

Now we move on to our section on retreat activities, starting with a chapter on strategic planning.

SECTION FOUR

The Facilitator's Activity Manual

Chapter 10

Leading a
Strategic Planning Retreat

You may wonder why in this chapter, in which we present practical activities you can use in strategic planning retreats, we aren't also providing our standard strategic planning retreat agenda. The reason: We don't have a standard strategic planning retreat agenda. We custom tailor every retreat (whether on strategic planning or not) to take into account the unique circumstances and needs of each client. Sometimes we focus more on creativity or on communication or on some other theme. It all depends on where the organization is starting from and where it wants to end up—the answer to, "What do we want to be different as a result of this retreat?" Feel free to mix and match exercises from this chapter with those from the following chapters to best meet your own needs.

Strategic planning is the most common reason organizations hold retreats. Organizations convene offsites to help them determine where they want to be in a year, two years, or three years; what route they want to take to get there; and what resources they'll require for the journey.

This is a tall order, and a single strategic planning retreat won't result in a fully formed blueprint for the future. But it can help participants make great strides in reaching agreement on the key elements of a plan to guide their business decisions.

Organizations are continually presented with unexpected opportunities and problems. They must make hard choices quickly, in an environment in which little is certain. It's easy to become distracted by these challenges, expending time, money, and energy in activities that divert people's attention from the organization's principal goals. To avoid that distraction, organizations need a keen understanding of what those goals are and a clear sense of what it will take to achieve them.

A strategic plan is like a pilot's flight plan. It specifies the destination, route, and amount of fuel required, taking into account weather conditions, characteristics of the aircraft, and passenger and cargo loads. A strategic planning retreat allows an organization to fill out its own flight plan in a setting that is conducive to thoughtful reflection, candid discussion, and purposeful decision making.

Before embarking on the strategic planning process, organization leaders must be clear about their own priorities. In planning such a retreat, we recommend that you ask the leaders to answer candidly the question: "What do I personally want to see happen?" It's not that you will try to guide the retreat group toward what the leaders want, but leaders' views do affect the range and scope of possible outcomes. In the end, if the plan doesn't match what the leaders are willing to support, it won't be implemented.

This is especially true in privately held companies or organizations headed by their founders. For example, in designing a retreat for a firm owned by two partners, we asked each of them to spell out the emotional, intellectual, and financial rewards they wanted from the company. Each declared that he wanted to retire in five years with a multi-million dollar cash buyout. When we pointed out that the company would have to grow eightfold to finance such large simultaneous buyouts, the owners realized that they had to redefine their own expectations before they could forge ahead with planning for the company.

Elements of Organization Strategy

There is no universal model of what should go into a strategic plan and no single "best" format. The planning model you use to guide the retreat discussions must fit the organization's circumstances, expectations, and needs.

Today's strategists, realizing the futility of predicting the future, tend to think less about complex analyses of past performance and more about imagining a new future and inspiring people to create it. Here is a strategic framework model we often use to help groups begin this process:

In this model, *purpose* is at the core of everything an organization does. It defines the kind of work the organization will do and, ultimately, how it will measure success.

Flowing out of purpose are four primary aspects of strategy that every organization must address: client selection, financial resources, differentiation, and scope of work.

Look for an activity about strategic purpose later in this chapter on p. 180.

Client Selection: Whom Will the Organization Serve?

Whom does the organization serve? For companies, this question implies difficult marketing considerations: Which customer segments generate the greatest sales volume? Which are the most profitable? Which have the greatest potential for future growth? Without answers, companies can fall victim to the tendency to seize every opportunity that comes along, regardless of its strategic value to the firm.

In the nonprofit sector, client selection can be even harder, because it implies that the organization will not serve all possible constituencies equally, if at all. Most nonprofits don't have the resources to serve everyone they would like to (or who would like to be served) and they frequently fall into "mission creep," adding a few more programs every year to address the needs of new constituent groups. Over time these organizations can lose focus and, in attempting to serve everyone to some extent, ultimately end up serving no one well.

This phenomenon isn't limited to nonprofits, however. Many corporations muddle their identities and tax their resources by trying to serve too many market segments.

Financial Resources

How will the organization ensure its future success? This issue is not simply a measure of profitability or growth. Strategically, looking at financial resources means understanding the economic drivers of the business—the determinants of financial success. If an organization is faced with insufficient financial resources to achieve its goals, it must examine how it generates revenue, how it charges for its products or services, and how expense budgets are allocated.

Differentiation

How will the organization distinguish itself from others in its field? An organization's basis of differentiation could be in the distinction of products, quality, pricing, service, philosophy, or the breadth and depth of its offerings. To get at what makes the organization stand out from others in its field, participants must ask themselves, "What do we do or know that is unique? Do we have any proprietary processes, systems, services, or products? What do we do (or can we do) better than anyone else?"

Too often an organization claims differentiation that is . . . well . . . not really different. To be significant, the difference must be part of the fabric of the organization's everyday work, and it must represent a true difference from the way competing organizations operate.

If identifying significant differences is difficult for businesses, it can be a particular challenge for nonprofits, but it's critical that they, too, be able to articulate what makes them unique. Unclear differentiation from other groups that do similar work denies current and potential funders and donors compelling reasons to support the work of that particular organization.

Scope of Work

What are the reach and focus of the organization's day-to-day operations? Does the organization concentrate on just one thing it can do particularly well, or are its activities highly diversified? Does it have sufficient financial resources to support all of its programs, or should some be scaled back or eliminated?

The organization's *structure* and *culture* are shown on the outer edges of the model, because together they restrict what is possible for an organization to achieve. And they're in the same ring because they are so interconnected that changing one almost always requires changing the other. Highly successful organizations may not need to delve deeply into these elements in a planning retreat. But organizations that are struggling will have to explore their structure and culture before they can make real progress in planning.

Finally, every organization operates in an environment it cannot control. Effective strategic planning demands a deep awareness of the rapid changes taking place outside the organization—in its field, in technology, in business, in the economy, in society, in politics, and in the world at large.

Most retreat processes fall into three phases: understanding the current state of things (scanning the environment), setting goals, and devising strategies to fulfill those goals. In *scanning the environment,* the organization examines both the external and internal factors that will have an impact on the success of its plans. In *setting goals,* the organization outlines in measurable terms what it hopes to achieve. Finally, in *devising strategies,* the organization determines what actions are necessary to meet its goals. The concepts and activities that follow will help you move the participants through the decisions necessary in each of these three planning phases.

The Flow of a Planning Retreat

1. Scanning the environment—understanding the current state of things.

2. Setting goals—establishing what is to be achieved.

3. Devising strategies—deciding on actions to fulfill the goals.

Mission, Vision, or Purpose?

Although many organizations like to begin a planning retreat by revisiting their mission statement or coming up with a new vision, starting there is like deciding to hike through a swamp. It's possible to get where you're going, but it's going to be very messy and take a lot longer than necessary.

The instinct to start with a mission statement isn't a bad one. Obviously, participants have to agree on the organization's core purpose before devising a strategy for achieving it. But the problem with most mission and vision statements is that they typically have been wordsmithed so thoroughly that they no longer reflect anything unique about the organization. They express the organization's commitment to such uncontroversial issues as quality, caring for people, satisfying clients, being environmentally responsible, and, oh, by the way, making a profit. They're often so bland that they obscure what the organization is really all about. (That's one reason few employees in most organizations can remember what their mission statement says, let alone what it means.)

Strategic planning retreats, however, should focus on the organization's core purpose and goals, not on how they're written.

If the organization needs a guiding statement, it should focus on strategic purpose: a single compelling direction. Jim Collins (2001), in *Good to Great*, calls this direction a Hedgehog Concept: "a simple, crystalline concept that flows from deep understanding about . . . what you can be the best in the world at,

The Trouble with Mission Statements

Several years ago we were conducting interviews in the conference room of a government agency that had just completed a lengthy process to define its mission. Pleased with the outcome, the planning team hung large, color posters with the mission statement all over the office.

In the course of an interview, we asked a mid-level manager to tell us what the department's mission was. "Um," she said, "I think we have one. I know we worked on it. I can't quite remember." Meanwhile, the mission statement was hanging just over her left shoulder on the conference room wall.

Hedgehog or Fox?

"The fox knows many things, but the hedgehog knows one big thing," wrote Archilochus, a Greek poet, circa 650 BCE. This quote was popularized by the British philosopher Isaiah Berlin, who used it to classify some of the great writers and thinkers of all time as either hedgehogs (single-minded visionaries) or as foxes (those who pursued a broader range of interests).

what drives your economic engine" and, "what you are deeply passionate about." Since such a mission statement doesn't pretend to spell out everything—only the single most important thing—it can be written in one sentence.

A widely understood strategic purpose informs the hundreds of daily decisions that, in the end, will determine what an organization can achieve.

No organization will be as effective as it might be until its people understand and support the organization's strategic purpose. A muddled sense of purpose leads to confusion and allows people to decide individually what's important, without any context to guide them. A clear and galvanizing purpose, on the other hand, focuses everyone's efforts and moves the organization forward in an unambiguous direction.

But a mission statement doesn't specify how the organization will get there. The "how" part comes from the strategic plan and the staff's commitment to it.

If your interviews have demonstrated that the organization's mission and vision statements are well understood and influence behavior and decision making, by all means encourage the group to use them as a framework for planning. If not, you'll conserve time and energy by helping the group agree on the organization's core purpose rather than trying to lead them through the swamp of drafting a mission statement as a group.

Here is an activity we use to help organizations identify their purpose.

Exploring Strategic Purpose

Description

In this activity, participants list their aspirations for the organization on individual Post-it® Notes, share their thoughts with the group, and post the notes on a flip chart. Participants work together to refine their choices and agree on a strategic purpose. They consider whether the purpose selected will help the organization make effective decisions.

> **Experiential Elements**
> - Individual and group reflection
> - Experimenting with ideas
> - Group discussion

Steps

1. Tell the participants: "This is your chance to be bold and creative in identifying the organization's core purpose. You will begin your thinking process in silence, recording each of your ideas on a *separate* Post-it Note.

   "Please complete the following sentence, using only concrete and observable actions, not attitudes:

   'Our future potential will be realized when . . .'

   "Examples of concrete actions or behaviors are 'we expand into Europe' or 'we win our industry's Company of the Year award.' Attitudes, such as 'we should treat our customers well,' do not easily translate into actions, although 'customer complaints drop 90 percent' would."

   In answering the question, the participants should consider the critical questions suggested by Collins:

   - What could we be the best in the world at?

   - What is the single best measure of our economic success?

   - What are we deeply passionate about?

2. When everyone has written down their thoughts, ask participants to come to the front of the room one at a time to read their Post-its and then stick them on a flip chart. Continue until everyone in the group has read their ideas.

3. Ask participants to look for common themes that can be combined into one or more expressions of core purpose. Group the Post-its by theme.

> **Setup**
> Prepare the sentence prompt "Our future potential will be realized when . . ." on a flip chart.
>
> **Special Supplies**
> A pad of Post-it Notes and a felt-tip pen for each participant.

> Read more about the importance of these questions in Jim Collins' book *Good to Great: Why Some Companies Make the Leap . . . and Others Don't.*

4. Write the themes on a flip chart and ask the group to discuss each as a possible core purpose for the organization. Help the group come to agreement on a brief core purpose statement for the organization.

5. Ask participants to suggest typical strategic issues that arise in the organization, for instance, "Is the timing right for us to expand into other geographic markets?" or "Should we increase our plant capacity or outsource new product manufacturing?" List the issues on a flip chart.

Facilitator Experience Required

This is a difficult activity to lead. The facilitator must guide senior executives in the process of making tough choices about complex issues and narrowing these choices down to a single strategic purpose.

6. Test the relevance of the purpose the group has agreed on by asking, "If this were our strategic purpose, would it help us address these issues?"

Facilitator Notes
- Don't get trapped into editing the participants' statements or debating the meaning of words. If you do, you may end up spending the entire retreat on this activity.

- The biggest mistake planning groups make is not thinking boldly enough. If the ideas aren't compelling, encourage the group to try again. Or ask the group why their ambitions are so constrained. Try to get at the underlying issues.

Discerning the Organization's Values

We discuss organizational culture in depth in Chapter 11.

Many organizations recognize the influence their culture and values have on how people work together and what they can achieve. While a discussion of values is not always part of a planning retreat, you may want to include such a topic if your interviews indicate that a lack of clarity about values is interfering with people's ability to work together smoothly.

No matter what is written in a values statement, the people who work in an organization know instinctively what the organization stands for. If a company allows a particular customer to abuse the staff because that customer gives the company a lot of business, employees will consider the organization's statement that "employees are our most important asset" to be a sham. On the other hand, if the organization grants liberal paternity leave and permits three people to leave on the dot of 4:00 p.m. every day to pick up their kids from pre-school, there is no need for a formal statement that the organization is "family-oriented." Everyone knows.

Many of the planning issues for a healthy organization center on making course corrections and taking advantage of opportunities. But if the organization is foundering and people seem to be working at cross-purposes, it's important to spend time at the retreat helping the group identify a guiding philosophy and governing values.

One way to determine an organization's values is for the senior managers to reflect individually and then collectively on what they believe in. Once they've agreed on a list of their core values, you can help them whittle the list down by asking, "If this value became a competitive disadvantage, would you cling to it anyway?" Only those values that receive a strong "yes" should be considered core values. Help the group identify values that are relevant to the work, rather than just lofty social goals.

Just as with a mission statement, you want a statement of values that people can recall. If an organization lists more than three or four values, chances are people won't be able to remember them. Encourage participants to hone their values list down—by combining similar values and eliminating those that are less central—to those they genuinely care about and would make personal sacrifices to achieve. And if senior leaders don't visibly exemplify the organization's values, the statement will be meaningless, or—worse—staff will ascribe to management the value of hypocrisy.

If an organization needs to examine its values, the following activity is a thought-provoking way to start.

Looking at Our Values

Description

In this activity, participants make collages to express in a visual manner their view of the values the organization practices and those that the participants aspire to.

Steps

1. Introduce the task: "We are going to explore the values that your organization practices and the values that you would like it to practice. We'll do this by making collages that express your thoughts visually. Making collages is a way to help you tap into your more intuitive right-brain thinking."

2. Divide the group in half. Show the two flip chart pages: "Our Current Values" and "The Values We Should Aspire To." Say, "The first group will consider Our Current Values in making their collages. You should think about what values seem to be in place now—even if unspoken—judging by the way people behave and get things done in the organization.

   "The second group will consider The Values We Should Aspire To. You will keep in mind the values that you think [the organization] should practice in its everyday work.

   "Each person will make an individual collage by cutting out pictures and words from these magazines and pasting them on a sheet of cardstock [show sample]. Choose your pictures and words by keeping in mind the statement you have been assigned. You will have half an hour to make your collage."

3. After the participants have completed their collages, ask them to give their collages titles. Then post all the collages on the wall. Ask each person in the first group to explain the meanings of their collages. Collect their thoughts on a flip chart. After looking at all the collages in the first group, ask the other group, "What values does this group see in the organization right now?" Make a list on the flip chart.

Experiential Elements
- Reflecting back on experiences
- Making collages
- Group decision making

Setup
- Write two flip chart pages that say, "Our Current Values" and "The Values We Should Aspire To."
- Prepare a sample collage for participants to look at.

Special Supplies

A selection of magazines with many photos and ads, at least three for every participant; scissors, glue stick, and an 11 inch x 17 inch sheet of heavy cardstock for each person.

4. Now ask the individuals in the second group to explain their collages. Take notes on a flip chart as they speak. After looking at all their collages, ask, "What values does this group wish the organization would have?" Make a list on the flip chart.

5. Compare the two lists. How closely does the Our Current Values list match the Values We Should Aspire To list? If they match closely, what are the three or four most important of these values? If the values don't match, facilitate a discussion of what would have to change for the organization to live up to the new values suggested.

Facilitator Experience Required

The facilitator should be comfortable working with visual images and helping people see multiple levels of meaning in the images they choose. Be prepared to overcome objections that this exercise is "childish" or "silly." (It *is* childish in a way or, more accurately, childlike, which is the whole point. Children know how to create with unfettered imagination, which this activity helps participants reclaim.)

Understanding the Environment

Even when an organization has a clear purpose and explicit values, participants cannot begin to plan for the future without first understanding the environment in which the organization exists. An organization's work may be affected by external economic, social, political, and technological changes. A retreat provides an ideal forum to reflect on what is changing externally and what impact these changes might have on the organization's future.

> The *Fifth Discipline Fieldbook*, by Senge, Roberts, Ross, Smith, and Kleiner, is an excellent resource for examination of values in the workplace.

When a change in the environment occurs unexpectedly, people often resist acknowledging it and therefore are unable to come up with strategies to address it. But when retreat participants start thinking about what might happen, these possible scenarios form what Swedish neuroscientist David Ingvar (1985) calls "memories of the future." According to Kees van der Heijden (1996), author of *Scenarios: The Art of Strategic Conversation,* when people practice developing such scenarios they learn to recognize new trends more quickly and can take more appropriate action in response to changes that occur. "Even if the specific rehearsed scenario never plays out in reality," he wrote, "the mind has nevertheless built up a readily available set of concepts" that will increase people's ability to see what's really happening and to respond accordingly.

Of course there's no way to predict the future, but you can help the group explore the potential ramifications of several possible future scenarios. We've found that the following activity often elicits dramatic pictures of possible futures that can help organizations make more informed strategic choices.

Glimpses into the Future

Description

This activity promotes discussion of present and future trends in the organization's external environment (including socio-cultural, economic, technological, legal, political, and international factors as well as trends affecting customers, competitors, suppliers, and the labor market). Participants list trends on large Post-it Notes; then, working in small groups, they choose several trends that might influence possible futures.

Experiential Elements

- Individual and group reflection
- Group discussion
- Experimenting with ideas
- Storytelling and group presentations

Steps

1. Introduce the activity: "Clues to the future environment [the organization] will be operating in can be found by looking at current trends and considering where they might lead in the future. These are the trends that occur in your professional field, trends inside the organization, and external trends (in economics, technology, politics, and society at large, for instance).

   "Refer to the three major areas of trends identified on the flip charts (see Setup): trends in our field, in our organization, and in society as a whole.

   "List as many trends as you can think of in each of the trend areas, writing *one idea per Post-it Note.*"

2. After the participants have written down their ideas, ask them to stick their notes on the appropriate flip chart sheets on the wall. Encourage them to take a moment to read what others have posted.

3. Divide the participants into breakout groups of four to six people, preferably mixed by department, discipline, or organizational level. Ask each breakout group to select four trends—including at least one from each of the three trend areas. The groups should take back to their tables the four Post-it Notes that represent the trends they've chosen.

4. Ask the breakout groups to address the following questions, using the trends they've selected, and to prepare a presentation for the entire group on flip chart paper. Hand out the Breakout Group Assignment sheet:

Setup

Prepare three "Trend" flip charts and post on the wall:
- Trends in Our Field
- Trends in Our Organization
- Trends in Society

Prepare and copy Breakout Group Assignment sheets for each group.

Special Supplies

A pad of 3 inch x 5 inch Post-it Notes and a felt-tip pen for each participant.

Breakout Group Assignment

What would be the implication for our organization if these trends increased in force and speed? What might the future look like in that case?

Invent a plausible future that is based on these trends. Make the description of that future as detailed and realistic as possible.

Give your "future" a name (for example, "Less Is More" or "The Clash of the Titans") and prepare a flip chart presentation about it.

In the light of the future scenario you imagined, what alternative actions or strategies might be called for, regardless of whether we would be able or willing to take those actions now?

5. Ask each breakout group to make a presentation of its assignment to the rest of the group.

6. Facilitate a discussion on the strategies the organization would need to pursue to thrive in the different possible futures.

Facilitator Notes

- Most strategic planning groups are composed of the managers who are responsible for having created the *status quo*. It can be hard for them to look critically at their own work, but solid planning must be based on a realistic appraisal of the current state of the organization. This activity helps participants learn to challenge their own assumptions and innate complacency and embark on a whole new way of thinking. Ask the participants: "If you keep operating the way you do now—even if you keep getting better at what you already do—could you survive and thrive should these possible future scenarios come to pass?"

Facilitator Experience Required

A strong understanding of the client's industry and of the business environment in general will allow the facilitator to ask probing questions that will help make the glimpses into the future compelling for the participants.

- Don't let the group get caught up in choosing among the possible future scenarios. The point of this activity is to encourage the group to think about all of the possibilities, not to try to predict the future.

The following two activities provide a framework for assessing the organization's current operations.

Rating Resources

Description

In this activity, the participants create a report card rating the organization's competencies. The ensuing discussion should address issues of how to improve performance and reallocate resources.

Experiential Elements

• Active decision making
• Individual and group reflection
• Shared dialogue and discussion
• Receiving and acting on feedback

Steps

1. Introduce the activity: "A critical piece of any organization's operational strategy is the scope of work it takes on and how well it performs that work. This activity will help you focus on how you rate [the organization's] competencies. The ratings will allow you to determine where improvements are needed."

2. Ask the group: "What kinds of clients (customers, members, or constituents) do you wish to serve in the future?" As they answer, write the list on a flip chart.

Special Supplies

Ten to fifteen small sheets of paper (approximately 3 inches x 4 inches) for each participant; two handheld calculators.

3. Ask the group: "Looking at this list, which competencies would help you best meet the needs of these clients you want to serve?" On a flip chart, list the competencies the group suggests.

4. Then ask: "Are there any competencies you now have that are not on this list?" Add those to the list.

5. Facilitate a discussion to group the competency suggestions into common themes. Limit the final list of competencies to no more than ten.

6. Hand out the small pieces of paper to each participant. Go through the list of competencies one by one. For each, ask participants to write on a slip of paper how they rate the organization on a scale of 1 to 10, 1 meaning that the organization has no competency in that area and 10 being perfection.

   Ask for two volunteers to help calculate the average ratings the group will produce.

   Ask participants to fold their sheets of paper and pass them up to the volunteers.

   Have the volunteers tally the ratings to derive an average score for each competency, while participants are doing their ratings on the next competency.

7. List the competencies and their average ratings on a flip chart, as shown below.

Competency	Average Rating
A	xx
B	xx
C	xx
D	xx
E	xx

8. Discuss the ratings. Any competency that scores a 7 or less should be considered deficient. Ask the group to consider strategies for improving the organization's rating in that competency.

Facilitator Notes

- It is often surprising how realistically an organization rates itself. Be prepared for the possibility that the average ratings will be significantly lower than what some senior managers might expect them to be.

- For some groups, it might be useful to have the group rank the competencies in order of importance before revealing the rating scores.

Facilitator Experience Required

This is a straightforward activity that is easy to facilitate unless participants become defensive about the ratings.

Our Stable of Clients or Resources

Description

This activity focuses on the characteristics of any one of the organization's resource areas—clients, programs, products, services, customers, or other stakeholders. Participants categorize each of the clients (programs, products, and so forth, depending on the resource area selected) according to its value to the organization. In the course of the activity, different opinions often arise, so the group develops a broad-based concept of how different people view the contribution of various resources.

Experiential Elements
- Group discussion
- Using metaphor to express ideas
- Individual and group reflection
- Experimenting with ideas

Steps

1. Tell the participants: "We are going to assess one of the resources available to your organization, your clients [substitute what you are assessing, if it's not clients], and what value these clients represent to [the organization]. We will be assigning each client to one of five categories in the 'Stable Matrix.'"

   Show the "Stable Matrix" chart (see the table on the next page for more detail on each category):

Setup
Prepare the "Stable Matrix" chart.

Special Supplies
A pad of Post-it Notes and felt-tip pens for the facilitator.

2. Ask participants to list the organization's current clients and write the name of each client on a Post-it Note.

3. Ask the participants to call out how they would assign each client to a "stable" category. Since not everyone will agree initially on the assignments, ask individuals to explain their assessments.

4. When the group has reached agreement on the category for each client, have the participants discuss the strategies the organization would have to pursue to turn more of the clients into long-term winners.

5. (Optional) Indicate each client's annual revenue value to the company. Total the revenues in each category, then calculate what percentage of the organization's revenues fall into each category of the stable. Ask the group: "What should these percentages be? What actions would you need to take to increase the number of high-revenue clients in the stakes winner category?"

Activity (continued)

Our Stable of Clients

Category	Description	Comments
Stakes Winners	Vital to our growth and future success	Ideal—profitable, have a solid growth pattern, and are good to work with. Value quality work.
Workhorses	Attractive for the moment, but not for the long run	Often have had a close relationship with the organization for years.
Yearlings	Unproven, but have the potential to become thoroughbreds	Represent the possibility of strong growth in the near future or of doing high-quality, profitable work.
Mules	Inconsequential for the organization's future	Neither particularly profitable nor large. May take more time than they're worth.
Nags	Detrimental to the organization's future success	Unprofitable, difficult to work with, don't value quality work. Actually consume more resources than they provide.

Facilitator Notes

- If any client or other resource falls into the "Nags" (detrimental) category, the organization should consider ceasing to devote resources to it because the group's judgment is that the client is actually hurting the organization. You may need to press this point with the group.

- Nonprofits can use a variation of this activity to focus on their programs. In that case, they would measure each program's capacity to advance the organization's mission vis a vis the resources it takes to run the program, as in the table shown on the next page.

- In the variation of this activity that focuses on products, for example, the group would put new and existing product lines into the categories.

Facilitator Experience Required

The facilitator must be able to help participants reach agreement on issues on which they may have very different perspectives. To be able to ask appropriate questions about which stable category a resource belongs in, it is helpful if the facilitator has an understanding of the underpinnings of the client's industry.

Our Stable of Programs

Category	Description	Comments
Stakes Winners	Ideal programs	Serve the right groups, operate well, and are well-funded, achieve their goals, align with the goals and values of the organization
Workhorses	Long-running programs	Often large programs with long histories, but whose effectiveness (or the need for the program) may be in gradual decline
Yearlings	New programs	Seem to have potential to become ideal programs, but it's too soon to tell
Mules	Programs that serve few people at high resource costs	May no longer be important to the organization's mission or may not be financially feasible to continue
Nags	Detrimental to the organization	Programs that don't serve the needs of constituents well and use up more resources than the value they create

It's difficult for many organizations—especially nonprofits—to decide which constituencies will receive priority attention. Organizations that don't establish such priorities can easily over-stretch their budgets and burn out their staffs, boards, and volunteers. As painful as the decision may be, organizations must often be explicit about whom they will serve and how.

If you sense that an organization is trying to be all things to all people, you might try the following activity to help participants sort out their commitments to various constituency groups.

Prioritizing Constituencies

Description

This identification and ranking activity allows participants to examine and evaluate a nonprofit organization's various constituencies. After working together to list constituencies, participants get out of their seats and "vote" by sticking colored dots onto their choices.

Experiential Elements
- Group discussion
- Individual and group decision making

Steps

1. Ask participants, working as a whole group, to list discrete categories of constituents that the organization serves or must answer to. List the constituent categories on a flip chart.

2. Tell the participants: "The categories of constituencies recorded on the flip chart must be prioritized to examine the organization's opportunities to serve them:

   - "The A Group receives highest priority for resources. This is an enormously important, primary constituency; they are probably familiar with much of what you do.

   - "The B Group receives targeted resources. This group is important for your future, but is likely to be less familiar with what you do now. They are infrequent or non-participants in your programs and activities, but have the *potential* to become participants without an extraordinary new effort.

   - "The C Group receives lower priority for resources. These may be smaller groups of people, perhaps with very specialized or narrow interests compared to your overall purpose, or groups whose needs do not align closely with your current abilities to serve them.

   - "The D Group (with no votes) receives no targeted resources. The organization doesn't have the resources to serve them in light of its obligations to members of the A, B, and C Groups."

3. Distribute a supply of blue, red, and yellow voting dots to each person. Show the flip chart sheet you have previously prepared with the dot groups. Explain: "The blue dots represent the A Group, red dots the B Group, yellow dots the C Group, and constituencies that receive no dots comprise the D Group. Using the dots as 'votes,' you should each place one dot on every constituent category you believe merits at least some of the organization's resources."

Setup

On a sheet of flip chart paper, make a chart that shows what each color dot represents:

Blue Dot = A Group
Red Dot = B Group
Yellow Dot = C Group

Special Supplies

Several large blue, red, and yellow voting dots for each person

4. Invite everyone to come up to the chart and place their dots on the constituent categories to indicate in which group they believe each constituent category should be classified.

5. After the voting, review the votes each constituent category received to see if the group agrees with the results. For each category, how consistent is the rating? Wherever there is a mix of dot colors, the mix indicates lack of agreement about the importance of that constituent category. Facilitate a discussion to resolve the differences of opinion.

Facilitator Notes

- Be sure to explain that the results of this activity will not force the organization to abandon any of its constituents. Rather, it helps the organization focus its resources to best meet the needs of its key constituents.

> **Facilitator Experience Required**
> This activity is easy to manage.

- Make sure you limit the number of voting dots of each color so that participants must make choices and cannot, for instance, rate all constituents as being in the A Group.

- This activity should spark a discussion about how much effort the organization can and should make to convert "the non-interested" into participants or whether it is a better use of their resources to deepen relationships with constituents who are already involved.

If participants have trouble articulating exactly what it is that sets their organization apart, you might use the following short activity.

Distinctive Competencies

Description

Participants are asked to role play a situation in which they must quickly and succinctly describe what is unique about their organization. By restricting responses to what can be written on the back of a business card, this activity forces participants to make difficult choices.

Experiential Elements
- Active decision making
- Participation in role play
- Shared dialogue and discussion

Steps

1. Distribute one or more blank "business cards" to each participant. Introduce the scenario: "Imagine that you are attending an important civic event and are introduced to the head of an organization you have been desperate to do business with. You start talking and really seem to connect when, suddenly, he looks at his watch and says, 'Whoops! I'm running late for a meeting. I've got to go. Give me your card.' Then he adds, 'You know, we're very happy with the organization we're already working with. Would you jot down on the back of your card what makes your organization different?'"

Setup

Prepare "business cards" for the activity. (You can use your office paper cutter to create "business cards" by cutting index cards or paper into 2 inch x 3 1/2 inch cards.) You will need one "business card" for each participant and one for each breakout group.

2. Give participants thirty seconds to write on the back of their "business cards" the one thing that makes their organization unique. Tell them to be sure to write clearly so this organization head will be able to read what they wrote when he gets back to his office.

3. Collect all the cards and read them aloud, without identifying the authors. Take note of the responses on a flip chart.

4. Review the responses. Ask the participants:

   - Do these cards say anything that others in our field couldn't say?

   - Is this our version of "all things to all people"?

   - Do we say things that everyone says, such as, "We care"?

   - Do these cards set us apart from our competitors?

5. Have the participants form small breakout groups and give each group a single blank business card. Ask them to decide how they could describe what makes their organization unique so succinctly that they could write it on the back of that card, and ask them to do so. Ask each breakout group to present its business card to the rest of the group.

Facilitator Notes

- The point of this activity is to help participants focus on what sets their organization apart from others: what differentiates their products or services from others in the industry—distinctive product features, exceptional service, new technology, and so on.

Facilitator Experience Required
This is an easy activity to facilitate.

- The real-life scenario of this short activity creates insights that can lead to a powerful debriefing.

- The immediacy of this activity helps participants re-examine their assumptions about the organization.

Evaluating Work Processes

When an organization is considering major changes such as reorganizing, adding new products or services, changing compensation structures, or moving to teams, it's helpful to have participants examine their current operating processes first.

In his book *The Process Edge,* consultant Peter Keen* (1997) posits that all work processes fall into one of five categories: *identity, priority, background, mandated,* and *folklore* processes. He suggests that determining which category an organization's work processes fall into will help leaders decide whether each is a net asset or a net cost (that is, does it generate revenue or other benefits to the organization, or is it an expense?).

Having retreat participants classify their work processes in this way will help them determine where process improvement would actually make a difference in the organization's ability to achieve its goals.

Identity Processes

These are the processes that define what the company stands for to its customers, its members, its funders, its staff—to everyone who has a stake in its success. These processes are almost always net assets; they are what attracts new clients to the organization.

For a history museum, for instance, one identity process might be the way it plans, produces, and promotes special exhibits. For a retail hardware chain, an identity process might be how it displays merchandise or how it designs its advertising and marketing campaigns.

Investing in these identity processes, says Keen, will usually result in a direct payoff in terms of improved operations and long-term viability.

*Adapted with permission from Harvard Business School Press. From *The Process Edge: Creating Value Where It Counts* by Peter Keen. Boston, MA, 1997. Copyright © 1997 by Harvard Business School Publishing Corporation, all rights reserved.

Priority Processes

These are processes that support an organization's identity processes. They're not necessarily visible to an outsider, but they're critical to an organization's success, because without them the organization wouldn't be able to maintain its identity processes.

An example of a priority process for a museum might be conservation of its materials. For a computer design firm, it might be its in-house programming ability. For an association, it might be its research capability.

Background Processes

These are the processes, such as billing, compensation, benefits, and accounts payable that help the day-to-day business run.

Most background processes are net costs. They're all necessary, but, says Keen, it can be a mistake to spend massive amounts of money to improve them, because no matter how much better they are, they won't bring revenues into the organization. Yet it is just in these areas where many organizations often spend the most in process improvement. That's not to say an organization shouldn't work to improve these processes and make them more cost-effective, but only after paying attention to their identity and priority processes.

Mandated Processes

These are the things an organization is required to do by law, such as filing employee withholding taxes. Mandated processes are almost always net costs. Spending money to improve them usually doesn't bring any significant return on investment.

Folklore Processes

These are the things an organization has always done, although the reason for doing them is lost in the mists of history. They no longer serve a real purpose and create no value for the organization. People have done them for so long,

Ask participants to work in small groups to identify their organization's current identity and priority processes. In the group as a whole, help participants come to agreement on their classification of these processes. They should ask themselves:

- Is there anything that should be on our list of identity or priority processes that is not?

- Are there identity or priority processes we should be very good at, but aren't doing at all, or are doing poorly?

- What are our folklore processes that we should let go of?

however, that it's almost impossible for them to see how they could get rid of them without changing the nature of the organization. Typical folklore processes are producing reports that no one has any use for or holding weekly meetings that take up more time than they're worth. One organization we worked with devoted many staff hours every spring to preparing a report that a previous CEO had demanded but that the current CEO couldn't have cared less about.

Folklore processes should be eliminated. They burn up the organization's time and money for little or no return.

Planning for Action

Once the group has worked through thinking about the organization's environment and possible futures and has rated current performance, participants will have a good sense of the areas in which change is called for. But it's almost certain that they won't be able to implement all the changes they've thought of.

Good strategy involves making tradeoffs. It's practically a law of nature that unless resources are increased, paying more attention to one thing means devoting less attention to another. If an organization tries to do everything equally well, it will be expert at none, and may fail at all. Venerable companies have gone out of business or been acquired by more successful firms because they bit off more than they could swallow.

Such tradeoffs are not only inevitable, but, according to strategy expert Michael Porter (1996), they serve a useful purpose for these three reasons:

- Making choices forces an organization to resolve inconsistencies in image or reputation.
- Different strategic choices require different activities, different types of people, and different ways to deploy resources. If an organization isn't willing to make hard choices, its energies will be dispersed.
- Strategic tradeoffs make organizational priorities clear to the staff.

Setting Objectives

Often when it comes to writing the plan, participants become entangled in discussions about vocabulary. Is there a difference between "goals" and "objectives"? What is a "strategy"? Is this idea a "tactic" or a "strategy"? In reality, the terminology isn't important; what's critical is the quality of the thinking. It may be helpful to remind the group of these simple definitions:

- *Goals* or *objectives* answer the question, "What do we want to achieve?"
- *Strategies* answer the question, "What major initiatives will we have to undertake to achieve our goals?"
- *Tactics* specify the action details within strategies.

It may take an organization several years to fulfill its strategic purpose. In the meantime, senior managers need to establish measurable shorter-term goals so they can monitor progress. Five-year goals, common in plans of several years ago, are practically useless in guiding people in making their day-to-day decisions about how to use their resources, so we recommend including shorter time-frames and milestones.

Goals outline what an organization (or work group) intends to accomplish, where the participants want to go, like the destination of a journey. If there isn't agreement on goals, people will pull in different directions and expend great energy while making little forward progress.

An organization's goals should answer the question, "What specific results do we want in the next year?" While a corporation's goals may generally be financial and those for nonprofits may relate more to the reach, quality, and effectiveness of the services they provide, objectives should always be expressed in terms that are measurable.

To help retreat participants determine the results they want, you will want to guide them in an exploration of these key areas.

Financial Results. For a company, you might ask: From the total gross revenue (or percent increases in revenue, profit margins, or changes in sources of business) will you achieve the results you want? If not, what could be done to change that? For a nonprofit organization, the question might be: What are the trends in total income, changes in sources of income, ratio of earned income to contributed income, or membership totals and what are the implications of those trends for your organization?

Products and Services. Are changes necessary in the products or services the organization now offers? Should new products or services be developed? To whom are or should the organization's services be directed? How satisfied are the people the organization currently serves with its offerings?

Internal Management. Does the organization need to take steps to improve organizational effectiveness? Are some operating ratios out of whack? Do certain operational processes need to be overhauled? Are any changes called for so that the organization can function more in accordance with its values?

Brief Activity

Remind the group that the list of goals should be short so people can remember them, dedicate sufficient resources to them, and work diligently to achieve them. You can help the participants refine their objectives by asking these questions:

- If you acheived this objective, would it move you toward your strategic purpose? (See "Activity: Exploring Strategic Purpose," pp. 180–181.) If not, why do you have it as an objective?

- Which of these objectives will make the greatest contribution to fulfilling the organization's most deeply held aspirations? Which will move the organization ahead faster?

- What would happen if the organization took no action on one or more of these goals? Would it make a serious difference in the long-term results you could achieve?

Learning. What new skills and knowledge must the organization obtain to thrive in the future? What competencies must employees possess or acquire?

Prioritizing Among Goals

One of the hard decisions organizations have to make is prioritizing among goals. You might use the following activity to help the retreat group do just that.

Targeting Core Priorities

Description
Participants use the power of visually prioritizing the organization's goals on a bulls-eye target, making forced choices to sharpen their thinking. Then they break into small groups to discuss the implications of their rankings.

Experiential Elements
- Group discussion
- Visualizing relationships
- Group decision making

Steps

1. Divide the participants into subgroups of five to seven people. Direct each subgroup to a flip chart on which you have drawn concentric circles, like a bulls-eye target, as shown in the sample on the right. On each chart, the group will find Post-its with the organization's stated goals or priorities placed in random order in the rings, one Post-it per ring.

2. Ask each subgroup to work *in silence* to rearrange the written notes, placing only *one* note per ring, from goals they judge to be the least core in importance in the outermost ring, to the most core in the bulls-eye.

    Tell the group, "The goals as written might not adequately reflect what any member of your subgroup believes they should be. You are all free to write new goals to replace the ones that are on the notes. (Again, working in silence.) If someone does this, he or she should move the original Post-it to the side of the flip chart. Don't add a new goal without removing another goal."

3. Have the subgroups consider these four questions when making their determination:

    - What is our strategic purpose?

    - Where can we make the biggest difference with our resources?

Setup
- Create a quadrant of a large bulls-eye target on flip chart paper for each subgroup. (A quadrant of a target is all you can fit on a sheet of flip chart paper because each concentric ring must be wide enough to accommodate a 3 inch x 5 inch Post-it Note, more or less. See the sample below.) Make sure you have one ring for each of the group's identified priorities (no more than six or seven).

- For each subgroup, write one of the group's identified priorities (these could relate to program areas, financial targets, types of activities) per Post-it Note. Place the Post-its in random order on the bulls-eye chart, one goal or priority in each of the concentric rings (see Step 1).
- Write the four questions outlined in Step 3 on a flip chart.

- What *must* we do that no one else can do?

- What can we give up to make the greatest impact in our core areas?

4. Encourage the participants to stay engaged in the activity until they are satisfied that the goals are arranged in priority order. Just because someone moved a note from where another participant thinks it belongs doesn't mean the activity is over. All participants should keep moving the Post-its into the priority order they believe is best.

5. When everyone can agree with the order of the placement of the notes, or if the subgroups are at an impasse, have the subgroups sit down. Ask each subgroup to tell the whole group: Why they put the priorities in the order that they did, where they got stuck, and why that happened. Facilitate a discussion with the whole group to see whether participants can come to common agreement on priorities.

Facilitator Notes
- If this activity follows the Setting Objectives discussion (see pp. 201–203 above), write the objectives the group came up with on the Post-it Notes. Otherwise, use the organization's previously stated general goals or priorities for the activity. You should be able to find these goals in your pre-retreat research. They are often listed on an organization's website or in an annual report.

- It's important to keep this activity lively and fun and encourage participants to keep pushing for what they'd like to see happen, even if it means moving notes back and forth several times. Remind participants to maintain silence when they are working in their subgroups.

- If this activity is debriefed well, it can be one of the most powerful focusing activities of the retreat. For this to happen, participants must keep pushing for their priorities in their subgroups and in the larger group.

Special Supplies
A pad of 3 inch x 5 inch Post-it Notes and felt-tip pens for each participant.

Facilitator Experience Required
This activity is moderately easy for most facilitators.

Checking Against Resources

Many strategic planning retreats are tied only loosely to an organization's formal budgeting process. But the answers to such basic questions as, "How much can we spend?" and "Will we be able to hire new staff to work on this project or must we re-deploy existing staff?" define (and limit) how ambitious a plan can be.

In every strategic planning retreat, you'll need to build in ample time for reviewing, at least in broad strokes, the current year's operating budget and revenue projections for the coming year. You can help ensure that this review happens by alerting the convenor well in advance that budget and revenue information will be required. Guide the participants in a discussion of such questions as these:

- How did you spend your financial resources this year (both in absolute dollars and in percentage of budget)?
- In which budget categories do you need to spend more?
- Which budget percentages must be reduced next year?
- (For corporations) Are you budgeting to hit your profit or margin goals? If not, where will you cut expenses or increase revenues to become more profitable?

In the end, every organization needs an operating budget that is consistent with its goals and strategies, but also goals and strategies that are consistent with its budget. Here's an activity we use to help organizations look at the impact of the goals that participants have identified and the resources needed to achieve them.

Resource/Impact Matrix

Description

This activity helps participants examine their organizational goals, considering both the resources needed to achieve the goals and the potential impact on the organization of meeting it objectives. The relative value of those two considerations becomes dramatically visible when participants create a large matrix and plot each goal on it.

Experiential Elements

- Using visual means to clarify ideas
- Discussion of ideas

Steps

1. Ask the group to list the organization's available resources (such as staff time, money, office space, brand recognition) and write them on a flip chart labeled "Resources."

2. Then ask the group to list the impact achieving a goal might have on the organization (such as increasing sales, raising brand awareness, attracting new clients) and write them on a flip chart labeled "Impact."

3. Present the "Resource/Impact Matrix" to the group, defining the labels on the matrix:

    - High Impact/Low Resource Usage = Winner (represents high return on investment)

    - High Impact/High Resource Usage = Future Potential (needs assessment to see if the high resource cost is justified)

    - Low Impact/High Resource Usage = Abandon (low return on investment)

    - Low Impact/Low Resource Usage = Small Potatoes (Can the impact be increased? Otherwise, it should also be abandoned, because it's probably a distraction.)

Setup

Create a large "Resource/Impact Matrix" using four sheets of flip chart paper, as shown below.

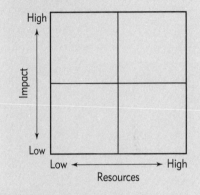

Special Supplies

Pad of 3 inch x 5 inch Post-it Notes and a felt-tip pen for the facilitator.

4. Write each of the group's previously determined goals on the Post-it Notes. Goals should include quantitative and qualitative measures.

5. Ask for a group of four or five volunteers to place the Post-it Notes with the goals into the appropriate squares of the matrix. The volunteers should keep working until they come to consensus on the placement of each goal. The rest of the group observes their actions and listens to their deliberations.

6. After all goals are placed, conduct a whole group discussion about what choices the volunteers made. Based on the discussion, rank the goals as:

   • Top priority

   • Secondary priority

   • Low priority

Facilitator Notes In addition to helping the group assess goals, this activity can be used when an organization wants to examine current programs, products, or services in terms of their impact and the resources they consume.

> **Facilitator Experience Required**
>
> The facilitator should be expert in formulating and working with goals. Familiarity with business principles in general and with the organization's operations and financial resources is a plus.

Devising Strategies

Once the goals are set, the group can start working on strategies that outline how they plan to achieve those goals. The goals should have answered the questions:

- What do we want to happen long-term?
- What do we want to happen short-term?

Strategies will address the question:

- What do we need to do to make these things happen?

When the participants reflect on the organization's strategic purpose and on their more immediate goals, the process may feel overwhelming. The best advice you can give them is: Don't try to do everything at once.

For each goal, ask the group, "What do you have to *change* to make this happen?" And, perhaps even more importantly, "Are you willing to make those changes?" The answers to these questions will help the group focus on initial strategies. There's no sense including something in the plan if the organization isn't ready to make it happen.

Encourage the group to list everything the organization needs to do to achieve its objectives. At this stage, you're still looking at broad-strokes ideas. For instance, the group might say, "Improve relationships with current clients," without having to specify that they're going to send front-line employees to customer service training.

Management consultant and author Peter Drucker (1999) also advises, "The first change policy . . . throughout the entire institution, has to be Organized Abandonment. The change leader puts every product, every service, every process, every market, every distribution channel, every customer and end-use, on trial for its life."

When you're facilitating this discussion, you have the difficult task of prodding participants to specify what they're willing to give up to get the resources to create something fresh. (You might find the Resource/Impact Matrix a useful tool.)

Testing Strategies

To make sure the recommended strategies are cohesive, ask the planning group these key questions:

- Have you planned at least one strategy for achieving each goal? (If you don't have strategies for achieving each of your goals, nothing will happen with respect to that goal.)
- Does every strategy contribute to at least one goal? (Make sure you haven't included strategies that are "nice to do" but don't really move you ahead aggressively.)
- Is each one of these strategies *necessary* for you to achieve your goals? (You don't want to spend resources on things you don't have to.)
- If you carry out all of these strategies, will they, taken together, be *sufficient* for you to reach your goals? (There's no sense in starting something that's doomed to failure because the planned actions won't lead you to achieve the goal.)

Go to Chapter 8 to review the action planning necessary to conclude the strategic planning retreat.

Once the participants are convinced they've ascertained the appropriate broad strategies, they need to stipulate the *tactics*—the specific actions individuals and work units will take to implement the strategies. The participants should assign responsibilities and deadlines—and sufficient resources—to the task. You'll probably have to help them be realistic. If most of the responsibilities are assigned to people who have little control over their workloads, the tasks are not likely to get done. Finally, help the participants determine how they will monitor progress toward the goals. What will happen if a person or department fails to accomplish its tasks?

In this chapter we have provided some theory and presented several activities designed to help facilitators lead strategic planning retreats. We've looked at elements of strategy and how to define the organization's mission, vision, or purpose. We discussed how to discern the organization's values in practice (whether the same or different from its declared values), how to gain an understanding of the larger environment in which the organization operates, and how to evaluate work processes. We explored how to approach action planning, how to prioritize goals, and how to check ambitions against available resources, and we concluded by examining how to devise and test strategies.

In Chapter 11, we'll focus on factors facilitators have to take into account when facing the challenges of changing an organization's culture.

Chapter 11

Leading a Culture Change Retreat

L et's be realistic: You can't take a bunch of people to an offsite retreat and expect a dramatic and immediate turnaround in the organization's culture. It isn't going to happen. A retreat, however, can be a significant event in the life of an organization, and as such can have a powerful effect on its culture.

An organization's culture builds up slowly over time. It starts back when a company is founded. The principles that the founders believed in probably still have some influence on how employees view events and react to them today. As people observed the founders and the decisions they made, especially in hard times, the organization's culture started to solidify. When those choices worked out well, employees learned, "This is the way we do things here." And when things went wrong, they learned what *not* to do. The culture is then handed down from each generation of the staff to the next, just as parents teach their children, by word and—arguably more significantly—by example.

Employees start learning the culture from their first contact with the company. How were the help-wanted ads worded? How was the interview handled? What were the conditions of employment? And as soon as they join the organization they're exposed to a barrage of stories, each one carrying the same cultural message: "This is the way we do things here."

New employees are taught the formal rules (regulations, policies, and procedures) while at the same time they begin observing for themselves how things *really* work. They quickly become aware of any disparity between what Harvard Business School professor Chris Argyris calls the company's "espoused" values—those it professes to believe in—and its values "in use"—those it actually practices. And it's the values that are practiced, rather than those that are merely preached, that have the most powerful effect on employees' perceptions of the organization's culture.

Although influenced powerfully by its founders, an organization's culture isn't static. It continues to evolve over time, based largely on major events in the organization's history and the leaders' responses to them. Take, for example, how a major layoff was managed at one company.

On a Friday morning, the organization announced a large layoff. Those who were affected were asked to clean out their desks and were escorted out of the building before lunchtime. They had little time to say goodbye to colleagues who were staying on.

Worse, when the remaining employees came to work the next week, they were confronted with the sight of tables in the hall piled with the telephones that had belonged only a couple of days before to their longstanding friends and associates. Employees looked at those phones and remembered the people they used to call.

Message: "We treat people like expendable office equipment."

Another organization, in contrast, established a job placement center in anticipation of staff cuts and permitted laid-off employees to use its facilities for several weeks to receive counseling and seek other jobs.

Message: "People really are important to us here."

Great Expectations: What Can Realistically Be Accomplished at a Retreat

Most retreats are convened to address particular business-related issues. Rarely are they intended specifically to influence the organization's culture. But it's hard to make significant changes in response to business needs without first addressing cultural issues. For example, a firm whose top managers seemed unable to work together cooperatively wanted us to focus on improving those managers' communication skills. In our pre-retreat assessment, we found that the managers were quite skilled at communicating with the employees they supervised and people above them in the chain of command, but not with one another. The problem was that the culture encouraged internal competition. The managers had learned that they had to protect their turf, and one way they did this was to withhold information from one another. The organization didn't have a communication problem; it had a culture problem.

To help an organization explore its culture while still focusing on specific business needs, include in your retreat design activities that will help participants:

- Discuss how they view the organization's culture and what they would like to be different
- Understand their own contributions to the prevailing culture
- Explore why various teams or departments work the way they do
- Examine why disagreements arise
- Identify and discuss strategies for changing their own counterproductive practices
- Assess obstacles to a more positive environment and generate ideas on how to overcome them

Remember that human beings tend to resist change, especially change to conditions they themselves have helped create and sustain. So it's important to help participants identify how the culture is contributing to the problems they are experiencing.

If the retreat is dedicated to cultural issues, you'll probably want to begin with a diagnostic activity that helps people see their culture more clearly. It's often difficult for groups to assess their own culture; they can't easily get enough distance from it to make objective observations. We've found that the following activity, which asks people to examine their culture—not from their own perspectives but from that of "anthropologists"—yields remarkable results.

Visit Our Village

Description

Participants are asked to observe the culture they work in by looking at its rituals and practices through an objective lens. They respond to questions anthropologists might use to study a culture and post their observations on a wall. All participants then review the postings and draw conclusions about their culture.

Experiential Elements

- Personal reflection
- Observing and reflecting on other people's actions
- Applying theories to real-life situations

Steps

1. Introduce the task: "As you know, anthropologists study cultures by living among the people of those cultures. To learn about the culture you are a part of, please imagine that you are anthropologists about to make a report on your village, Village X [use the name of the organization or department].

   "You have been living in and studying this village for some time. What observations have you made about how things work here? Answer some of the questions I will give you shortly [see Anthropologists' Questions below] for your report. You won't have time to answer all of them, so pick the ones that interest you the most. Write your answers, one idea per Post-it, and when you have written several, walk up to the board and stick them under the appropriate questions. Then write and post your answers to more questions. You have twenty minutes to write and post your answers."

2. After twenty minutes, ask the participants to walk along the wall and read the notes.

3. When everyone has read the notes and is seated again, ask, "What themes emerge from your observations?" Facilitate a discussion to help the group agree on five or six themes.

   For each theme ask: "Is this a positive or negative aspect of your culture? If it's positive, how can you support it? If it's negative, what changes must you make to reduce or eliminate it?"

Setup

- Print out a list of Anthropologists' Questions (see Step 4) and make a copy for each participant.
- Select a long wall with ample space for participants to walk along it to post and review written material.
- Print each question separately on 8 1/2 x 11 inch paper in 48 point type. Tape these Question Sheets on the wall, with space around each to affix the participants' Post-it® Notes.

Special Supplies

A pad of Post-it Notes and a fine-point felt-tip pen for each participant; a list of Anthropologists' Questions for each participant; Question Sheets (see Setup).

Here is a sampling of questions you may wish to choose from to present to the participants. We recommend selecting no more than ten to fifteen questions.

Worship

What is worshipped here?

What are the rituals of worship?

Voice of the Elders

Who are the elders?

How are they treated?

What do they say?

How does one become an elder?

Legends and Stories

What stories and legends do people hear when they first join our village?

Whom do they hear the stories from?

What new stories have they heard lately?

Communications

What are the formal channels of communication?

What informal communication channels exist and who uses them?

How is reality communicated?

Who is included and who is left out of the communication patterns?

Politics

How important is politics in the life of the village?

What are the various internal political factions or affiliations?

Which political factions are currently in power?

What do the groups that are out of power do to get attention?

Fighting

Who are the enemies?

What weapons are used?

How does the village fight internally?

What determines who wins?

Good News

What is good news?

How is it communicated?

Is good news celebrated? In what ways?

Laws

What are the primary laws?

Who can make or change laws?

Are the laws obeyed?

What are the consequences for breaking the law?

Children

Who are the children?

Who raises them?

How are they treated?

Rites of Passage

How are new members initiated into the village?

What rites of passage must people go through to be fully accepted into the village?

What do people have to do to become leaders in the village?

Learning

Is learning new things important in the village?

How does the village learn?

Who are the teachers?

What's the most important thing people learn?

Decisions

How are decisions made?

Who participates?

Who has the final word?

Are decisions abided by?

What are the penalties for not abiding by them?

Outsiders

Who are the outsiders?

What principles guide relationships with outsiders?

Neighborhoods

What physical neighborhoods exist?

What differentiates the neighborhoods?

Are some neighborhoods thought of as better or worse than others?

Where do people gather and talk informally?

Do people cross neighborhood lines?

How can people move from one neighborhood to another?

Facilitator Note   The key to the success of this activity is to have the participants discuss how cultural issues and perceptions affect their behavior back at work. Sometimes it's helpful for participants to understand how the culture they've described in the Visit Our Village activity evolved in the first place so they can determine what can and ought to be changed. Because shared experiences build culture, you can help the group explore the impact of those experiences with either of the next two activities.

Facilitator Experience Required
The facilitator must be skilled enough to manage potential defensive reactions from leaders who don't like the image of the culture that may emerge from this activity.

Timeline of Our History

Description

This activity encourages participants to identify the defining events that have shaped their organization's culture and explore how those events have influenced their (and others') subsequent beliefs and behaviors. They write their own thoughts on large sheets posted on the walls, then walk along the "timelines" to see how others perceived the same periods and events in the organization's history.

> **Experiential Elements**
> - Personal reflection
> - Discussion
> - Listening to the ideas of others
> - Observing while walking around the room

Steps

1. Distribute an "Events in Our Organization" note sheet to each participant. Introduce the task: "We're going to look at how your reactions to important events have shaped your working culture. Thinking about what has happened here in the past ten years, write down the events that are most significant to you and approximately when they took place."

2. After five or six minutes, invite everyone to transfer what they have written on their note sheets onto the big timeline taped around the room.

Setup
- On a fifteen-foot long (or longer) sheet of paper, write the heading that is on the participants' note sheets: "Events in Our Organization." Tape the long sheet of paper horizontally on a wall.
- Across the top of the sheet, write the years that the timeline will cover, leaving space between years. A typical timeline might cover ten years; allow more space between the most recent years. For example:

Events in Our Organization

93	94	95	96	97	98	99	00	01	02

Special Supplies

A roll of newsprint or butcher paper; one marker for each participant; one note sheet for each participant, titled "Events in Our Organization" and marked with the dates covering the period of time that will be considered.

3. After they write their comments in the appropriate places, invite the participants to tour the timeline and read what others have written. Facilitate a discussion around these questions:

- Are there any significant themes suggested by this timeline?

- How would you complete this sentence: "Judging from our timeline, we are an organization that. . . ."

- What similarities did you see in the events other people chose, compared to the ones you selected?

Facilitator Note Rarely do two individuals assess the impact of a specific event in the same way, so walking along the timeline can be a profound learning experience.

Facilitator Experience Required

The facilitator must be able to ensure that all viewpoints expressed get a fair hearing, including those not shared by most members of the group.

Significant Stories

Description

Small breakout groups are asked to identify and tell the story of an event inside the organization that they believe illustrates an important principle about the culture. After the small groups report out, everyone discusses their reactions to the stories and what they learned.

Experiential Elements

- Storytelling
- Personal reflection
- Listening to others

Steps

1. Create subgroups of four to six participants. Define the task: "Each group will tell us a story about an event that happened in this organization [or department] in the past two years. Choose an event that you believe exemplifies how things work here. Each subgroup needs to agree on a story and be prepared to tell the story to the rest of the group. Avoid mentioning names if possible. Please tell us what rewards and punishments—both formal and informal—occurred as a result of this incident and what this story says about what this organization values and how it operates."

2. After they have heard each subgroup's presentation, ask participants how these events might be interpreted differently by different people or departments in the organization. Guide the participants in a discussion of the underlying meanings of the stories they chose. Ask such questions as:

    - Why is this story significant to you?

    - What does it represent?

    - Is it significant to other people as well?

    - What impact have these events had on the culture and on your perception of the way things work in this organization?

3. Invite the group to suggest the stories they would prefer to be telling about the organization: "What do these stories say about the group's aspirations?"

Facilitator Experience Required

The facilitator must be able to work with individuals sensitively to ensure that their stories don't go on too long, are relevant to the task, and don't embarrass any individual, whether present in the room or not.

Facilitator Note

This activity encourages participants to identify and study significant events in their organization's history. The discussion is likely to surface divergent perspectives on the same events.

Working with Sensitive or Controversial Issues

Many leaders are reluctant to have controversial issues come up at a retreat for fear that they might lead to open conflict. And even if top managers are willing to discuss sensitive topics, very often participants are hesitant to speak openly. They may not want to hurt anyone's feelings. They may worry that candid comments about how the culture is perceived will be taken as a criticism of management. Also, some people just don't have the skill to speak articulately about delicate issues. These are legitimate concerns.

When it's important for participants to address issues they believe are "undiscussable," you may have to structure an activity that allows them to raise their concerns less directly. The following activity helps people bring difficult issues to the surface by working through them in small groups and in silence. It almost always elicits responses that go straight to the heart of people's concerns.

Silent Dialogue

Description

Participants express their reactions to a sensitive issue in the organization by drawing a picture together. Small groups work together in silence, using line and color to express feelings. The post-drawing discussion of the "pictures" opens the door for the group to speak honestly about the issue.

Steps

1. Seat four to six participants at each table. Introduce the task: "This is an activity that addresses [state the organization's issue]. Please think about all the ways you might answer the question that's on the flip chart."

   Show the flip chart with the question to be covered, such as "How well do you feel the layoffs were managed?" Take a moment to ensure that everyone understands the question.

   Tell the group, "Using the paper and markers on your tables, you will draw your thoughts and feelings in silence to make a group picture that answers this question."

2. Show the rules on a second flip chart.

   The Rules
   - No talking
   - No writing words
   - No drawing pictures

   Explain the task: "We are going to do this activity in silence. Please don't speak or communicate with anyone else in any way. In fact, don't even make eye contact with anyone while you are working on the picture.

   "You are going to use color and line to express your thoughts and feelings, independently and simultaneously.

Experiential Elements
- Personal reflection
- Giving feedback
- Using drawing to express thoughts and feelings
- Listening
- Group discussion

Setup
- Create a double-sized sheet of flip chart paper for each table by placing two blank sheets of paper side by side and taping them together. Then draw an oval a couple of inches inside the edges of the paper—freehand is fine.
- Put one of these double sheets in the center of each table. Place art markers in glasses or mugs on the table.
- Write on a flip chart page the question the group will address.
- Write the rules on a second flip chart page.

Special Supplies

Sixteen art markers (such as Prismacolor® markers) in various colors for each table (see Facilitator Notes); four glasses or mugs per table.

"Don't write any words or draw a picture of anything. For instance, if I wanted to express feeling hopeful, I might use a yellow color and draw lines like this [demonstrate], but the rules say I couldn't draw a happy face. Or if I were angry, I might take a black marker and make short powerful lines like this. But I wouldn't draw pictures of lightning strikes.

"After we start, I'll come by and move the paper, but just continue working after I do that. Don't change where you are sitting."

3. Make sure everyone understands the task; then ask the group to begin drawing in silence. After three or four minutes, turn the paper so that participants are now sitting as far as possible from what they were drawing. (It doesn't matter that the corners of the paper might be in front of someone or hanging off the edge of the table.) Participants will begin adding to whatever art they find in front of them.

4. After three or four more minutes, rotate the paper at each table again so participants are working on an entirely new section of the drawing.

5. After four more minutes, make the final move, turning the paper once more so that participants are working on yet another section that is new to them.

6. Finally, after another few minutes, ask the group to bring their silent drawing to a close.

7. Instruct each group to spend some time talking among themselves about their pictures. Suggest that each participant start with, "Here's where I first began drawing" and then explain what the drawing stood for. For example: "I was drawing these little purple dots to represent that I feel that everybody is very separated here. And this black line indicates how senior management watches over us. Then the paper turned and I got this big blue wavy thing. I thought that it looked like indecision, so I started putting yellow lines around it to illuminate our thoughts. Then I saw that Loretta was drawing overlapping circles all around my purple dots, and I thought maybe we could all overlap with each other so I made big yellow circles showing that we should all work together to solve our problems."

8. Ask each group to develop three or four major themes that their picture illustrates and write them on a sheet of flip chart paper. Each group should then title its picture and post it with the summary of themes on the wall.

9. Each group should describe its picture and tell the others in the room the title and the themes it surfaced.

10. Facilitate a discussion about what the group has learned about the issue as a result of the Silent Dialogue. Sample questions:

- What do the themes and how you worked together in this activity say about [the organization]?

- How did you feel when other people started drawing on your work?

- Did your group decide to draw outside the oval line? Does the way that decision was made mirror the way decisions are commonly made in [the organization]?

- How does this experience reflect your behavior back at work?

Since every picture will have its own harmony of appearance, you might also ask participants how they achieved that harmony without talking.

Facilitator Notes

- Working in silence allows participants to access more intuitive thinking.

- This activity does not work well with ordinary felt-tip markers. We recommend you use art markers or another medium that offers a large variety of colors. (Prismacolor® Double-Ended Markers are an excellent choice. They come in 144 colors and are available at art supply stores.) Other materials you might consider include art pastels (although they smear easily) and crayons (a low-cost alternative). Art markers will create the most striking pictures, however.

- There will be a few moments at the beginning of the activity when no one knows what to do, but eventually someone at each table will pick up a marker and start drawing. Soon, everyone will join in.

> **Facilitator Experience Required**
> This activity requires skillful facilitation. Some participants may react negatively to your request that they engage in what they see as "therapy." Some may need help translating their visual expressions to verbal ones. In addition, the facilitator must have the skill to deal with the possibility of uncomfortable revelations that may emerge during the debriefing of the drawings.

- Remember: Don't speak to the group during the double-sheet paper moves—this reinforces the "no talking" rule.

- Some people will confine their drawing to a space they have defined for themselves. Others, however, will reach over into other spaces and draw outside the oval line (the oval line has no purpose other than for people to decide whether or not they want to cross it). Sometimes a group will even add more paper and extend the drawing. Let every group work in its own way. Don't give any further instructions.

- Very often groups want to bring their pictures back to the workplace and hang them up. Some even decide to have the pictures laminated or framed. Displaying these dramatic and emotional works in hallways or gathering places helps remind people of the power they have to create beauty out of confusion.

Reward Structures Help Shape Culture

Another important element of an organization's culture is the effectiveness of its reward structure. (Keep in mind that rewards aren't limited to salary and benefits. They can also include a variety of things that make work more enjoyable, from an office with a door to an extra day off to celebrate particularly hard work.)

Do the organization's rewards produce heightened commitment and a strong sense of loyalty? Or are the rewards inappropriate or inadequate, leading to cynicism, apathy, and high turnover?

In one large nonprofit organization, performance awards were centralized in the human resources office, which processed nominations from supervisors. This office decided which candidates would receive recognition and what form that recognition would take. Employees didn't consider the process to be fair. They believed that some people received performance awards who should not have and that some people who deserved awards were passed over. Many also thought that awards were often given for the wrong reasons. They didn't take the awards seriously, so the awards didn't serve as incentives for improved performance.

In the course of a retreat, the organization's senior managers heard that employees thought the current award system was counterproductive. The leaders asked retreat participants how they would design a more equitable incentive program. Employees suggested that anyone, rather than just supervisors, be able to nominate someone for an award and that a wide range of employees, not just a central office, be involved in deciding who would actually receive awards. And they suggested that additional categories of recognition be established.

Management accepted the proposition. Employees formed committees and designed and administered the employee recognition system with the blessing of the organization's leadership team. Awards soon came to be seen as legitimate recognition for excellence. Recipients appreciated them, and others aspired to them.

Here's an activity to help the group assess whether the organization is rewarding what it intends to reward.

What Gets Rewarded Here?

Description

This activity provides an opportunity to explore the current reward systems, both formal and informal. In addition, participants examine other ways in which people might be rewarded.

Experiential Elements
- Group listing and ranking
- Group presentations
- Listening

Steps

1. Divide the participants into groups of five to eight people. Half will be designated "A" groups and half "B" groups. Give each group a flip chart and markers.

2. Introduce the task: "We're going to explore all the ways in which this organization might reward or reinforce certain actions. The A groups will list all the elements of the formal reward system—promotions, raises, awards, and so forth—and the B groups will list the components of the informal reward system—personal attention, recognition of achievements, peer group opinions, top management interest, and so forth. Recognition and reinforcement might come from inside the organization or from outside.

   "You have five minutes to make a comprehensive list of all the rewards an employee might receive."

3. After five minutes, ask the groups to discuss: "What would a person have to do to earn each reward you listed?" Give the groups ten minutes to write their answers on flip charts.

4. In round-robin style, have each group report to the other groups one of the behaviors or actions they chose and why they chose it, until all groups have reported what they came up with. (*Note:* To avoid repetition, groups should only report on behaviors and actions that were not previously addressed by other groups.)

5. Discuss the implications for the organization or office based on what emerges from the group reports. Ask, "What might need to change so that the organization actually rewards or recognizes what it intends to?" and "What type of reward or reward system would you find most motivating?"

Facilitator Experience Required

This activity will be moderately easy for most facilitators.

How Individuals Foster Cultural Change

Experts differ on how long it takes to change an organization's culture, but everyone agrees it can't be done overnight. The biggest mistake a group can make at a retreat is to try to change everything at once.

Often when people talk about their organization's culture, they speak in terms of attitudes: "Nobody really cares about quality around here," "We're all obsessed with what the CEO thinks," or "If we could just move beyond office politics, we'd all work together better." Colleagues typically make assumptions about one another's motivations and attitudes. And although they behave as if these assumptions were the truth, no one can know for sure what is going on in another person's mind.

In the retreat, then, you'll need to help participants translate their *assumptions or perceptions of attitude* into *observations of behavior*. Ask, "What does it look like when people are obsessed with what your department head thinks? How does that play out in your work?"

The culture won't change because someone says, "Let's stop being obsessed with what the department head thinks." But people can change some of their behaviors. You might ask the group about the impact of that perception in meetings, for instance. If it means that people aren't willing to state an opinion until they see which way the wind is blowing, ask participants to suggest ways to change that behavior. They might decide, for example, to have everyone write down their opinions and read them aloud (or have others read them aloud) before the department head declares himself on an important issue.

Remember, too, that all organizational cultures contain positive and supportive elements. It will be reassuring to the participants if you take time to help them focus on what they appreciate and want to maintain in their culture, not only on what they want to change.

Recognizing and Removing Obstacles to Change

Even after participating in the decisions on how to foster changes in the organization's culture, many people still won't make a wholehearted commitment to modify their own behaviors. It's easy for people to see insurmountable obstacles, both for themselves and the organization. "Oh, we've tried to change things before, but it never works," some people say. "Here we go again." Such sentiments obstruct forward movement because they can become a self-fulfilling prophecy.

In a retreat for the online department of a national magazine, the participants readily identified specific changes that were within their power to make. They agreed that they would work better together if they made these few changes. But when we asked what obstacles stood in the way of implementing these changes, they quickly generated a list of more than forty reasons why these changes couldn't happen.

See "Participants Are Resisting New Ideas," Chapter 9, pp. 165–168, for techniques to manage resistance when it emerges.

This group wasn't any more negative than the participants in an average retreat. It's easier for most people to think about why things won't work than to figure out how to make them work. So you'll probably want to include time for people to confront the impediments they anticipate. The following activity offers a structured way to address these concerns.

Obstacle Busters

Description

Working first in small groups, participants discuss what might hamper their ability to achieve their goals. After identifying the obstacles, they discuss ways to eliminate them or reduce their impact.

Experiential Elements

- Reflecting back on experiences
- Listening to the ideas of others
- Envisioning possibilities and generating new ideas

Steps

1. Create subgroups of six to eight people. Introduce the task: "Too often we get in the habit of thinking we can't achieve things because there are too many obstacles in the way. Some of these obstacles are real, but very often we find that what we perceive to be obstacles can be removed. And some are simply embedded in the way we usually do things."

2. Ask each group to take ten minutes to list on a flip chart every obstacle they can think of that might interfere with achieving the desired goals.

Setup

Write the three obstacles questions on a flip chart (see Step 3).

Special Supplies

A pad of Post-it Notes and a felt-tip pen for each participant.

3. Reassemble the groups, but don't review their work yet. First show them a flip chart with these questions:

   - Which obstacles could be removed or minimized by group effort and agreement?

   - Which obstacles are insurmountable?

   - Which obstacles exist primarily in our minds?

     Define the next task: "Sort the obstacles you've identified into these three categories: Obstacles in our power to remove or minimize, insurmountable obstacles, and obstacles that exist primarily in our minds."

4. Ask each group: "Choose at least six major obstacles and determine specifically what the people in this room can do to eliminate or reduce them. Consider only the actions that are within the power of the people here, not actions that you wish others would take. You have thirty minutes to work."

5. After thirty minutes have each group report on its findings. Facilitate a whole group discussion of what actions the group should take to address the obstacles. Help the group come up with an action plan of three to ten items. (Keep it simple.)

6. Tell the group: "Since we can't eliminate obstacles that are out of our control, we'll skip that category and go on to obstacles that are in our heads. Using a separate Post-it Note for each idea, answer the question: "What assumptions can we get rid of?" After participants have written down their ideas, they should read their thoughts aloud in turn and post them on the wall.

7. Facilitate a discussion of these questions:

- How will we implement the obstacle-busting ideas back at work?

- In the future, how can we avoid making erroneous assumptions about what's possible?

Facilitator Experience Required

The facilitator must be skilled enough to prod reluctant participants to take personal responsibility for addressing the obstacles and negative attitudes that are identified in this activity.

Feedback for Senior Executives (and Others)

A retreat is a great opportunity for executives to learn about the impact of their behavior on the organization's culture. How open are they to new ideas and to adapting their leadership styles to best serve the organization? How willing are they to try new approaches, help others grow, and encourage risk taking? Do they foster internal cooperation or competition?

It's very hard for leaders to get honest feedback from employees who may fear the consequences of speaking out. Thus, executives often lack valuable perspectives that could help them lead their organizations more effectively.

When we conduct retreats, we often ask senior executives if they want feedback from the people they supervise. If they do (and most *say* they do), we give them the feedback about them and their leadership styles that emerged from the interviews and surveys we conducted (while being very careful to protect the sources) and discuss the implications of this feedback with them. We encourage leaders to talk with the participants about what they've learned, what they're willing to change, and also where their boundaries are firm.

Talking about this feedback at the retreat gives executives the opportunity to clear up misconceptions that can arise when people ascribe erroneous motives to their leadership practices. When participants see it is safe to request changes from their leaders, trust improves exponentially. Executives often find that by making small changes they can make significant improvements in the working environment.

In addition to hearing feedback, any management group can benefit from personal reflection on the impact of its behavior on others. The following activity is a simple but extremely memorable way to guide such reflection.

Metaphorical Management

Description

Using visual symbols, managers first discuss how they would like to be perceived by their colleagues. Then in small groups, again using metaphors, participants receive feedback about the impact of their management styles and can explore ways to modify them to be more effective.

Experiential Elements

- Personal reflection
- Using metaphor to express thoughts and feelings
- Giving and receiving feedback
- Active decision making

Special Requirements

This activity works only in retreats where there are three or four people with whom the participant who is receiving feedback works daily—an intact team, members of the same department, a management group, or an *ad hoc* committee, for example.

Steps

1. Introduce the task: "This activity will help you look at the impact of your management style on others and think about the style you aspire to. We're going to use metaphors—visual symbols—for this exploration. Using metaphors helps people come up with more creative and intuitive ideas. And having a visual symbol will help you organize your thinking and remember these ideas back at the office.

Setup

Prepare two flip charts: "My Ideal Management Style" (see Step 2) and "Differences Between My Two Metaphors" (see Step 5).

"First, let's begin by thinking about your ideal management style. Think about the kind of work you do and what's critical for success in that work. You might want to make some notes. Then, think of a metaphor—a symbol—that represents your ideal management style."

To help participants understand the task, offer a personal example: "For instance, I might say that my ideal management style would be symbolized by an eagle [the facilitator should substitute his or her own metaphor here]. Why? An eagle is farsighted and sees the big picture. She flies high above all the activity on the ground and doesn't worry about the little stuff. The eagle is also very target-directed. She sees her prey, zooms in on it, and swoops it up quickly. I like the symbol of the eagle because I think I get too wrapped up in the minutia of my job and don't look up often enough to remember the big picture. I want to focus on more important projects, instead of always chasing after little details that don't seem to make much difference in the long run."

2. Display the first flip chart on Ideal Management Style, as shown here.

   My Ideal Management Style

   - Metaphor (visual symbol)

   - Five or six reasons why this metaphor represents my ideal style

   Have participants select a symbol that represents their ideal style. The symbol can be anything—an animal, a place, an object, a tool, even an admired person. Tell participants not to worry if their symbol isn't a perfect fit; the idea is to choose something that helps them remember the essence of their ideal style.

   Ask participants to list five or six reasons why they chose this metaphor.

3. Break the participants into groups of three or four people. Tell the groups to focus on one person at a time in each group and to choose a metaphor to describe that person's style. When the group agrees on a metaphor, one of the members should write it down and the reasons the group chose it. After the metaphor is discussed, the selected person reveals the metaphor she chose for herself and the reasons for choosing that symbol.

4. Have each group talk about the differences between the symbol the group chose and the symbol the group member chose for herself. Repeat this process with each member in turn.

5. Display the second flip chart.

   Differences Between My Two Metaphors

   - What are the differences between my ideal style metaphor and the metaphor the group chose for me?

   - What actions can I take to close the gap between the two?

   Ask participants, working alone and in silence, to reflect on what they learned from their group. The participants should write the answers to the two questions for their own use on a sheet of paper they can take back to the office.

Facilitator Notes

- This activity is less threatening than a direct discussion of management styles. People feel safer talking about a personal issue, such as management style, through metaphors, and the activity can be fun, which nearly always reduces tension. The visual symbols become memory hooks that enable participants to remember what they've learned long after the session.

- You might encourage participants to find a picture or object when they get back to the office that illustrates the metaphor they chose. At the next staff meeting, retreat participants might show their symbols and explain how they remind them of the changes they are hoping to make. You might even recommend that people keep the picture or object visible in their offices. We've seen executives with stuffed eagles and bears on their bookshelves as a result of this activity.

- We have focused here on providing feedback to senior executives. But top executives aren't the only people who have an impact on organizational culture. This activity can be adapted so that other managers and staff can also learn about the effect of their behavior on the organization.

In Chapter 11 we focused on the challenges of changing corporate culture and provided activities to help the group take responsibility for bringing about change. We explored ways to deal with sensitive and controversial issues and discussed the sometimes thorny topic of rewards. We also examined how to recognize and remove obstacles to change and the influence of senior executives on an organization's culture.

In the next chapter we're going to explore how a retreat can be a springboard for improving relationships back in the workplace.

Chapter 12

Leading a Relationship–Building and Teamwork Retreat

When employees seem to be working at cross-purposes, when too many things keep falling through the cracks, when one department head won't cooperate with another, or when managers find themselves spending an inordinate amount of time mediating subordinates' disputes, executives often conclude that it's time for a teamwork retreat.

There are other reasons for convening a teamwork retreat as well. If staff members are just beginning to work in formal teams or if different working units are being merged, a retreat can help the group get off to a good start.

If You're Asked to Lead a "Teamwork" Retreat

It's often tempting for executives and employees alike to believe that most of an organization's problems would disappear if people would only stop behaving badly and learn to cooperate with one another. In such situations, management sometimes calls for a "teamwork" retreat, although the word "teamwork" in this case may not relate to the work of a formal team. What management wants is to have people work more effectively together.

While the behavior of individual employees often contributes to an organization's problems, it's rarely the root cause. A perceived lack of teamwork may really stem from a fundamental disagreement about where the organization is heading or trust issues rather than from "difficult" employees. Teamwork retreats are unlikely to produce lasting results if they over-focus on interpersonal issues when the real problem is something else entirely. That being said, we've seen many instances of relationships that changed dramatically for the better as a by-product of work that was done at a retreat.

Many dysfunctional relationships, often ascribed to "personality differences," result from the assumptions people make about each other and the conclusions they draw from those assumptions. When participants work to address real issues in a retreat setting together with others with whom they have had difficulty in the past, they can learn to see one another in a new light. Their new insights often lay the groundwork for more constructive professional relationships. Although a retreat is unlikely to be the most effective setting for resolving a longstanding personal issue between two individuals, it can establish a frame-

Teamwork Retreat, Team Training, or Team-Building Experience?

A retreat that addresses what is hampering effective teamwork is quite different from team training or formal team-building experiences. Team training tends to concentrate on teaching specific skills that relate to people's jobs, such as how to use the new accounting software. Training to improve communication might teach participants specific techniques they could use back at work. In a retreat to improve communication, participants would explore what lies behind their miscommunications and engage in activities to help them come up with their own answers to improve the situation. Even after training, people often need a framework within which to explore their new skills. An offsite retreat is intended to create that framework.

In what are often called "team-building experiences," people take part in structured activities, working together to solve problems such as how to navigate an outdoor ropes course. The content of the experience is a metaphor for the kinds of issues people deal with in the office, but—in contrast to a retreat as we use the term in this book—the issues aren't addressed directly and benefits of the experience may not translate well when applied to problems back at the office.

work for dealing with that issue more effectively back at work. It can also be a forum to begin to address issues that rankle work groups and departments.

Exploring How Things Are and How Participants Would Like Them to Be

People often express what they want to be different in the workplace by complaining about what's wrong. But it's not possible to deal constructively with "what's wrong" unless people have a full view of the larger picture, which also includes what's right. A gripe session, however satisfying it might feel in the moment, won't change anything (and could make things worse).

That's why it's important to have participants take a balanced look at how things *really* are. People typically come away from such an activity with a greater appreciation for all the things that are "right" with their working relationships and a clearer sense of where to focus their energies to make things better.

Vehicle for Change

Description

This activity uses vehicles as a metaphor to stimulate thinking about what working relationships are like now and what they could be like in the future.

Experiential Elements

- Using metaphor to express thoughts and feelings
- Personal reflection
- Drawing
- Group presentations
- Giving and receiving feedback

Steps

1. Divide participants into subgroups of four to five people. Introduce the task: "Imagine your organization [or department, as appropriate] as if it were a vehicle of some kind. Take a moment to picture the organization as it is now—its characteristics and its environment—in terms you might use to describe an automobile, a truck, a cement mixer, an 18-wheeler.

   "I will be asking you to draw a vehicle that represents the organization, but first, here are some questions you should consider." Show participants the flip chart.

Setup

Prepare: "Questions" (see Step 1), "The Rules," (see Step 2), and "Organizational Characteristics" (see Step 2) flip charts.

Questions

- What kind of vehicle is it? (For example: Bus? Sports car? Unicycle? Minivan? SUV? Motorcycle? Front loader? Dump truck? Tank?)

- What does it look like?

- Is it in good condition?

- Who is driving?

- Who are the passengers? What are they doing?

- What else is on the road?

- What obstacles might the vehicle be facing?

- What's in the surrounding landscape that might affect the vehicle's forward progress?

2. Ask participants to take a moment—without talking—to get a clear picture in their minds of a vehicle. Show participants the following flip chart and explain the rules.

The Rules

- Work in silence—no discussion about what goes on the page.

- Everyone in the subgroup must draw on the page.

- Everyone in the subgroup must participate in giving the group's report.

Advise participants to look for symbolic ways to convey their organization's (or department's) characteristics. Show the participants the following flip chart that should help guide the elements they include in their drawing.

Organizational Characteristics

- Achievements

- Reputation

- Available resources

- Work atmosphere

- Work methods

- Use of each person's talents

Now have each subgroup work *in silence* to draw a vehicle on a sheet of flip chart paper.

3. After calling time, have the members of each subgroup describe in turn their picture to the larger group and explain what each element of the drawing means. Note: Since participants will have been working in silence, they themselves won't know what it all means until they hear other members of their group report out loud.

4. Explain the task: "Now, draw another vehicle, or the same vehicle under different conditions, that represents your organization [or department] *as you would like it to be*. This time, you can talk with each other as you design your vehicle."

Activity (continued)

5. After calling time, have the subgroups, as before, describe their pictures to the larger group and explain what they mean. Ask such questions as:

- Were there any themes common to most of the drawings? What do those themes say about this organization [or department]?

- What would this group like to be different in this organization?

- What steps can you take to move from the vehicle you're in now to the vehicle you'd like to be in?

Facilitator Notes

- This activity can help a group discover and sort out issues that may be causing confusion and anxiety. Using the symbol of the vehicle, the group can quickly see what is on everyone's mind and come up with strategies for change.

- The use of metaphors and silent work in groups can help the participants surface difficult issues in relative anonymity.

Facilitator Experience Required
This activity requires skilled facilitation to draw groups out on the real significance of their pictures.

Clarifying Individuals' Roles and Responsibilities

No one person in an organization can be responsible for doing everything, but everything that has to be done must be someone's responsibility. Most organizations struggle to achieve the proper distribution of responsibility. Typically, some people are given or take on too much, while others are assigned or are willing to undertake too little. The result can be resentment, frustration, duplication of effort, and important work slipping through the cracks.

You'll find two excellent activities on responsibility charting and workflow mapping in *The Fieldbook of Team Interventions: Step-by-Step Guide to High Performance Teams*, by C. Harry Eggleton and Judy C. Rice, pp. 161–178.

Individuals' expectations for themselves and for others should advance the organization's or work group's overall purpose, and individual roles should be clearly defined and understood by all when actions are planned and tasks are assigned. The more people know about what their colleagues are doing, the better able they will be to collaborate with one another, complement each other's efforts, and provide one another appropriate support and assistance.

Improving Work Processes

Often, circumstances change over time, but an organization's work processes do not keep pace.

Take the case of a federal government agency that found it could not respond adequately to the great number of requests for information it received. Agency officials were deeply concerned about the increasing number of complaints from irate customers (and members of Congress) about backlogs and slow processing times.

The agency had recently lost approximately 15 percent of its workforce (including many of its most experienced employees) in government-mandated downsizings at the same time the demand for information was increasing steadily. To make matters worse, the agency had not modernized its databases in years, so its technology was woefully out of date.

Agency leaders convened an offsite retreat to look at fundamentally redesigning the work processes. By giving employees information about the urgency for the change and involving them in redesigning the work processes, they were able to generate commitment for a new course of action.

When the participants grasped the full picture of how the work was being done, they were surprised to discover that they were undertaking many unnecessary tasks, with much duplication of effort. By focusing their attention on eliminating or reducing these redundancies, they were able to come up with new processes that significantly increased their productivity and reduced their response time—and complaints.

Here's an activity that can create a framework for discussing work process improvements.

Decorations Factory*

Description

This activity is a simulation that engages participants in a start-up project that requires cooperation and business decisions up, down, and across organizational lines. As participants interact in the simulation, they learn more about how they typically work together.

Steps

1. Divide the group into four or more teams of two to four participants each. (To the extent possible, arrange these teams so that each is made up of members from various levels and divisions in the organization.) Designate one team the Executive Team, another the Sales Team, and the rest Production Teams.

2. Distribute the instruction sheets and tasks to the appropriate teams. (*Facilitator's note:* You will adjust the number of prototypes the group is required to produce based on what would be a difficult number for the group to reach in the amount of time they have. We suggest twenty units per team if the teams are small.)

3. Give the construction supplies to the Executive Team. Tell the teams they'll have fifteen minutes to complete their initial tasks. Ask if there are any questions and then start the activity.

4. End the work period by calling for order and asking the Executive Team to announce the company name. Then ask each Production Team to present the designs that passed the Sales Team's quality control standards for presentation to the CEO.

   You, the facilitator, should take on the role of the CEO and ask for all the designs to be brought to a central table. Pick a design at random to serve as the prototype. (We suggest closing your eyes so there will be no hard feelings about the design you chose.)

This activity requires at least twelve participants.

Experiential Elements
- Group planning and cooperation
- Group problem solving
- Giving and receiving feedback
- Participating in role play and improvisation

Setup

Prepare instruction sheets for the Executive Team, Sales Team, and Production Teams. (See Instructions on pp. 250–252.)

Special Supplies*
- Miniature marshmallows
- Toothpicks
- Scissors
- Felt-tip markers in a variety of colors
- Masking tape
- Paper and pencils
- Multi-colored plastic straws
- Multi-colored paper clips
- Other construction supplies as you might determine
- A timer

*Note: Limit the quantities so that the teams don't have a sufficient supply to do the work as efficiently as they might.

---

*This activity, originally created for *Games That Teach Teams* by Steve Sugar and George Takacs, has been used with permission and reformulated for this book.

5. Tell the group that they will have fifteen minutes for the next part of the activity.

   - Ask each Production Team to produce as many copies of the selected decoration as it can and quickly route them to the Sales Team.

   - Ask the Sales Team to carry out the quality control function by accepting only those decorations that match the selected model and rejecting those that do not and to have some of its members prepare its marketing plan for presentation to the rest of the group.

   - Ask the Executive Team to do what it can to encourage as much production as possible of decorations that meet its exacting standards of quality.

6. The more communication and cooperation there is among the teams, the more likely it is that the company will be able to manufacture marketable products for sale to the public. Each team must interact well with the others if the task is to be accomplished. When debriefing the activity, consider using the following sequence:

   a. Have each team rate its own efforts on a flip chart on a scale of 1 (least) to 5 (most) in terms of:

      - Efficiency

      - Effectiveness of its work processes

      - Communication among fellow team members

      - Communication with other teams

      - Cooperation among fellow team members

      - Cooperation with other teams

   b. Ask each team to present its ratings in turn and explain to the group why team members rated themselves as they did.

   c. After each presentation, ask other teams to provide feedback on what they think that team did well and what team members might have done differently to make it easier to accomplish the task.

   d. Once all teams have presented their ratings, received feedback, and discussed their performance, facilitate a discussion around these questions:

      - When there was competing pressure between high quality and high production, how did you personally handle it? How did other members of your team handle it? From what you observed, how did other teams handle it?

- What conditions made it harder or easier to communicate and collaborate with others on your team? With other teams?

- For the Production Teams, how did you make decisions about how to produce a high quality product in large quantities? Did you work as a team or as individuals? What effect might working more closely with your fellow team members as well as with other teams have had on the quality of your work and on the number of units you produced?

- Did your team receive enough supplies? Did other teams? If you perceived any imbalance or unfairness, how did you handle it?

- Were you confused at any time about what you should be doing to move the production along? If so, how did you handle it?

- How accurately did what happened in this activity reflect what typically occurs back at work? (If participants respond, "There's no relationship; we don't manufacture products back in the office," probe more deeply.)

- What might you do differently when several departments or teams are working on parts of a large project?

Facilitator Notes

- During the activity, you may find that some teams are confused or far behind in their tasks. Let the activity continue.

- The purpose of this activity is to create an environment in which teams must rely on one another to produce the best possible product. The activity provides an excellent framework for the group to explore communication, cooperation, and work processes as they affect particular work groups and their interactions with other work groups.

Facilitator Experience Required

The facilitator must be able to manage a complex and fast-moving activity while observing the patterns of behavior that emerge.

- It is very important that you spend some time in the debriefing process helping participants understand what happened during the activity. Not every person will have seen or heard what happened in the other teams. Before the participants can start drawing lessons from this activity, they must have a common frame of reference for understanding what took place.

Executive Team Description and Instructions

The Executive Team is made up of the executives in charge of a new company that needs to design and produce a highly original decoration for the Independence Day holiday. The CEO wants to choose from among sixty viable prototypes.

The Executive Team must encourage the Production Teams to create as many high quality models as possible. In addition, the Executive Team will develop a plan for naming this new company and manage the production and sales of the product, which includes allocating all the supplies needed by the Production Teams.

Executives have many and varied tasks in an organization. The main task of the Executive Team in this activity is to make sure that the company is moving in a predetermined direction. Some of the problems facing the Executive Team are:

- The company has no name.

- The supply distribution system has broken down.

- There is no marketing plan for the Independence Day decoration.

- There is no design for the Independence Day decoration.

- There are not sufficient resources for the Production Teams.

- There appears to be some hostility between Sales and Production.

You may also have to perform tasks that are not listed in these instructions. It's up to you to decide what you need to do.

Sales Team Instructions

You are members of the sales force for a new company whose current plan calls for designing, manufacturing, and marketing a new decoration for the Independence Day holiday. It is the Sales Team's mission to provide quality control of the manufacturing of the product, market it, and sell it.

In addition, the Sales Team is to create a marketing plan for the Independence Day decoration. In carrying out quality control, the Sales Team will guide the Production Teams on which designs are acceptable to submit for the CEO's approval. This decoration could represent a great deal of business in the future, so the Sales Team must rigorously enforce high standards of quality.

Some of the tasks facing the Sales Team are:

- Devising a marketing/sales plan and obtaining Executive Team approval for it

- Obtaining cooperation from the Production Teams to produce large quantities of high quality decorations

- Carrying out quality control in the design and manufacturing stages

- Approving items manufactured by the Production Teams that meet company standards and rejecting those that do not

You may also have to perform tasks that are not listed in these instructions. It's up to you to decide what you need to do.

Production Team Instructions

The Production Teams are to design and produce a highly original decoration to be sold to consumers for the Independence Day holiday. The CEO wants to see sixty viable prototypes, so you are to work as fast as you can while not sacrificing quality. The task for each Production Team is to produce at least twenty different high quality decorations.

Some of the issues facing the Production Teams are:

- The Production Teams must design and produce as many high quality models of Independence Day decorations as possible.

- You've heard rumors that supplies are scarce.

- The models must be presented to the Executive Team and Sales Team for approval.

- Once the CEO accepts a prototype, the Production Teams must produce as many decorations that match the prototype as possible.

- The company has a very high and exacting standard of quality.

You may also have to perform tasks that are not listed in these instructions. It's up to you to decide what you need to do.

Strengthening Communication

If you learn in your preliminary interviews that people in the organization share information freely, follow through on their commitments, and give and receive helpful feedback, it's likely that communication is not a major issue.

If, however, there's an atmosphere of secrecy, mistrust, and gossip; if employees feel they're not getting the information they need and want; or if internal and external customers receive mixed messages, you'll want to focus some attention at the retreat on improving communication.

Here's an activity to help participants examine the effectiveness of their organization's communication processes so they can take steps to improve how they share information with one another and with outsiders.

How We Communicate

Description

In this activity participants focus on how they and their colleagues typically communicate by taking on the viewpoint of outsiders—sociologists sent to study their organization. Their observations will inform discussions about the positive or negative value of various communication patterns.

> **Experiential Elements**
> - Personal reflection
> - Discussion
> - Giving and receiving feedback
> - Observing other people's actions
>
> **Setup**
> Prepare a flip chart with How We Communicate on it as shown below.

Steps

1. Give this introduction: "Imagine you're a group of sociologists sent to study communication in [the organization or office]. As you consider what you have observed, what patterns do you see in the ways people convey, withhold, distort, use, misuse, understand, and misunderstand information?

"Concentrate on the way *most* people communicate, not on individual communication styles. Look for anomalies—disparities between what people are trying to communicate and how they're going about it.

"For example, do managers praise subordinates in private but not in public? Could a subordinate wonder whether the manager really means it?

"Pay attention to patterns, not to individual styles. You might observe, for example, that 'Most people avoid confrontations,' rather than 'Arlyne and Jim avoid confrontations, but Shari and Daniel love to mix it up.' If there's no clear pattern, note that, for instance, 'Many people seem to dislike confrontations while an equal number seem to relish them.'

"In a moment, I'm going to divide you into small groups. In your group, you'll make a list of the five to ten most important questions you want to study from a sociologist's perspective. Look over the examples I'll show you in a moment to get some ideas, but feel free to add to them or make up your own list." Now show everyone the flip chart: How We Communicate.

How We Communicate

- Who talks to whom?

- How can we tell who's important?

- When and among whom is communication more formal or less formal?

- Do people prefer communicating face-to-face, over the telephone, in written memos, or via e-mail?

- Do people tend to communicate directly or through third parties?

- Do subordinates feel free to communicate with higher ups? How do they do so? What sorts of things do they communicate about?

- Where do people congregate?

- How do people communicate in meetings?

- Are there observable differences in communication patterns related to gender, age, ethnicity?

- How do people disagree?

- Is dissent encouraged or discouraged?

- Is confrontation favored or disfavored?

- Do people ask for permission to do things? How?

- Do people talk behind one another's backs? Is there an active "rumor mill"?

- Do people ask for help?

- Do people offer to help one another?

- Do people share information readily?

2. Have participants work in groups of three to five to determine and then answer their five to ten most important questions.

3. Ask each group to identify the top three answers that seem to give the best idea of what communication is like in the organization and then write those answers on a flip chart.

4. Invite participants in each group to explain to the whole group why they chose the examples they did and why they think people communicate in the ways they identified.

5. Explore in a group discussion the implications for the organization. What might need to change to foster better communication throughout the organization?

Facilitator Experience Required
This activity needs particularly skilled facilitation to guide the group in addressing previously unarticulated—and sensitive—communication issues.

Exploring the Importance of Feedback

"You're cold. You're getting warmer. Now you're hot!" You probably played that guessing game as a child. Without feedback, people may reach their destinations accidentally—and they may not even know it. More likely, they'll wander aimlessly, never attaining their goals.

People need to know in a timely manner specifically how they're doing, what's working, and what's not. And feedback must be well-timed and respectfully delivered. If not, it's not likely to be very effective.

You can use the following activity to help participants (and you as facilitator) receive immediate feedback on the impact of their words and behavior.

Snowball*

Description

This activity provides a means of giving feedback in the moment by having participants toss crumpled paper balls at anyone who violates behavioral norms in the agreed-on ground rules. Whoever tosses a paper "snowball" must then explain what statement or behavior prompted him or her to do so.

Experiential Elements

- Giving and receiving feedback
- Participating in physical activities
- Interpersonal dialogue

Steps

1. Ask for a volunteer. Take the volunteer aside for a moment. Explain that you will intentionally do something (and say what that will be) that violates the ground rules. Ask the volunteer to wad up a piece of paper and toss it at you when you do.

Special Supplies

Several pieces of scrap paper for each participant.

2. Do something that is an obvious violation of the ground rules, such as cutting a participant off abruptly. The volunteer will then toss his or her "snowball" at you. (If the volunteer misses the cue, prompt him or her right away.)

3. Ask the volunteer to tell you what triggered the snowballing and model appropriate behavior when receiving feedback from the volunteer. (Listen to understand, ask clarifying questions if necessary, take the feedback under consideration, thank the volunteer for giving you the feedback.)

4. Explain to the group, "For the remainder of this retreat, when anyone, including me, makes a comment or engages in behavior that you believe breaks one of the ground rules or otherwise inhibits the group, make a snowball and toss it immediately at the offender, and then, when the offender asks, explain what prompted the snowballing, just as [the volunteer's name] and I modeled a few moments ago."

5. Later in the retreat (after some snowballs have been thrown), ask participants these questions about feedback:

   - How do you feel when you throw a snowball?

   - How do you feel about being hit by snowballs?

   - How can you implement this idea at work?

*This activity, originally created as a feedback activity for *Games That Teach Teams* by Steve Sugar and George Takacs, has been used with permission of the authors and reformulated for this book.

If no snowballs are thrown during the rest of the morning or afternoon, ask participants why:

- I noticed that no snowballs have been thrown. Why do you think that is?

- Would it be too threatening to toss a snowball at someone?

- Are you saying that no one has violated the ground rules?

- Do you think that the possibility of being snowballed might have anything to do with that?

Facilitator Notes

- The purpose of this activity is to show that feedback given right after something has been said or done can be a light-hearted but effective and non-confrontational way of reminding people of agreed-on behavioral norms.

- If you do not want the participants to toss paper at you, do not use this activity. Everyone—including you—must be a potential target for the snowballs.

- Every time a snowball is tossed, collect it and place it in a special receptacle to underscore the number of times feedback was given during the retreat.

Facilitator Experience Required

This is a very easy activity to facilitate as long as the facilitator has a good sense of humor and is willing to be snowballed if he or she violates the ground rules.

Probing for Sources of Conflict

In many organizations, conflict is a taboo subject, as if denying its existence would make it go away or acknowledging it would destroy the illusion of a happy family of co-workers. But conflict is inevitable in any relationship, and it's actually an asset when it's expressed openly and respectfully. Open conflict can provide a reality check on decisions and directions.

Where there is no apparent conflict, there may be apathy. Or conflict may have gone underground where it can fester and, like a hidden abscess, re-emerge in damaging ways at the worst possible times. When dissent and disagreement are not allowed to surface, the organization becomes inflexible and unable to respond to opportunities that might arise. On the other hand, you don't want unbridled conflict that turns into open warfare, personal animosities, name calling, and active or passive resistance.

Conflict is a natural and healthy consequence of people dealing with issues that are important to them. To try to suppress it is as futile as it is counterproductive. Conflict leads to tension when it is ignored or denied or when an organization's culture demonizes it as a "bad thing" to be avoided.

Organizations that create a climate of trust at a retreat allow difficult issues to surface. Greater trust helps participants discover better and more satisfying ways of doing their work, which often translates into enhanced collegiality, communication, and cooperation back in the workplace. Managed effectively, the energy that drives conflict can be channeled to foster greater understanding and more respect among colleagues.

Following is an activity designed to generate discussion about the impact of conflict on retreat participants.

How Conflict Affects Us

Description This activity is a facilitated discussion, both in small groups and in the group as a whole, about how people respond to conflict. The design is simple, but the questions will provide participants with a framework for discussing difficult issues.

Experiential Elements
- Personal reflection
- Discussion
- Giving and receiving feedback

Steps

1. Distribute one worksheet to each participant. Introduce the task: "Please write your answers to the questions on the worksheet I just passed out. You'll have ten minutes."

   Questions on Conflict

   - How is conflict usually dealt with in your organization [or office]? Why do you think this is so?

   - What impact does the way conflict is dealt with have on the quality of your organization's work?

   - What impact does the way conflict is dealt with have on the quality of your relationships at work?

   - What's working and not working about how people in your organization [or office] manage conflict?

   - What's the one thing you would most like to change about how conflict is managed in your organization? Complete the sentence: "I wish. . . ."

2. After the participants complete the worksheet, divide them into subgroups of three to five people and have them discuss what they wrote. Have each group record its members' responses on a flip chart and report to the whole group.

3. Ask the participants to explore the similarities and differences in the various subgroups' responses. Ask: "What do these similarities and differences tell you about the perceptions of conflict in your organization [or office]?"

Setup

Prepare a worksheet listing the questions about conflict as shown in Step 1, leaving sufficient space between questions for participants to write their answers. Make one copy for each participant.

Facilitator Experience Required

This activity is moderately easy to facilitate. It's particularly important for the facilitator to discourage blaming others as the source of conflict.

The following activity can help retreat participants get to the root of a deep-seated conflict and make a commitment to change for the better.

Taking Responsibility

Description

This activity causes people to reflect individually and in groups about the impact of their own behavior. The group reports are often surprising—and occasionally moving.

Experiential Elements
- Personal reflection
- Active listening
- Giving and receiving feedback

Steps

1. Divide participants into groups of people who usually work together, in specific departments or teams, for instance. Introduce the task: "Everyone here is aware that we have a particular issue we need to grapple with: [name or describe the issue]. Before we can begin to resolve it, we have to understand everyone's role in making this an issue.

   "Working individually and silently, write down your Sources of Satisfaction, that is, the contribution your department made toward resolving or reducing the conflict. Use one Post-it Note for every new idea, and write down as many Source of Satisfaction items as you can come up with. Then have one person in your group collect all the Post-its."

Setup

Prepare three flip chart pages with the following titles: Sources of Satisfaction, Sources of Regrets, Good Intentions and post them on the wall.

Special Supplies

A pad of Post-it" Notes and a felt-tip pen for each participant.

2. Continue the activity: "Just as you might be pleased about many things your department has done, there may also be actions your department has taken in relation to this issue that you regret or wish you had done differently. Please list the things that you or your department has done that you regret, again using one Post-it Note for each Sources of Regret item. Give all your ideas to a person in your group (not the same one who collected the Sources of Satisfaction)."

3. Ask the person who collected the Sources of Satisfaction Post-its in each group to read aloud all the items and post them on the appropriate flip chart. Then ask the person who collected the Sources of Regret Post-its to read them aloud and post them on the appropriate flip chart.

4. Now ask each group to list their Good Intentions for the future—the specific actions or changes they are prepared to undertake. Again, each item should be written on a separate Post-it.

5. Have a third representative from each group collect and read all the Good Intention items and post them on the appropriate flip chart. Then ask the group, "What have you learned from hearing how other groups or individuals view their contributions to this issue? Did you hear anything that surprised you?"

After facilitating the discussion on contributions and surprises, ask, "Are there some Good Intentions that you can all agree on?" Record participants' ideas on a flip chart.

Facilitator Note This activity is an easy one to integrate into the workplace after the retreat. Bring the three flip charts listing the Sources of Satisfaction, Sources of Regrets, and Good Intentions back to the office and post them on a wall where people can see them. Leave the sheets posted for a week or two. Suggest that the organization use the format of Sources of Satisfaction, Sources of Regrets, and Good Intentions to begin meetings about issues in which people or groups have different views and have taken opposing positions.

Facilitator Experience Required

This activity is moderately difficult to facilitate. You'll need to be prepared to deal with any defensiveness that might crop up during the discussions about Sources of Regret. In addition, you may need to prod the group to come up with specific actions they will commit to take during the Good Intentions discussions.

Exploring How Individuals Can Change Their Own Behaviors

The following activity will help individuals and work groups bring to the surface issues that may have blocked effective working relationships.

Star Performers

Description

Participants are asked to list the individual talents that help them be effective at work and the individual traits that hinder their effectiveness. They then participate in a role play, presenting themselves to others in the group as one of the hindering characteristics. Individual reflection and group discussion follow about what might be different for the participants and the organization if people didn't feel a need to hide the hindering characteristics.

Experiential Elements

- Personal reflection
- Participating in role play and improvisation
- Experimentation

Setup

Prepare two flip charts: My Talents and Things That Hinder Me.

Special Supplies

For each participant, a brightly colored sheet of paper on which you have printed the outline of a large five-pointed star on the front and back.

Steps

1. Distribute one sheet of star paper to each participant. Introduce the task: "We will be looking at some of the talents we possess that help us do our work successfully, as well as some of the traits we have that may hinder our effectiveness." Display the first flip chart.

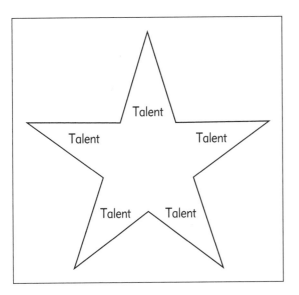

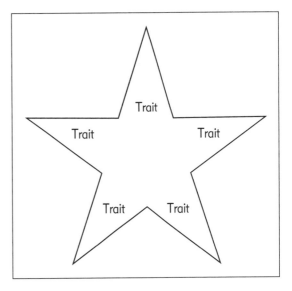

My Talents

Write one talent you have that helps you be more effective at work in each point of the star.

Explain: "Write one of your five most significant personal talents on each point of the star on your paper. Choose the five that most help you achieve success in the workplace. For instance, you might write things like 'helpful to others,' 'good presenter,' 'creative thinker,' or 'positive outlook.'"

2. After the participants have written their five talents, say: "Now flip your papers over. Write a trait that helps define a bit who you are but may hamper your effectiveness at work on each point of the star on the other side of your paper. For instance, you might write things like 'perfectionist,' 'dislike details,' 'impatient with others,' or 'avoid conflict.'"

Display the second flip chart:

Things That Hinder Me

Write one trait that hinders your effectiveness at work in each point of the star.

3. Introduce the next task: "Even if we recognize that certain traits do not help us at work or in life, most of us are aware of at least one that defines a bit of who we are. For example, I might say, 'I'm a perfectionist [substitute your own example here], and although I know I stay up too many nights fussing over the details of some project, I'm kind of proud of my high standards.' Or, I might say, 'I need to be right, and I know that sometimes my co-workers see me as a know-it-all, but the truth is, I do like to be right.' Or, 'I'd rather be spontaneous than plan ahead.' So think about what that principal hindering characteristic is for you and circle it on your star."

4. After participants have filled in the points of both stars, ask them to engage in an interpersonal activity: "Now pretend that this gathering is a party and that you want to meet as many people as possible. Everybody stand, mill about, and introduce yourself to everyone in the room, not by your job title but as the hindering trait that most gets in your way. So I might say, 'Hi, my name is Carol, and I need to be right.' 'Hi, I'm Frank, and I'm a perfectionist.' 'Hello, my name is Ken, and I don't plan ahead.' After introducing yourself, move on as quickly as possible to the next person at the party." Verify that everyone understands the instructions.

5. After two or three minutes, have the participants return to their seats. Ask them to write down their personal reflections: "Take a moment to write down how you felt when you introduced yourself to others as a characteristic that you perceive hinders you. Also write down the feelings you had when others introduced themselves to you as a characteristic that hinders *them*. Finally, write down the feelings you had if someone introduced himself or herself to you as a characteristic you share."

6. Ask participants to take a moment to reflect on why a particular characteristic seems to exert an influence over them and whether this is a characteristic they would normally disclose about themselves. If not, why not?

7. Ask the participants to think about how the energy changed in the room when people started introducing themselves by characteristics that hinder their effectiveness. Ask them to imagine what would happen if they all could be more forthcoming about acknowledging areas in which they could stand to improve:

   - How might things change for you personally?

   - How might your relationships with colleagues change?

   - How might this enhance your effectiveness at work?

8. Finally, invite participants to share their experiences: "Would a few people be willing to tell us what they have learned when reflecting on this activity? Might you deal with some of the traits that hinder your effectiveness in any other way based on what you learned?"

Facilitator Notes
- This activity requires that participants open up to one another. Don't use it in a group where there is low trust.

- Suggest that people report occasionally to others (at meetings, for example, or informally) on progress they have made in letting go of habits that hinder their effectiveness.

Facilitator Experience Required

This activity requires particularly sensitive facilitation to encourage people to disclose their talents and hindering traits. When led in a light-hearted judgment-free manner, participants get a lot out of this activity.

A Special Case: A Peers-Only Retreat to Call a Cease Fire in Interdepartmental Turf Battles

Often employees see their colleagues in other parts of the organization not as partners but as competitors, and they resolutely defend their turf against all who would encroach on it. Some executives even consciously encourage this behavior by fostering internal competition as a way of keeping subordinates "on their toes."

If you discover in the preliminary interviews that the organization is having problems getting different departments to cooperate, you might discuss with your client the possibility of holding a retreat of managerial peers only (all department heads, for instance), with none of the higher-ups present. The goal of such a retreat would be for colleagues to figure out better ways of working together, thinking together, resolving problems together, sharing information, and taking collective responsibility for the organization's success.

Early on in a peers-only retreat, participants need to talk about what's working and what's not working in each part of the organization, which collectively they represent. From this discussion, they will gain a comprehensive view of what is happening throughout the organization.

As participants get to know each other and come to realize that they have common interests, aspirations, and concerns, they can begin to break down artificial barriers that have been inhibiting cooperation and interfering with communication. They will then be able to make decisions or recommendations that benefit the entire organization, not just their piece of it. The more they work to support one another's goals, the more likely they are to overcome the mistrust and competition that can hobble an organization.

But better relationships don't happen automatically. Participants must make a commitment to address explicitly not only how they would like to work together but also what currently hampers effective collaboration.

For example, a hotel management company held a retreat in which only mid-level managers took part for the first two days, before the senior managers joined them for a third day of discussion. The middle managers discovered common problems they had not realized were affecting them all. In the course of the retreat, the participants shared information and cleared up misunderstandings. They made several joint recommendations when the senior managers came on the third day of the retreat. Most importantly, they decided to keep meeting as a group when they returned to their office.

The middle managers were pleased to find that they could communicate quickly and directly with each other, problem solve together, and share best practices. This new cooperation allowed them to develop consistent policies and resolve many issues at their level rather than having to buck everything up the chain of command. Executives, freed from having to deal with these issues, were pleased because they were now able to devote more time to the larger issues they were supposed to be

You'll find a more detailed explanation of how working relationships can be improved in *Seeing Systems: Unlocking the Mysteries of Organizational Life* (1996) by organization consultant Barry Oshry, who refers to it as "middle integration."

Suggested Activities for a Peers–Only Retreat

- Exploring Strategic Purpose (See Chapter 10)

- Glimpses into the Future (See Chapter 10)

- Distinctive Competencies (See Chapter 10)

- Targeting Core Priorities (See Chapter 10)

- Visit Our Village (See Chapter 11)

- Timeline of Our History (See Chapter 11)

- Significant Stories (See Chapter 11)

- Obstacle Busters (See Chapter 11)

- Metaphorical Management (See Chapter 11)

- Vehicle for Change (See Chapter 12)

- How We Communicate (See Chapter 12)

- How Conflict Affects Us (See Chapter 12)

- Multiple Perspectives (See Chapter 13)

- Expert Opinion (See Chapter 13)

- Considering Risk (See Chapter 13)

dealing with. Even the middle managers' subordinates were pleased, because the organization was more responsive to their concerns, quicker at getting back to them after they'd raised an issue, and more consistent in its policies across departmental lines.

Chapter 12 focused on improving relationships at work—increasing teamwork, making things better, clarifying individuals' roles and responsibilities, enhancing work processes, and making communication more effective. We looked at the importance of feedback, how to surface sources of conflict, and how individuals can change their own behaviors. Finally we examined a special case—the importance of improving communication and cooperation among managerial peers to end turf battles.

The next chapter takes us into the realm of creativity, as we explore how retreats can be used to tap into and take advantage of the group's gifts for imagination and innovation.

Chapter 13

Leading a Creativity and Innovation Retreat

One hallmark of a successful organization is that it continually seeks innovative ways to improve its products, services, and processes to retain current customers and attract new ones. But where will the creative thinkers come from? Chances are they're already working in the organization. And not just in jobs that are generally thought of as requiring creativity.

Human brains are wired for creativity, and each of us is a natural problem solver. Watch young children at play: Everyday objects become spacecraft. A spoon is a snowball catapult. A cardboard box is a sports car. But by the time most of us enter the workplace, we've learned to follow rules and procedures. We are often too self-conscious to risk suggesting an unconventional idea. Moreover, most of us tend to see ourselves as either creative or not. If we don't think we're creative, we'll likely leave the innovation to others.

Yet creative thinking is a skill that can be recaptured and improved with practice. Just as people learn to drive a car, play soccer, or win at bridge—and to become better at these things by doing them over and over—they can learn to improve their creative thinking skills.

In a retreat structured around creativity and generating new ideas, the activities you will use may cause some participants to worry about appearing foolish. But you can help them see that, just as stretching is important to an athlete before exercising, playing with unusual ideas is critical to loosening up the thinking muscles and releasing people's innate ability to exercise their creativity.

Most people's primary experience with creative thinking is through "brainstorming" (a method for generating ideas developed in the 1950s by advertising executive Alex Osborn), so chances are the convenor will assume that a creative thinking retreat is basically a long brainstorming session. If this point comes up in your discussions, encourage the convenor to think back to the last brainstorming session she participated in. She probably enjoyed the fun and high energy and thought that the session generated lots of ideas. But chances are, the group didn't come up with nearly the quantity and breadth of ideas it was capable of.

Why not?

Because people are often so concerned with what others will think that they don't articulate their most audacious ideas. Because groups fall in love with an idea too soon and stop pushing themselves for more. Because quieter, more reflective people can easily be ignored or "hide out" in a group setting. Because people who are in positions of authority or who are the most aggressive often intimidate others and carry the day, even if they don't have the most original or useful ideas.

Perhaps most importantly, because people are *talking*. When do you get your best ideas? Many people say, "In the shower," or "Driving in my car" or, "Just before I fall asleep." In other words, when they're *not talking*. Recent research provides a neurological explanation for this phenomenon. Human speech centers are primarily located on the left side of the brain, while intuitive and creative thinking are right-side functions. The more we talk, the less likely we are to come up with big new ideas. Basically, the left side of the brain drowns out the right side. To be creative, we need some silence.

Here is an alternative to traditional brainstorming, a way of fostering creative thinking that uses the power of silence and gets everyone's ideas on the table.

Wide Open Thinking

Description

This activity introduces a new way of coming up with solutions to a problem. Individuals write their ideas on Post-it Notes *in silence*, generating as many ideas as possible. Then, in small groups, participants share their ideas and post them on flip charts. This is an extremely lively activity that generates lots of good humor, while still addressing real issues.

Experiential Elements
- Writing down ideas individually
- Envisioning possibilities and generating new ideas
- Breakout group discussion
- Listening to others

Setup

Prepare Organizations flip chart (see Step 3). Each subgroup will need its own flip chart or a couple of blank flip chart pages taped to the wall near their table.

Special Supplies

A Post-it˝ Note pad and a felt-tip pen for each participant.

Steps

1. Divide the participants into subgroups of five to eight people. Introduce the task: "Coming up with lots of new ideas should be easy, but usually it is not. Typically, we think of a few ideas and then dissect, evaluate, and either accept or reject them. What we end up with is rarely the best we could do if we knew more about idea-generation techniques, which is what we're going to focus on in this activity."

2. Introduce the issue by presenting a current problem or simple question for the group to think about. For instance, let's take a look at. . ." [Insert a real issue for these participants, such as: '. . . how you can improve employee morale.' The issue must be open-ended enough to have many possible solutions.]

3. "I'd like each of you to write the names of five organizations that you feel have a lot of character and personality *and* that anyone in the room would recognize. For instance, Nike or *The New York Times* would probably conjure up a vivid image for anyone here, but a small company in my hometown or my local newspaper would not.

   "You can choose any organization, in any area of human endeavor. Here are some examples." Show the prepared flip chart.

   Organizations

   - Companies (Coca-Cola, Microsoft, Apple Computer, McDonald's)

   - Sports (National Hockey League, New York Yankees, Chicago Bulls)

- Nonprofits (Girl Scouts, Red Cross, Salvation Army, Make a Wish Foundation)

- Entertainment (Rolling Stones, Beastie Boys, Fox TV Network, National Public Radio)

- Politics (African National Congress, National Rifle Association, Common Cause, NAACP, AARP)

- Government (the British Parliament, the Supreme Court, the CIA)

- History (the Spanish Armada, Attila and his Huns, the French Revolution, World War I)

- Fiction (Peter Pan and the Lost Boys, Knights of the Roundtable)

"Write your list of five organizations on one sheet of Post-it paper." After individuals write their lists, have them set them aside.

4. Define the procedure: "Each of you will *work alone and in silence* to generate ideas to address [the issue the group identified]. 'In silence' means not talking and not even making eye contact with each other. Stay in your own little bubbles. Your silence will facilitate more creative, intuitive, right-brain thinking.

"You will write one idea per Post-it. Each of you should be able to come up with at least thirty ideas. Please note that I didn't say, 'thirty GOOD ideas.' We're looking for *quantity* at this stage, so *any* idea will do, including silly, impossible, illegal, ridiculous, even tasteless ones.

"If I gave you the issue and you started right now, most of you would come up with only six or seven ideas and then get stuck. Here's how we're going to make sure you *don't* get stuck. Give your list of organizations to someone else in the room. You should each end up with a list you didn't write. You will use this list of organizations to help spark new ideas.

"Start with the first organization on the list you received and ask yourself, 'How would this organization go about solving this problem?' and 'What does this organization remind me of?' For instance, if the problem were how to improve morale in the accounting department, and you have 'CIA' on your list, you might write, 'Give rewards when somebody *spies* accounting employees doing something helpful,' which could be a good idea. You could also write 'Give them truth serum to find out what the real problems are.' Now that is an outlandish idea, but ridiculous ideas are not only acceptable but very valuable at this stage of the process. When you run out of inspiration from the first organization on your list, move on to the next one.

"Remember to write one idea per Post-it and keep your pen moving. Don't censor your ideas. Focus on quantity, not quality, of ideas. Try to come up with at least thirty fresh ideas."

5. Allow the participants to work in silence for seven to eight minutes.

6. Participants should listen to all the ideas generated within their subgroup by having each person read his or her ideas aloud in turn and then stick the Post-it Notes on a flip chart. When people read their ideas, others may keep writing, as new ideas are sparked by what they're hearing.

7. After all the ideas have been read and posted, suggest to each group that they discuss those that are the most appealing to them.

   • Are there common themes?

   • Could some ideas be combined?

   • Can you improve on some of the ideas?

   • Can you take a really bad idea and turn it into a good one?

8. Ask each subgroup to share their best ideas. Facilitate a discussion around these questions:

   • Which ideas might be implemented?

   • What conditions helped you be more creative in this activity?

   • Is there anything about how you worked that you want to take back to the office?

Facilitator Notes
   • Using the names of organizations helps spur new ideas that people might not normally feel free to express—or even think of. Suggest that participants tell other members of their breakout groups which organizations they had in mind as they generated their ideas.

   • The target of thirty ideas is given only so that people won't stop working after they have a few ideas they like. Stretching to reach thirty ensures that they will come up with some illogical ideas. Most people, however, will not actually reach the target of thirty ideas in the time allotted.

   • It's important to celebrate the potential usefulness of the "bad ideas." Encourage participants to take their most bizarre ideas and turn them into good ones.

Facilitator Experience Required
This is a moderately easy activity to facilitate. Create a light-hearted atmosphere that helps participants enjoy the playfulness of this activity.

For help in evaluating new ideas and deciding which ones to act on, see the activity "Resource/ Impact Matrix" in Chapter 10, pp. 207–208.

   • A variation of this activity can be done by having the facilitator generate the lists of organizations in advance and cutting them into strips that are scattered around each table. In this variation, when the participants have exhausted the possibilities that one name triggers, they grab another from the table.

A revered ballet master was once asked whether—while looking at a class of young three- and four-year-old girls taking their first dance lessons—he could predict which would become great dancers. "Oh, yes," he said, "it's quite simple. You look for the ones who fling themselves around the room and make utter fools of themselves. They are the ones who will do *anything* to be great."

Wacky ideas generated when people are mentally flinging themselves around the room often contain the germ of something brilliant. This next activity helps reinforce participants' willingness to take the risks necessary to come up with extraordinary ideas.

Really Bad Ideas

Description

Participants identify an issue or problem and come up with possible solutions by first reversing the problem and thinking about how to make the situation worse before thinking about how they can make it better.

Experiential Elements
- Small group discussion
- Listening
- Reflecting on prior experiences
- Envisioning possibilities and generating new ideas

Steps

1. Have the whole group agree on a clear and concise statement of a vital problem or issue. For example: "Our procedures for dealing with customer complaints are too labor-intensive."

2. Reverse the problem statement and present it to the whole group. For example: "Our customer relations procedures are not labor-intensive enough."

3. Divide the participants into subgroups of three to five people. Have the participants—working alone and in silence—write down as many ideas as they can that would solve the reverse of the real problem, that is, how to make the real problem worse. (In this example you might say, "How can you make your customer relations procedures as labor-intensive and unproductive as possible?"). Allow five minutes.

   Encourage people to be really silly in generating these ideas. (For this example, ideas might include such things as ordering minute-by-minute reports on customer complaints, requiring that every customer complaint be routed to a supervisor for assignment back to someone to work on the problem, or urging customers to set up picket lines at your company's headquarters until their issues are resolved.)

4. Have participants read their ideas to one another, with one group member recording the ideas on a flip chart. Then each group should take two or three of the ideas and discuss how their opposites might generate practical ideas to address the real issue. For example, if making the problem worse would require minute-by-minute reporting, maybe there's a way to eliminate some routine reports that take a lot of time to produce. If requiring a supervisor's approval in advance would make things worse, maybe freeing employees to solve more problems themselves would help improve the process.

Facilitator Experience Required

This is an easy activity to lead as long as the facilitator can create an environment in which participants feel free to come up with "really bad" ideas.

5. Lead a whole group discussion about the ideas that were raised in the subgroups.

Minimizing "Groupthink"

"Groupthink" is a phenomenon that occurs when people are more interested in getting on with things or gaining others' approval than in challenging themselves to come up with breakthrough ideas. It's important to encourage the participants to remain independent, not to agree with the first good idea that comes along.

To minimize groupthink, use the following activity, which forces people to come up with their own ideas and interpretations.

Impressions

Description

This activity helps participants think in fresh ways by having them imagine relationships between a random picture and an existing issue.

Experiential Elements
- Using visual materials
- Individual reflection
- Experimenting with ideas

Steps

1. Distribute one Issue Sheet to each participant. Define the task: "We're going to use visual stimuli to give us new perspectives on this question. Think for a few moments about the question. Then, in silence, walk over to the table and pick up a picture. Make your choice quickly. Don't analyze the pictures; just select the first one that attracts you.

   "When you sit down again, continue to maintain silence. Look at the picture and consider how it suggests answers to the question at the top of your issue sheet. Write down your thoughts, using these questions to guide your thinking." Show the flip chart below.

   How to Look at Your Picture

   - How does the issue resemble this picture?

   - Why did I pick this particular picture?

   - What structures in the picture relate to the structures in the issue?

   - What is unknown in the picture? In my issue?

   - What does the picture reveal about the issue?

   - Where is the light coming from in the picture? Where might the light at the end of the tunnel be for the issue?

   - What do I resist in this picture? What do I resist about the issue?

Setup
- Cut as many large pictures with as wide a variety of subjects as you can find from magazines such as *National Geographic* or from remaindered books of photographs. You will need at least three photographs for each participant. Put each picture, backed by blank paper, in a transparent sheet protector.
- Place all the pictures face up on a large table so that participants can walk around it and view them.
- Prepare one Issue Sheet per participant. These are sheets of paper containing one question that everyone will answer, such as, "How can I help create a climate of innovation in my department?" or "What kinds of insights or ideas would help me achieve my goal?"
- Prepare How to Look at Your Picture flip chart (see Step 1).

Special Supplies

One copy of the Issue Sheet for each participant.

- How does the picture change when I turn it upside down? If I looked at it from another angle, how might the issue change?

It is helpful to demonstrate to the group how you might get ideas from a picture. Choose one from the table yourself and tell the group the messages you read from it. For instance: "This picture is of very straight rows of trees, very orderly. And that tells me that I must plan in a more ordered and organized way how I can encourage more interdepartmental cooperation among my staff. I can't just expect it to happen spontaneously. These trees look old; someone planted the seeds a long time ago. So I have to plant the seeds and be patient, not expect everything to change all at once. There are some people in the background having a picnic, and that reminds me that I must make the changes fun for people. When I turn the picture upside down, I notice how the trunks of the trees connect to the ground, and I think about keeping us all rooted in the good things we have already achieved."

While participants are writing, mix up the remaining pictures and turn them all face down on the table.

2. After seven or eight minutes, ask participants to return to the table, still in silence, and pick up another picture, this time without looking at it. Ask participants to respond to these questions: "What do I typically overlook concerning this issue? What does this picture remind me of that I must not forget?"

3. After a few minutes, ask for volunteers to show their pictures and share what they wrote with the rest of the group.

Facilitator Notes
- It's important that you use neutral pictures. Don't choose pictures that are related to the group's industry or issues.

- Some people may be initially reluctant to use the pictures in this way, but they will eventually join in.

- Participants should not be pushed to talk publicly about their reactions. Often people who are initially reticent will—after hearing others speak—become eager to explain their pictures.

- Sometimes one or two participants have such a significant response to their pictures that they wish to take them home. We encourage you to let them do so if you can spare the photos.

Facilitator Experience Required
This activity requires a strong ability to model the imaginative use of visual stimuli. It requires comfort in debriefing nonlinear and occasionally highly personal data.

This activity was derived from the authors' experience at the Center for Creative Leadership's Leading Creatively program. The center offers a collection of photographs and illustrations for use with groups in their Visual Explorer® product. The package includes instructions on a number of different ways to use visual stimuli. It can be purchased at www.ccl.org.

Cultivating the Creativity Habit

We all have our habits and our ruts—our established ways of doing things. A certain amount of routine is fine; otherwise we'd start each day by reinventing the proverbial wheel. But we can become so accustomed to operating in particular ways that we can't imagine any other possibilities. It may be difficult for us even to acknowledge that there could be better ways.

Not only that, but when we look at something new, we tend to make assumptions based on what we already know. These assumptions can be very useful (We wouldn't want to have to wonder what to do with a chair every time we saw one), but they also limit our thinking (What other uses could we make of this chair? What other forms can a chair take? What else can I use as a chair?).

How can we break out of this limited way of thinking? "The important thing," Albert Einstein once said, "is to never stop questioning." The more questions we ask, the closer we come to understanding the problem. A creative thinking retreat provides an opportunity for participants to ask the all-important question Why? And also Who, What, Where, When, How, and Why not?

Here is an activity that helps participants move beyond their assumptions and generate new ideas.

Isolated Words

Description   In this activity, participants use a simple verbal manipulation to help them challenge the way they habitually see things and find new solutions to familiar problems.

Experiential Elements

- Individual reflection
- Whole group discussion
- Applying theories to real-life situations

Steps

1. Divide participants into subgroups of three to five people. Introduce the task: "We are going to work on coming up with new ideas in relation to [specify issue and write it on a flip chart].

"Sometimes we become so caught up in what we know about a problem that we have difficulty getting a fresh perspective on it. So we must reframe the issue, that is, try to reposition it to see it differently. In your group, write down your assumptions about what characterizes this issue. For instance, if our issue were, 'How can we increase repeat sales to our customers?' some of our assumptions might include: 'Customers don't read our direct mail. Our product line lacks variety. Our prices are too high. Our competition sells harder.'"

2. "Now, challenge your assumptions by placing emphasis in turn on each noun, verb, adjective, or term in your statement, for example: 'Customers don't read our direct mail.' Each time you do this, write down how the issue or problem might be different if another word were substituted for the stressed word. What new ideas do you get for solving the problem?

"In the example, 'Customers don't read our direct mail,' if *customers* won't read it, will someone else in the customer's organization read the mail? The customer's assistant? His boss? A purchasing agent? An IT specialist? The CEO?

"If customers don't *read* our direct mail, what else could we get them to do with it? Pass it along to someone else? Post it on a bulletin board? File it? Scan it into their computers? Eat it like candy? Listen to it on their CD players?

"If customers don't read *our* direct mail, whose direct mail might they read? A celebrity's? A friend's?

"If customers don't read our *direct mail*, what would they read? Personal letters? Technical white papers? Journal articles? News releases? Faxes? E-mail?"

Allow fifteen minutes for the groups to work through their lists of assumptions.

3. Ask the subgroups to present their ideas. What other ways can participants think of to view the problem differently? Can they invent a fresh solution?

Facilitator Notes
- Many of us create self-limiting assumptions that constrain how we look at a problem, issue, or process. Here participants are given a way to challenge their assumptions by revisiting and reframing their observations.

- This is a quick activity that can spur participants to eliminate the self-limiting assumptions that may be hampering their success.

Facilitator Experience Required

The facilitator must be able to generate multiple options easily and give the subgroups examples to help them move ahead if they are stuck.

Besides being too entrenched in our own assumptions, we often fail to realize that others see things through different lenses. Being able to view a situation from other people's perspectives can help retreat participants devise solutions that work for all concerned. The following activity will help participants gain various perspectives on an issue.

Multiple Perspectives

Description

This activity requires participants to view an issue from their own perspectives and then to adopt the points of view of other stakeholders. To encourage empathetic listening, participants must write in someone else's "voice."

Steps

1. Write an issue or problem that affects the group on a flip chart. Define the task: "Take a look at the issue on the chart and then consider where you stand on the issue in your own words. On a Post-it, complete this sentence: 'What I wish would happen is. . . .' You don't have to be comprehensive. You need only cover one facet of the issue, but choose one that really concerns you.

   "For instance, if our issue were, 'How can we make our sales presentations more effective?' I might write: 'What I wish would happen is that we start a presentations training class for our sales reps.'"

   Allow time for participants to write their sentences.

2. "Now, on other Post-its, complete that same sentence about the issue as you think it would be answered by at least four other people involved—a customer, a vendor, your spouse, your supervisor, someone from another department, and so on. Note whose perspective you think this is and state it in quotes, as if the sentence were in the person's own words.

   "So, in the example, I might write: 'Sales Manager: . . . our reps would learn to listen better to customer needs.' 'Spouse of Sales Rep: . . . my wife would get home at a reasonable hour every night.' 'Customer: . . . my sales rep would understand our industry and wouldn't ask me such elementary questions.' 'Sales rep's assistant: . . . I never had to prepare another boring PowerPoint presentation.'

   "Please work independently _and in silence._"

   Allow five minutes for people to write their responses.

3. Have participants stick their Post-its on flip chart paper mounted on the wall.

> **Experiential Elements**
> - Individual reflection
> - Imagining other people's interests
> - Listening

> **Setup**
> Tape several sheets of flip chart paper, each titled, "What I wish would happen is . . ." (see Step 1) to a wall.
>
> **Special Supplies**
> A pad of Post-it Notes and a felt-tip pen for each participant.

4. Ask participants to choose three perspectives from the wall that do not reflect their own opinions. Have them work individually to come up with new ways to address the issue, inspired by the various perspectives they chose.

5. Invite participants to share their ideas. Ask: "What new ideas or insights come from looking at the problem through the eyes of other people?"

Facilitator Note   This activity can be conducted in one large group or in breakout groups.

Participants won't come up with good ideas if they are paralyzed by fear of failure or of appearing foolish. If the corporate culture looks askance at anything that diverges from "the way we've always done things," chances are participants will be reluctant to come up with truly creative ideas to address pressing issues.

Sometimes you can encourage new thinking by giving people "cover" for their new ideas—by asking them, for instance, to project what they believe someone else would think. This activity makes it easy for reluctant participants to imagine new solutions.

Expert Opinion

Description

This activity helps participants think creatively by having them imagine what an expert would say about an important issue or problem.

Steps

1. Present a problem or issue in the form of a question to the entire group. For example, "How can we gain an advantage over our low-price competitor who's cutting into our market share?"

2. Ask each participant to think of *someone they've never met* whom they believe would be a good person to consult about this question. This expert could be someone they know by name (such as Steve Jobs of Apple Computer) or just by a title (such as the marketing director of the Ritz Carlton Hotels). The person can be an inspirational figure outside of business (the Dalai Lama, for example) or someone who is deceased (such as Leonardo Da Vinci). It could even be a fictional character (like James Bond, Agent 007). Each participant selects his or her expert without disclosing the identity of that person to anyone else in the group.

3. Define the task: "Working alone, imagine that you run into your expert. Think up a story of how you meet (on a plane, at a coffee shop, attending an imaginary conference for geniuses). You strike up a conversation about the issue. And your expert says, 'I've been thinking about that very issue. Let me tell you what I've learned and what I think your company should do.' Write down the advice the person gives you, focusing specifically on what he or she tells you to do to resolve the issue."

Allow fifteen to twenty minutes for people to imagine their conversations and make notes.

4. Have participants read aloud their invented conversations. A notetaker should collect all the ideas on a flip chart. Ask participants to consider the ideas they've come up with:

   - What were the themes that came out of your stories?

   - What did your choice of expert tell you about the way you view this problem?

Letting Go of Judgment

We've all learned to analyze, evaluate, critique, and pass judgment on anything new. But while the ability to think critically is a valuable attribute, critical thinking is not creative thinking. Throughout the retreat, you'll need to encourage participants to suspend their inclination to look for what's wrong with a new idea and instead focus on how they might make it work.

What are the risks of coming up with new ideas? Actually, if you have created an environment of trust at the retreat, there are few risks associated with idea generation. The difficulty rarely lies in "creative thinking." The challenge is to move those ideas to "creative doing."

One way to help the participants find the courage to try new things is to have them assess the risk realistically.

Considering Risk

Description

Participants first consider the nature of personal and organizational risk. Then they each work on a proposed action to evaluate the risk and formulate strategies to reduce it.

Steps

1. Divide participants into subgroups of three or four people. Introduce the task: "In your groups, describe to one another in turn the biggest risk you have ever taken, either personally or at work. Tell whether taking the risk turned out well or not. Either way, what did you learn from having taken the risk?"

2. Bring the whole group together. Ask the participants: "Did taking your risks mostly turn out well? What contributed to successful risk taking? What lessons did you learn from the risks that did not turn out well?"

3. Present the Considering Risk flip chart to the whole group.

   Considering Risk

   • The risk I'd like us to take is . . .

   • The possible downsides are . . .

   • I still consider it worth taking because . . .

   • We could minimize the downsides by . . . (for example, by having time limits, money limits, and fallback strategies)

   Ask participants to write down their responses to these four statements as completely as they can.

4. Divide participants into subgroups of three to five people (not the same groups as in Step 1). Have participants read their ideas to one another. After each participant has presented his or her ideas, ask the group to explore whether there are other possible downsides and, if there are, to come up with strategies to minimize them.

5. If the participants aren't members of the senior leadership team, make sure they know that they cannot decide for themselves what is an acceptable level of risk for the organization to assume. Ask the subgroups to choose one of the risks they discussed and prepare a case for management that lays out the key points.

6. Have the subgroups present their cases. Facilitate a discussion about the information senior managers need to make intelligent assessments of risk.

Experiential Elements

• Reflecting back on experiences
• Applying theories to real situations
• Group discussion
• Experimenting with ideas

Setup

Prepare the flip chart page, Considering Risk (see Step 3).

Facilitator Experience Required

This is an easy activity to facilitate.

Typically people are trained from their first day at school to make judgments about themselves and others. The work is good or bad. The answers are right or wrong. The ideas are smart or dumb. And thus *they* are good or bad, right or wrong, smart or dumb. Most managers climb the corporate ladder on the basis of their ability to assess a situation accurately and rapidly and to exercise good judgment. Indeed, people's capacity for sound judgment *is* important. But it can also stifle their ability to think creatively.

How? When someone offers a fresh idea, people tend to evaluate it, make a snap judgment about it, and begin to marshal their arguments for or against it. Usually people judge their own ideas before they express them—"How will this sound to others?" "Will this really work?" "What will people think?"

But the process of *generating* ideas is the polar opposite of evaluating them, and the two poles produce opposite effects as different as north and south. Idea generation works best when people come up with as many ideas as possible. Great minds do *not* think alike.

In contrast, *evaluation* is the process of culling the best ideas and eliminating the rest. Idea generation is inclusive; evaluation is exclusive. If retreat participants engage in both processes at once, they won't do either well.

The best way to help the group come away from the retreat with great ideas is to encourage people to put lots of ideas on the table, build on one another's proposals, and defer judgment for as long as possible. Evaluation and selection can wait.

This chapter contained several activities designed to help foster innovation and creativity at a retreat. In Chapter 14, we discuss how to close the offsite in a way that will help the participants recall the distance they've traveled and remain mindful of their commitments to take action. A fitting closing also helps participants make the transition from the somewhat special atmosphere of the retreat to the more familiar environment of the workplace.

Chapter 14

Closing the Retreat

No matter how well-planned and well-run a retreat is, it is unlikely to result in significant change if participants don't make concrete commitments for action (and honor those commitments back in the workplace). Before leaving the retreat, as we noted in Chapter 8, they must assign responsibility for action, determine interim and final target dates, and devise ways to measure progress toward meeting the goals they set.

The purpose of a formal retreat closure is to help participants reflect on what they've learned, make commitments to specific actions, and think about how they will integrate back at the office what they accomplished at the retreat. You might use one or two of the following activities to close your retreat.

See Chapter 8 for a full discussion of action planning.

The Messy Room

Description

The facilitator presents the "Four-Room Apartment" model (see Step 1). Participants discuss how the model might help them anticipate and deal with adverse reactions that might occur as they attempt to implement the changes they've recommended or decided on at the retreat.

Read more about the theory and application of the Four-Room Apartment in *Productive Workplaces* (1987) by Marvin Weisbord.

Steps

1. Present The Four-Room Apartment flip chart.

Illustration by Sachia Long.

Experiential Elements

*   Shared dialogue and discussion
*   Personal and group reflection
*   Experimenting with ideas

Setup

*   On a flip chart, draw The Four-Room Apartment as shown in Step 1.
*   Write the questions in Exploring the Rooms (see Step 3) on a flip chart.

Introduce the activity with this mini-presentation: "Imagine yourselves living in a metaphorical four-room apartment. You as individuals, and your group, team, department, and organization as entities, move from room to room in response to things that happen inside and outside your organization. As shown by the arrows in the diagram, the movement is cyclical and continual—meaning that it is a process that you continually revisit, not something you 'just experience and are done with.'

"The first room is the Room of Satisfaction, where you are pretty happy with how things are and content to leave them be.

you come back from this retreat and recognize that you need to make some changes. Or some changes are imposed on you from outside your organization [or department]. Acknowledging the need for or the inevitability of change impels you to leave the Room of Satisfaction and enter the Room of Denial.

"In this second room, you feel anxious about the possible change or even deny the need for change, although you may not be conscious of why you're feeling that way. You have to stay in this room, though, where you may be perceived as resisting change, until you come to terms with your denial. Once that takes place, you move to the Messy Room.

"If any of you have teenagers whose rooms you don't like to walk into, you know what a messy room is like. In this room, you start to question everything. You feel unsure of yourself and your environment. Thoughts that once were neat are now disorderly. Things that you once held to be true now do not seem so true, and you do not yet know what *is* true.

"Although it is extremely uncomfortable for most people to hang out in the Messy Room, it is probably the most important room in the apartment. For it is in the Messy Room that you are open to new ideas and perspectives. Only by passing through it can you get to the fourth room, the Room of Renewal.

"In this last room you are able to embrace change, to see how it benefits you and others and the organization as a whole.

"Organizations often try to institute changes after retreats by trying to push everyone straight from contentment to renewal. But change doesn't happen that way. If you don't work through the resistance in the Room of Denial and the doubts and discomfort of the Messy Room, you will not reach the Room of Renewal. So the key to reaching this last room is recognizing that change is a process and developing strategies for managing the process that are appropriate for the room you are in.

"Remember also that change is a cycle. Even if you were able to implement every change you have imagined at this retreat, eventually you would move back into the Room of Satisfaction and the cycle would start over again."

2. Ask the group what room they think they are now in with regard to the changes they want to make and why they believe they are in that room. Discuss similarities and differences among participants' responses and ask for preliminary thoughts about what those differences might mean for the success of these changes.

3. Divide the participants into four subgroups and assign each group the task of exploring one of the four rooms. Present the following flip chart:

Exploring the Rooms

- How will we know when we are in this room?

- What are the advantages and disadvantages of being in this room for the success of our change initiatives?

- What strategies might help us live better in this room and move on to the next when it's appropriate?

Ask each group to write their answers to the questions on a flip chart.

4. Have each subgroup present its work. Facilitate a discussion based on these questions:

- How might being aware of the dynamics of the change process help you back at work?

- How can members of this group help one another when some are struggling in the Room of Denial or the Messy Room, or staying in the Room of Satisfaction even though things aren't as rosy as they might seem?

> **Facilitator Experience Required**
> This is an easy activity to lead.

If the participants came up with a number of action steps, as they likely will, they will have to plan how to accomplish them and decide on their relative priority. The next activity helps the group focus on what needs to be done to achieve the greatest impact.

Top Priorities

Description

This activity requires participants to focus on their top three priorities and reach agreement on the actions they will take to accomplish these priorities.

Experiential Elements
- Shared dialogue and discussion
- Personal and group reflection

Steps

1. Introduce the activity by saying: "Based on everything we have talked about in the retreat, what are your top priorities for change?" Facilitate a discussion that concludes with agreement on the top three priorities.

2. Divide the group into three subgroups. Have each subgroup address one of the top priorities by answering the questions listed on the following flip chart.

Setup

Create the flip chart, What Can the People in This Room Do . . . ? (see Step 2).

What Can the People in This Room Do to Accomplish These Priorities?

- Who will do what by when?

- How will you communicate this priority to others?

- How will you encourage your stakeholders—internal and external—to embrace this priority?

- How will you handle pressure to spend time on non-priorities?

- How will you stop distracting one another from priority work to spend time on less important projects?

Have each subgroup report back to the rest of the group.

3. Discuss with the whole group how realistic its priorities are, given what it will take to accomplish them. Ask, "Can you accomplish all three of these priorities? Do you need to scale back to one or two?"

Ask the group, "Would some actions support more than one of the priorities? Should those actions be undertaken first?"

Facilitator Experience Required

Although this is not a difficult activity, the facilitator may have to press participants to make hard choices.

The next five activities all wrap up the work of the retreat in different ways. They may be used singly or in combination.

Closing Thoughts

Description

In this activity, participants write on individual Post-its and then share their thoughts in three areas: something they've learned, something they will commit to do, and a hope they have for the whole group.

Experiential Elements
- Reflecting back on experiences
- Writing down ideas individually
- Listening

Steps

1. Introduce the activity: "You have taken time away from the office to consider issues that you identified as important. This time should pay off as an investment in making things better in your organization. But change will only take place if the people in this room make commitments to change how you have been doing things.

   "So based on everything we have discussed in the retreat, write on *three separate* Post-it Notes:

   - One thing you have learned.

   - One thing you personally commit to doing differently.

   - One thing you hope the whole group will do differently."

2. Have participants read their resolutions aloud and post their notes on the appropriate flip chart.

Setup

Create three flip charts:
   I have learned . . .
   I will . . .
   I hope we all will . . .

Special Supplies

A pad of Post-it˝ Notes and a felt-tip pen for each participant.

Facilitator Note

This is a closing activity, not an opening for further discussion. No one should comment on what any individual says. Encourage participants to listen and absorb the ideas suggested.

Facilitator Experience Required

This is an extremely easy activity to lead.

Letter to Myself

Description

In this activity, participants write letters to themselves about the commitments they have made during the retreat. The letters are sealed in envelopes, collected, and later sent back to the individuals who wrote them.

Experiential Elements
- Reflecting back on experiences
- Writing down ideas

Steps

1. Distribute the sheets of stationery and envelopes to the participants. Ask them to write their names and office addresses on their envelopes.

2. Introduce the activity: "Please write a letter to yourself that summarizes what you commit to do differently as a result of this retreat. Be as specific as possible in making your commitments.

   - What will you do?

   - By what date will you do it?

   - How will you know when you have done it?"

   - Inform participants that you will send the letters to them to remind them of their commitments within the next week or two. Make sure they know that no one will see the contents of their sealed envelopes but themselves.

3. Give participants ten minutes to write their letters and seal them in envelopes.

4. Collect the letters. A week or so later, send the letters to the participants.

Special Supplies

Several sheets of organization stationery and one envelope for each participant; postage stamps (if the envelopes will be mailed rather than delivered).

Facilitator Note

Having participants write letters to themselves reinforces their commitment to the decisions they've reached at the retreat. When they receive their letters, they will be reminded of their intentions even as they are faced with competing priorities back at work.

Facilitator Experience Required

This is an easy activity to lead.

Appreciation

Description

In this activity, participants take turns openly expressing appreciation to each other for the contributions they have made during the retreat.

Experiential Elements
- Personal reflection
- Listening
- Conversations with others

Steps

1. Have the group sit in a circle. (If the group is very large, have people sit in two or even three concentric circles.)

2. Introduce the activity: "Please look around the room. Everybody here has made a contribution to the success of this retreat. When we are busy at work, we don't often take the time to appreciate one another's efforts. So we are going to take some time to do that.

This activity works best for groups of twelve or fewer participants. Variations for larger groups are given in the Facilitator Notes.

"Throughout this retreat, you worked with each other in new ways. You now have the opportunity to express your appreciation for something that people in this room did—taking a risk by bringing up a difficult subject, clarifying a misunderstanding, suggesting an idea for the group to consider, and so forth."

Demonstrate an appreciation: "For instance, 'I want to express appreciation to [Nancy. Nancy, I really appreciated how you didn't just go along with a decision you thought would be bad for customer relations. Your persistence—in the face of some frustration from colleagues who wanted to come to closure—helped the group make a better decision].'

"Notice that while I was expressing my appreciation to [Nancy], I made eye contact with her."

3. Invite other participants to contribute: "Now I would like to ask the rest of the group to think about [Nancy's] contributions over the course of the retreat, whether in small group discussions, in the whole group, or even on a break. We will all take a turn appreciating something that [Nancy] did.

"[Bob], why don't you start? And then we will go around the circle."

4. When everyone has appreciated that person, repeat the process with others until everyone has been appreciated by everyone else.

Facilitator Notes

- This is a wonderful activity to end a retreat in which the participants have grappled with really tough issues. It helps participants reflect on the hard work everyone has done and leaves people feeling good that others recognize their contributions. Only use this activity, though, if you feel confident that participants will recognize one another's contributions willingly, without feeling manipulated or forced.

- After starting the process, you should stay out of the circle. While it might be nice to bask in participants' comments about your work, it is more important to have the participants focus on their appreciation for one another and what *they* did to make the retreat a success.

- Very often people find being openly acknowledged for their contributions a moving experience. Be prepared for the possibility that some participants (both men and women) may become teary-eyed when being appreciated.

- This version of the activity will take too long if the group is larger than twelve people. Other variations for larger groups include:

The circle. A quicker version of this activity is just to have participants go around the circle and give an appreciation to the person on their right.

The Koosh™ ball. Another variation is to use a Koosh ball, a small, soft, easily caught rubbery object found in toy or novelty stores. One person tosses the ball to someone in the group while expressing appreciation for what that person contributed. Then that person tosses the ball to someone else in the room and expresses appreciation for that person, and so on, until everyone has had the ball and received an appreciation. (Remind participants not to toss the ball to someone who already has received it. In the interest of time and equity, one appreciation per participant.)

The yarn ball. Another variation is to introduce a ball of yarn, with each participant holding on to the string of yarn when they toss the ball. This creates a memorable visual (the "web of appreciation") that demonstrates how the whole group is interconnected.

Expectations and Outcomes

Description

This activity really starts at the beginning of the retreat. Participants write down their expectations for the retreat as an opening activity, then put these notes into envelopes and seal them. At the end of the retreat, their envelopes are returned, and participants reflect on the difference between what they thought would happen and what actually took place.

Experiential Elements
- Personal reflection
- Writing down ideas
- Personal and group discussion

Setup

Prepare the My Expectations form (see Step 1) and make copies for the participants.

Special Supplies

One envelope for each participant.

Steps

1. *Part I: At the beginning of the retreat:*

   Distribute the My Expectations form and an envelope to each person.

   My Expectations

   I think this retreat will accomplish . . .

   If difficult issues come up, I think this group will . . .

   I'm worried that . . .

   It would be incredible if . . .

2. Introduce the activity: "We are going to reflect on your expectations of this retreat we are about to begin. Please fill out the form with the first thing that comes to mind. Don't censor yourself in any way. No one else will see what you write."

   Allow five minutes for participants to fill in their forms.

3. Have the participants place their forms in the envelopes, write their names on the envelopes, and seal them. Collect the envelopes and tell participants that you will return their unopened envelopes to them later.

4. *Part II: At the end of the retreat:*

   Give the envelopes back to the participants. Ask them to open the envelopes and read to themselves what they wrote at the beginning of the retreat.

5. In small groups of three to five people, ask participants to reflect on what they wrote. Do they still see things the same way as they did at the beginning of the retreat? If not, what accounts for the change?

    Ask for volunteers to tell the whole group how they saw things at the beginning of the retreat and how they see them now.

Facilitator Note This is an excellent way to demonstrate how individual and group perceptions can change when a group puts in a good effort. Be aware, however, that there is always the risk that some people will express disappointment rather than approval.

> **Facilitator Experience Required**
> This is a moderately easy activity for most facilitators.

The Road We've Traveled

Description In this activity, small groups of participants draw road maps of the progress made in the retreat.

Experiential Elements
- Personal reflection
- Personal and group discussion
- Visual expression

Steps

1. Divide the participants into groups of three to five people. Introduce the activity: "We have traveled a long way over the course of this retreat. The road may have been bumpy, with a few blind curves, but we are now in a different place than when we started.

   "While it's important to remain focused on the future, on the road ahead, it's also important to glance over our shoulders to see how far we've already traveled. In your groups, draw a road map of this retreat on a flip chart, showing graphically what the journey was like, what landmarks we passed along the way, and where the road seems to be leading." Allow ten minutes for the groups to work.

2. Ask each group to post its road map on a wall around the room. Facilitate a discussion around these questions:

   - What are some of the most striking features of the road maps?

   - What picture do they collectively paint of what was accomplished at the retreat and where the group seems to be heading?

Facilitator Experience Required
This activity is easy to lead.

Writing the Follow–Up Report

Before you leave the retreat site, as everyone else heads for their cars, take a few minutes to separate all the flip charts that chronicle decisions and action steps from those that just reflect group brainstorming. Organizing the charts in this way while everything's fresh in your mind will be a big help to whomever will be writing the retreat report. Ideally, the report should be completed within a day or two of the retreat, so be sure to give the sorted charts to that person before he or she leaves the site.

Read more about "Capturing the Work Product" in Chapter 5, pp. 63–89.

Because it's so important to write and distribute the report quickly, a simple record of what happened at the retreat is far better than elaborate documentation that takes weeks to produce. If a strategic plan will come out of the retreat, the plan can be written based on the retreat report, but the report is not the plan.

The report should not be a chronological record of everything that took place at the offsite. A more useful structure for the report might include a few points, in the following order:

- Key decisions
- Action steps
- Pending items
- An appendix of the flip chart notes and handouts

Key Decisions. These should include the goals and the strategies for achieving them that the group has agreed on. This section of the report is, in essence, the executive summary, so it should be short, clear, and easy to read.

Action Steps. These provide the detail of what people will actually do: who will take what action, by what date, and with what resources. You may want to put the action steps into a chart that makes it easy for individuals and departments to find and track their assignments.

Pending Items. These include those topics that were never fully discussed. They should go on the agenda for a later meeting or a future retreat. Other pending items might be information still needed before a decision can be made or a decision that requires the involvement of people who were not at the retreat.

Transcriptions. These are the actual words from the flip charts created at the retreat and copies of the handouts. These records are important so participants can go back to the in-the-moment notes for the details of the various discussions. These documents also provide a resource for people to refer back to in case of later questions. The best place for them is in an appendix at the end of the report. We put them in chronological order or by topic so that readers can find them easily.

In capturing flip charts of open discussions, we generally try not to record those notes in a bullet-point fashion, because bulleted lists often connote order of importance. Especially if you've used Post-it Notes, organizing them into lists distorts the impression of free-flowing communications. You might consider using graphics software to present the Post-its as rectangles floating on a page.

We presented several activities in this chapter that focus on ending the retreat in a manner that's both satisfying for the participants and likely to motivate them to implement the decisions they reached and the recommendations they made. These include how to make the transition to the everyday world of work, determine top priorities, and create an opportunity for participants to make personal, yet public, commitments to action. Finally, we discussed how to prepare a follow-up report.

If the retreat generates a lot of interesting talk, including expressions of commitment, but no follow-through back at work, it can't be considered a success. Thus, Chapter 15 focuses on ensuring that the retreat plan is implemented.

An inexpensive software program that allows you to present ideas graphically is Inspiration, available at www.inspiration.com.

EPILOGUE

The Convenor's Guide to Keeping the Work of the Retreat Alive

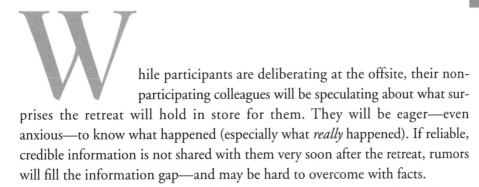

Chapter 15

Assuring That the Action Plan Is Implemented

While participants are deliberating at the offsite, their non-participating colleagues will be speculating about what surprises the retreat will hold in store for them. They will be eager—even anxious—to know what happened (especially what *really* happened). If reliable, credible information is not shared with them very soon after the retreat, rumors will fill the information gap—and may be hard to overcome with facts.

Thus it is critical that people who were not at the retreat be brought into the loop as quickly and completely as possible. The failure to carry out this crucial step may undo some or all of the hard work that was carried out at the retreat.

A common impulse at the end of a retreat is for everyone to agree not to say anything specific "until we work out the details." Another common comment is, "We have to make sure we all say the same things." Both ideas sound good, but they inhibit immediate communication and undermine confidence and trust. The longer people go without hearing something specific, the more time they'll have to speculate about why they aren't being told what happened.

And the sooner everyone in the organization knows what actually took place, the sooner fears will be allayed and the collective energy of the whole can be brought to bear on implementing decisions for change.

Retreat participants, like witnesses at a crime scene, will recall events differently. We all remember best those things that affect us directly or provoke an emotional reaction, while our recollections of things we are less interested in are fuzzier. This phenomenon can influence and distort how participants remember what took place. This is why the convenor and the facilitator need to take time at the retreat to guide the group in a collective discussion of the context for the various recommendations and decisions. Otherwise, participants will tell their own versions of events and the people back at the office will hear highly individualized (and sometimes contradictory) accounts.

While you don't want participants to reveal any information that they agreed was confidential or to tout a "company line," you as convenor should encourage them to speak informally with their staffs the very first morning back in the office. Participants can certainly give their colleagues an idea of the broad outcomes—for instance, "We spent most of the day talking about strategies and budgets for next year. It looks like we're going to spend a lot more energy on developing our brand. The details aren't finished yet, but you should know that branding will be the general thrust when the report comes out." That's far better than, "As soon as we get the report back and the executive committee meets, then we can tell you what we talked about, but not before." A reluctance to speak can stimulate suspicion that bad news is ahead.

If you did anything particularly unusual at the retreat, people will want to hear about that too: "After dinner we played charades till one in the morning, and I had no idea how well so many of our board members could act!" Also, be aware that if there were any dramatic events at the offsite—a shouting match between two executives or someone who insulted the CEO—you can be sure that those stories will immediately leak to the non-attendees. If such an event did occur, it's important that participants discuss it with one another before returning to the office. The group should decide how to put the event in context for the people who weren't there. That way no one has to respond on the spur of the moment to the people's questions about the meaning of the event.

Announcing Retreat Outcomes

Even with the casual reporting back to colleagues that each participant will do, everyone in the organization needs a formal announcement of the retreat's outcomes. The guideline here is: Over-communicate! People process information differently, and if you use only one communication mechanism, some people won't fully grasp the message.

Some ways to get the word out quickly include:

- Immediately send out an e-mail with an overview of the retreat proceedings and results.
- Post some of the key flip charts in convenient public locations where people can read them, in a common space, such as a break room, for instance. One organization not only posted the charts from the retreat, but left some charts blank, with Post-it Notes and pens on a nearby table, so non-participants could add any comments they might have.
- If there is a written report, distribute it to those who weren't at the retreat as well as those who were. (That's one reason such reports should be written as soon after the retreat as possible.)

A written report that summarizes major issues, recommendations, conclusions, decisions, action assignments, and timetables is essential, but not sufficient. The convenor should also plan to hold a meeting (or a series of meetings) with non-participating employees.

This meeting should be conducted in the spirit of the retreat itself. Instead of merely listening passively to oral reports, people who come to the meeting should be encouraged to ask questions and contribute ideas about implementation.

The meeting should not be announced as if it were an afterthought. It's a critical element in implementing decisions that were reached at the retreat, and it's best if it's scheduled even before the retreat takes place. You should encourage the widest possible attendance so that people who did not participate in the retreat will still be able to participate in the process. While you may want to lead this meeting, you need not be alone in presenting information and responding to questions; ideally, some of the retreat participants would share this task, or even take the lead while you act as moderator, moving things along and fielding questions.

As work on action steps proceeds, everyone needs to be kept well informed of progress, delays, glitches, and alterations. It's a good idea to set up communication channels for frequent updates, answering questions, and responding to rumors. E-mail can be a particularly effective means of accomplishing this.

Translating Decisions into Action

Once everyone has heard about the "What"—what occurred, what was discussed, what was recommended, what was agreed on—the next key step is involving employees who weren't at the retreat in the "How"—how we will get things done and who is responsible for doing what and by when.

It's important to involve as many people as practical in the change process, of which the retreat was only one step. Employees who did not take part in the retreat should have the opportunity to participate in task forces or special work groups charged with implementing the changes that were agreed on at the retreat. But they shouldn't be expected merely to be good soldiers who salute and say, "Yes, Sir!" (or "Ma'am"). Their views should be sought and taken into account as the change initiative takes shape.

The architectural plans for even the most well-designed buildings are nearly always modified during construction. The same is true for the implementation phase of a change initiative. Plans may be drawn up at the retreat, but the structure has to be built in the real world. Modifications are inevitable and even desirable because it's important to take into account anything the retreat participants didn't foresee. (This doesn't mean, of course, that decisions made at the retreat should be revisited *ad infinitum,* just that you should expect and welcome modifications as the change initiative progresses.)

Once the implementation plan is underway, it's important to celebrate progress by acknowledging significant milestones. People involved in change initiatives tend to focus their attention on the road ahead, which may seem endless. It's important that they look back from time to time to appreciate how much distance they have already covered.

You might want to draw on the facilitator's expertise as you carry out your plan. Sometimes a little outside assistance can help jumpstart a stalled change initiative.

A high tech company, for example, wanted to find a way to maintain the positive momentum growing out of its retreat. An external consultant helped them set up a peer support network that fostered better information sharing and collaboration among the various department heads.

Similarly, an accounting firm established several task forces to work on specific aspects of their action plan. The company kept its external consultants involved with the process to help task force members sharpen their creative thinking skills, learn how to plan and conduct more effective meetings, and master various decision-making techniques.

Avoiding Post-Retreat Letdown

A successful retreat can be a peak experience for everyone involved. People come back to work excited about new initiatives, about the collegial spirit they've experienced, about everything they've learned. Then they have to go right back to work on the same old stuff that was on their desks before they left.

When the bubble of the retreat environment bursts, participants may feel deflated. But you can take some steps to keep the retreat group engaged. These include:

Giving Participants Mementos of the Retreat. A useful or decorative object sitting on someone's desk can serve as a reminder of the spirit of the retreat. It might be as simple as a portfolio distributed at the beginning of the retreat, printed with the organization's name and the dates, for participants to use during the retreat, or a coffee mug with a theme on it, delivered a day or two later back at the office. Some groups have made a point of taking a group photo and having copies made for all the participants. Sometimes the mementos are more unusual. One group we facilitated in the Deep South had enjoyed an uproarious dinner at a catfish restaurant one evening of the retreat. When they returned to work, the CEO sent them all very tacky stuffed catfish plaques, which participants proudly displayed on their office walls.

Holding Periodic Post-Retreat Updates. Schedule regular times to bring the group together to talk about the status of the change initiatives. The get-togethers can be weekly, bi-weekly, monthly, or quarterly, whatever makes sense for you, but get the dates on people's calendars right away. These meetings can also provide an excellent forum for devising solutions to problems that arise in the implementation phases. And this doesn't preclude calling ad hoc meetings when necessary.

Convening Mini-Retreats. A half-day session with the retreat group can help keep the work moving forward. Each mini-session should focus tightly on one topic. The group can mobilize to get some targeted work done and maintain the special relationships they've formed.

Acknowledging Accomplishments and Celebrating Milestones. Look for ways to reward individuals and groups for the extra efforts they have made. Acknowledge progress often. Talk about large and small achievements in staff meetings and special "change champions" meetings. Send e-mails and personal notes to everyone who has made a special contribution to the change efforts. Help people see how far they've traveled as well as what remains to be done.

The Role of Senior Management

A retreat is over when it's over, but, as we have pointed out, it will be judged a success only if it initiated a process that continues to unfold back at the office. For this forward momentum to continue, senior management must take the participants' recommendations and decisions seriously and be committed to implementing those they've agreed to.

There are several ways you personally can champion change. You might, for instance, give staff members time to work on various retreat-related tasks. You might decide to reduce or redistribute people's regular duties, budget funds for training and professional development, or offer rewards and recognition to staff who contribute to achieving the goals agreed to at the retreat. And you might look critically at your own management style and modify your behavior as necessary to help foster desired change.

If change is difficult for staff members, it's much more difficult for executives. Executives typically (and usually correctly) credit their management styles for their ascension to the upper rungs of the organizational ladder. So they're often reluctant, unwilling, or unable to modify them.

But altering your management style to fit new demands doesn't mean becoming a different person, any more than altering a jacket makes it a different suit. It merely means accepting that you, like everyone else, could do some things better and that if you improve elements of your management style you will help foster the changes that you want to take place.

A retreat affords you a valuable opportunity to learn what you are doing right and what you could be doing better. Altering course in response to feedback is the hallmark of a successful leader.

> The Center for Creative Leadership conducted a study of promising employees whose career paths flattened out or even took a nosedive. The number one factor holding them back was inability to hear honest feedback about their performance or respond appropriately to such feedback.

Changing Cynicism to Support

One of the greatest impediments to making things better at work is cynicism—the belief that "You can't change human nature" and that nothing, therefore, will ever improve.

Well, you *can't* change human nature, but you *can* change behavior, and that's what can make things better.

For example, Patricia, the newly appointed director of a large government bureau was dissatisfied with the way her office operated. Staff took too long to respond to customers. New ideas weren't bubbling to the surface. Employees weren't motivated. Patricia recognized that this was the kind of bureau that gave "bureaucracy" a bad name. To remedy the situation, Patricia declared her commitment to change, introduced new concepts, held retreats to give employees a forum to decide how to make things better, and vowed to accept their recommendations.

Some employees were enthusiastic about the possibilities, but most were indifferent ("We've seen this all before") or even hostile ("None of this will ever amount to anything"). "I don't trust this new boss," said one employee, "and I'm not going to get my hopes up only to be disappointed."

Patricia took seriously what she was hearing. She realized that she would have to manage very differently if her experiment were to succeed. She worked diligently to modify her management style. In time, she overcame the resistance that accompanies any change initiative and won over the nay-sayers. In fact, by the time the bureau's new way of doing business was challenged a couple of years later by newcomers, some of the original critics who had opposed the changes most vocally had become its most ardent advocates.

Change cannot be imposed from the top down, but the role of the leader in a change process is critical. If the leader's attitude is, "I can keep managing the old way; everyone else will have to change," the effort is almost certain to fail. The cynics will dig in their collective heels and try to outdo each other in proving themselves right.

But when leaders can see and hear—*really* see and hear—they can initiate and manage change efforts that transform their organizations.

Overcoming cynicism is not easy. It will require you to hear things that may be discomforting, embarrassing, even painful. You may have to re-examine and perhaps abandon some of the management principles you have successfully employed over the years in pursuit of the positions you have attained. You may have to change your style in light of new economic conditions, new attitudes among employees, new trends in society, or new goals and objectives.

When you ask for candor, you have to mean it. When you encourage subordinates to take risks, you must reward risk taking. When you demand honesty and loyalty from the staff, you also have to return honesty and loyalty to the staff.

You won't transform cynicism to support for positive change overnight (and you may have to ask hard-core cynics who actively oppose or undermine the initiative to move on). If, however, you gain a reputation for listening to others, saying what you mean, and doing what you say you'll do, things are far more likely to change for the better.

Making the Plan Stick

The most common reason a retreat fails to spark lasting change is that everyday events overtake good intentions. People start remembering the retreat as an occasion—something we experienced—rather than a launching pad for their real work.

When they return from the retreat, participants must immediately make time to do the necessary follow-through. They have to make time in their schedules *regularly*, not just every now and then. That may mean giving up some other tasks or reordering some priorities.

Most important is the ongoing communication with everyone involved about where the organization is now headed and how it will get there. In our experience, some of the most critical actions the leaders must take are these:

Make the Outcomes Important. People will not change if they don't think it's really necessary and important to change. Leaders must make the reasons for change dramatic, compelling, and even urgent.

Design a Clear and Simple Implementation Plan. The more complex the ideas are that come out of the retreat, the harder they will be to remember—and the less likely they are to come to fruition. Make implementation strategies simple, clear, and explicit, and show people how these strategies apply as they set their everyday priorities and make decisions.

Demonstrate Support and Commitment Among Top Management. If a leader disparages any part of the plan, in public pronouncements or in private conversations with colleagues or outsiders, people will start perceiving the whole thing

Critical Leadership Actions for Retreat Follow-Up

- Make the outcomes important.

- Design a clear and simple implementation plan.

- Demonstrate total commitment among top management.

- Be unrelenting in pursuit of the goals.

- Keep everyone involved.

- Remove obstacles.

- Report on progress frequently.

as full of holes. And if leaders don't keep their commitments, others will see such commitments as meaningless. Everyone will watch top management's behavior for clues to what's important. It's not only what leaders say but also what they do that matters.

Be Unrelenting in Pursuit of the Goals. Leaders must not accept excuses and delays. They should be rigorous in demanding that people adhere to the new strategies and actions (with allowances, of course, for necessary modifications; wise leaders don't carve their plans in marble, but butter isn't a good medium either).

Keep Everyone Involved. Leaders must be very clear that nothing will happen without everyone's efforts. Create opportunities for people to get involved and take action at their own levels to advance the overall goals.

Remove Obstacles. Remove barriers to organizational success. Be willing to change systems and structures if necessary. Encourage risk taking in pursuit of the goals.

Report on Progress Frequently. People need a sense that their efforts are worthwhile. Hand out lots of praise and thanks for participation. If something derails, be up-front about the problems and engage with others in devising solutions.

Look Ahead, Plan Ahead

A retreat need not become an annual event, as predictable as Thanksgiving and the 4th of July, but regular offsites can help an organization continue to evolve.

It's a good idea to build retreats into the annual budget, although not into the calendar. In other words, you'll want to have the resources available to convene a retreat when the time is right. But the right time will not necessarily be the same week every year. You don't want your retreats to become routine.

Remember that holding a retreat will not guarantee an organization's success. Retreats are not cure-alls. A retreat should never be an end in itself.

Rather, a retreat is a means. It's an event in the life of an organization that can refocus and re-energize it. It's a means to determine an organization's future destination and delineate the route to reach it.

Make sure the retreat is genuinely supported by the organization's leaders, well-designed and well-led, and appropriate for the participants who will take part. If that's the case, you will have prepared the groundwork for a retreat that works.

Afterword

We hope you found the stories and examples in this book—all of which came from our experience or that of friends and colleagues—interesting and useful.

In return, we invite readers to share your stories with us—tales of triumphs, amusing anecdotes, interventions that fizzled—that we might include as lessons learned and illustrations in future publications.

We would also love to hear from our readers with questions, suggestions, and comments about this book or the subject of retreats in general. And, if you know of any great places to hold an offsite, let us know that as well.

You can communicate with us at the Retreats That Work website: www.retreatsthatwork.com. The site will feature the best lessons learned, answers to questions submitted to us, and other information for convenors and facilitators.

Whether you have something to contribute or are just interested in learning more about retreats that work, c'mon by.

Sheila and Merianne

Appendix

Checklists for the Convenor

1. *Overall Retreat Logistics*

☐ After selecting the facilitator, consult with him or her on the appropriate length for the retreat.

☐ Determine when the facilitator is available for your retreat.

☐ Check available dates with senior managers whose participation in the retreat is critical to its success.

☐ Select a retreat facility and determine dates when it is available for your group. (Your facilitator may have suggestions for appropriate facilities.)

☐ Announce the retreat and give participants two or three options for dates. They should tell you which dates, if any, *do not* work.

☐ Contract with the retreat facility for the dates you choose.

☐ Make arrangements for transportation, meals, lodging, and audiovisual support required.

☐ Announce the dates of the retreat and provide participants with the information they need, including lodging arrangements; directions to the site; recreational options, if any; the dress code; and how family members can get messages to them during the retreat.

☐ Ask invitees to confirm their participation, indicate any food preferences or limitations, and supply emergency contact information.

2. Assessing Facilitators

When you check facilitators' references, try to find out as much as you can about their ability to do the following:

- ☐ Listen accurately to what others are saying without injecting their own biases.

- ☐ Be neutral (and be perceived to be neutral) about the outcome of the discussions.

- ☐ Suspend judgment of retreat participants.

- ☐ Understand multiple perspectives, help bring them to the surface, and resist colluding with the group in avoiding thorny issues.

- ☐ Encourage participants whose viewpoints may not be popular to speak out, and urge others to listen.

- ☐ Help retreat participants recognize and deal with any behavior that might be hampering the group's work.

- ☐ Deal skillfully with the members of the group who might not want to accept their guidance.

- ☐ Empathize with others.

- ☐ Analyze and summarize key issues.

- ☐ Remain comfortable with ambiguous situations and those they do not control.

- ☐ Recognize and manage differences that may stem from the diversity (cultural, racial, gender, age, sexual orientation, and so forth) of the participants.

- ☐ Hear feedback from the participants without becoming defensive.

- ☐ Adjust their approach, acknowledge missteps, and ask for help when they need it.

3. Finding the Right Retreat Site

Look for a retreat site with:

☐ Soundproof rooms, so you won't have to compete with a speaker with a microphone on the other side of a thin wall.

☐ Hard-surfaced, easy-to-move tables that don't have to be covered by table-cloths.

☐ Comfortable chairs—either padded, rolling executive style or comfy sofas and upholstered chairs.

☐ Enough room in the main meeting space to allow participants to circle the chairs and work away from the tables when needed.

☐ Space to use for breakout groups: either a main room with moveable chairs, large enough for groups to move away from each other, or smaller rooms adjacent to the main space or very close by.

☐ Ample supplies of flip chart easels and pads, masking tape, and markers.

☐ Space where people can congregate informally to talk or grounds where they can walk.

☐ Snacks and drinks available all day, rather than just at scheduled breaks.

Checklists for the Facilitator

1. Structuring the Interview Questions

The success of the retreat will depend in large measure on your ability to ask questions that get to the heart of the issues. Here are some questions we often ask, which we recommend you modify to suit the needs of the organization you are working for.

☐ What do you think is most important to accomplish at this retreat?

☐ What might impede the group's ability to achieve that outcome?

- [ ] [If this group has held retreats before:] What did you find most helpful at the last retreat? Did you find anything troubling or frustrating about the last retreat and the actions that resulted from it?

- [ ] What words would you use to describe your experience at [your organization]?

- [ ] What do you think is going well at [your organization]? What do you like most about it?

- [ ] How would you describe relationships among the staff? Between staff and management? [Or between the staff and the board?]

- [ ] In every organization there is some conflict, disagreement, or difference of opinion. How is conflict or disagreement handled at [your organization]?

- [ ] If you had the power to change anything at [your organization], what would you change?

- [ ] Of the changes you said you'd like to see, are there any that you think would not be possible? Why not?

- [ ] How do you feel about taking part in this retreat?

- [ ] Do you have any concerns about what might take place?

- [ ] Is there anything else you think I should know, anything I haven't thought of asking, or anything you'd like to add to something you've already said?

2. *Matching the Retreat Design with the Convenor's Expectations*

Is your design:

- [ ] Suitable for the participants, taking into consideration their level of experience and expertise and their comfort level with certain types of activities?

- [ ] Focused sharply on delivering the expected outcomes?

- [ ] Likely to engage the participants so they are strongly committed to the decisions they make?

- [ ] Attentive to using participants' time wisely?

☐ Adaptable enough to allow for changes if something unexpected happens, but still able to move the group toward the desired outcomes?

☐ Flexible enough for participants to have time to discuss how decisions reached at the retreat will be implemented and integrated into the organization's work?

3. Setting the Conditions for Design Success

Have you:

☐ Come to clear agreement with the convenor about mutual expectations?

☐ Interviewed participants and other relevant stakeholders in advance?

☐ Provided enough variety in the retreat activities?

☐ Included in your design opportunities for people to think before they speak?

☐ Allowed for spontaneous changes to the retreat plan?

☐ Built in unstructured time?

☐ Devised activities that will force participants to make hard choices?

☐ Left adequate time for action planning?

☐ Provided an appropriate close?

4. Inspecting the Meeting Room

☐ *Room Arrangement.* Are the chairs and tables set up exactly as you planned? If not, move them now.

☐ *Your Materials.* Is there a table for your notes and supplies? Has the facility provided the supplies you requested, such as pads of writing paper or masking tape?

☐ *Wall Space.* Where will you post flip chart pages as they are filled? Is access to the walls blocked by tables, chairs, or lamps? Will you have to post them on windows? Where will you put charts as the walls fill up?

☐ *Equipment Supplied by the Facility.* Do you have the right number of easels and pads of flip chart paper? Are the pads full, or do some only have a few sheets left? Is all the AV equipment you ordered in the room and set up properly? Does it work? Do you have extra bulbs for your projector?

☐ *Markers.* If you haven't brought boxes of new markers, have you tested every marker supplied by the facility and discarded those that are dried out?

☐ *Facilities.* Do you know where the bathrooms are? Where the snacks will be set up? Where lunch and dinner will be served?

☐ *Participant Place Setups.* Are the supplies—markers, writing pads, and pens or pencils—and handouts that participants need in place? Do you have extras in case they're required?

5. The Facilitator's Toolkit

No matter how dependable the retreat facility seems, we always bring these things with us:

☐ Several sets of fresh markers, in black, blue, green, and red.

☐ Two sizes of Post-it® Notes, in multiple colors, one of each for every participant, plus about 20 percent extra.

☐ Name tags for the participants.

☐ Several rolls of masking tape.

☐ Colored labeling dots (for "voting" on choices).

☐ Pocketknife or box cutter for opening boxes of supplies, if you ship them ahead. (*Note:* You'll have to check these items if you are flying to the retreat site.)

☐ Bell, chime, whistle, or whatever you like to use to indicate the beginning and ending of timed exercises.

☐ A timer (so you won't have to keep looking at your watch during timed exercises).

References

Amabile, T.M. (1995). *KEYS: Assessing the climate for creativity.* Greensboro, NC: Center for Creative Leadership.

Amabile, T.M., Burnside, R.M., & Gryskiewicz, S. (1997*). User's manual for KEYS: Assessing the climate for creativity.* Greensboro, NC: Center for Creative Leadership.

Argyris, C. (1993). *Knowledge for action: A guide to overcoming barriers to organizational change.* San Francisco, CA: Jossey-Bass.

Argyris, C., & Schön, D.A. (1974). *Theory in practice: Increasing professional effectiveness.* San Francisco, CA: Jossey-Bass.

Block, P. (1981). *Flawless consulting: A guide to getting your expertise used.* San Francisco, CA: Jossey-Bass/Pfeiffer.

Briggs, K.C., & Myers, I.B. (1998). *Myers-Briggs Type Indicator: Self-Scorable Form M.* Palo Alto, CA: Consulting Psychologists Press, Inc.

Collins, J. (2001). *Good to great: Why some companies make the leap . . . and others don't.* New York: HarperBusiness.

Cooperrider, D.L. (1995). Introduction to appreciative inquiry. In W. French & C. Bell (Eds.), *Organization development* (5th ed.). Englewood Cliffs, NJ: Prentice Hall.

Cross, E.Y., Katz, J.H, Miller, F.A., & Seashore, E.W. (Eds.). (1994). *The promise of diversity: Over 40 voices discuss strategies for eliminating discrimination in organizations.* Burr Ridge, IL: Irwin Professional Publishing.

Drucker, P. (1999). *Management challenges for the 21st century.* New York: HarperBusiness.

Eggleton, C.H., & Rice, J.C. (1996). *The fieldbook of team interventions: Step-by-step guide to high performance teams.* Amherst, MA: HRD Press.

Esty, K., Griffin, R., & Hirsch, M.S. (1995). *Workplace diversity: A manager's guide to solving problems and turning diversity into a competitive advantage.* Holbrook, MA: Adams Publishing.

Goleman, D., Boyatzis, R., & McKee, A. (2001, December). Primal leadership: The hidden driver of great performance," *Harvard Business Review,* pp. 43–51.

Hall, E.T. (1983). *The dance of life: The other dimension of time.* Garden City, NY: Anchor Press/Doubleday.

Hamel, G. (2000). *Leading the revolution.* Boston, MA: Harvard Business School Press, p. 250.

Hamel, G. (1996, July/August). Strategy as revolution. *Harvard Business Review,* p. 78.

Hammond, S.A., & Royal C. (Eds.). (1998). *Lessons from the field: Applying appreciative inquiry.* Plano, TX: Practical Press.

Hofstede, G. (1997). *Cultures and organizations: Software of the mind.* New York: McGraw-Hill.

Ingvar, D.H. (1985). Memory of the future: An essay on the temporal organization of conscious awareness. *Human Neurobiology, 4,* 127–36.

Keen, P.G.W. (1997). *The process edge: Creating value where it counts.* Boston, MA: Harvard Business School Press.

Kirton, M. (1991). *Kirton Adaptation-Innovation Inventory.* Berkhamsted, UK: The Occupational Research Centre.

Kiser, A.G. (1998). *Masterful facilitation.* New York: AMACOM.

Kotter, J.P. (1995, March/April). Leading change: Why transformation efforts fail. *Harvard Business Review,* p. 60.

Marshak, R. (1995, September 15-17). *The introvert's protection act.* Classroom lecture, Organizational Dynamics, American University.

Maurer, R. (1996). *Beyond the wall of resistance.* Austin, TX: Bard Books.

McCall, M.W., & Lombardo, M.M. (1983). *Off the track: Why and how successful executives get derailed* (Technical Report No. 21). Greensboro, NC: Center for Creative Leadership.

Nevis., E.C. (1987). *Organization consulting: A gestalt approach.* Cleveland, OH: Gestalt Institute of Cleveland Press.

Oshry, B. (1996). *Seeing systems: Unlocking the mysteries of organizational life.* San Francisco, CA: Berrett-Koehler.

Oshry, B. (1999). *Leading systems: Lessons from the power lab.* San Francisco, CA: Berrett-Koehler.

Owen, H. (1995). *Tales from open space.* Available: www.mindspring.com/~owenhh/publication.htm

Owen, H. (1997a). *Expanding our now: The story of open space technology.* San Francisco, CA: Berrett-Koehler.

Owen, H. (1997b). *Open space technology: A user's guide.* San Francisco, CA: Berrett-Koehler.

Porter, M.E. (1996, November/December). What is strategy? *Harvard Business Review,* pp. 68–69.

Schwarz, R.M. (1994). *The skilled facilitator: Practical wisdom for developing effective groups.* San Francisco, CA: Jossey-Bass.

Senge, P.M., Roberts, C., Ross, R.B., Smith, B.J., Kleiner, A. (1994). *The fifth discipline fieldbook.* New York: Doubleday Currency.

Slater, R. (2000). *The GE way fieldbook: Jack Welch's battle plan for corporate revolution.* New York: McGraw-Hill.

Sugar, S. (2000). *Games that teach teams: 21 activities to super-charge your group!* San Francisco, CA: Jossey-Bass/Pfeiffer.

Thomas, K.W., & Kilmann, R.H. (2002). *Thomas-Kilmann Conflict Mode Instrument.* Palo Alto, CA: Consulting Psychologists Press, Inc.

Thomas, R.R. (1996). *Redefining diversity.* New York: AMACOM.

Van der Heijden, K. (1996). *Scenarios: The art of strategic conversation.* New York: John Wiley & Sons.

Varner, I., & Beamer, L. (1995). *Intercultural communication in the global workplace.* Chicago, IL: Richard D. Irwin.

Weisbord, M.R. (1987). *Productive workplaces.* San Francisco, CA: Jossey-Bass.

Weisbord, M.R., & Janoff, S. (1995). *Future search: An action guide to finding common ground in organizations and communities.* San Francisco, CA: Berrett-Koehler.

About the Authors

Sheila Campbell is president of Wild Blue Yonder, Inc., a consulting firm centered around creative thinking, strategy, change, organization behavior, and corporate culture. Campbell designs and leads offsite retreats for numerous organizations every year in the United States, Canada, and the Far East; her retreat clients include the Boston Museum of Fine Arts, National Geographic Television, Goodyear Tire and Rubber Co., the U.S. Department of Energy, and Kodak.

She also conducts training sessions on creativity in the workplace, strategic thinking, and leadership skills for the American Association of Advertising Agencies, OppenheimerFunds, AlliedSignal, and *Business Week* and *Barron's* magazines.

Campbell teaches both strategy and creativity in the MBA program at Johns Hopkins University. She has also served on the faculty of the University of Maryland and as director of the Mid-Atlantic Institute for Advanced Advertising Studies co-sponsored by the American Association of Advertising Agencies (AAAA). Also for AAAA, she conducts workshops in strategic planning and account management relationships for ad agency groups around the country. She has a master's degree in organization development from American University.

Merianne Liteman is president and CEO of Liteman Rosse, Inc., a consulting firm that specializes in designing and facilitating offsite retreats and presenting workshops on strategic planning, creative thinking, leadership development, communication skills, and other issues that may be hindering an organization from realizing its full potential.

Liteman designs and conducts retreats and workshops in the United States and Latin America, Africa, Canada, and Europe. She speaks regularly at national and international conferences and has been published and profiled by national journals interested in organizational effectiveness issues.

Liteman's retreat clients include Mitsubishi Electric America, Fannie Mae, the Boston Museum of Fine Arts, the Corcoran Gallery of Art, the International Monetary Fund, the U.S. Military Academy at West Point, the Red Cross of Mexico, the YMCA of Uruguay, and the U.S. Department of State.

Liteman has a master's degree in organization development from American University and completed a post-graduate training program in group facilitation from the same institution. She is a member of the NTL Institute for Applied Behavioral Science.

Steve Sugar is a writer and teacher in the use of activities that create a joyful learning environment. He is the author of *Games That Teach* (Jossey-Bass/Pfeiffer), co-author of *Games That Teach Teams* (Jossey-Bass/Pfeiffer), and the developer of three instructional game systems used across the world (HRD Press). Sugar has been interviewed by *Personnel Journal, Training & Development,* and *TRAINING* magazines. Sugar has contributed articles on game design to *The 1999 and 2000 Team and Organization Development Sourcebooks* (McGraw-Hill) and *The 2000 Annual, Volume 2, Consulting* (Jossey-Bass/Pfeiffer) and has served as editor-contributor to several (ASTD) INFO-Line publications. He has contributed chapters on instructional game design to *The ASTD Handbook of Instructional Technology* (1993: McGraw-Hill) and *The ASTD Handbook of Training Design and Delivery* (1999: McGraw-Hill).

Sugar has taught experiential learning in the graduate curriculums at Johns Hopkins University and the New York Institute of Technology. He has also been on the faculties of the University of Maryland, University College (UMUC), the Leadership Program at the Federal Judicial Center, the Human Resources Faculty, the Johns Hopkins University, and the Education Development curriculum at the USDA Graduate School.

Index

A

Acknowledging accomplishments/milestones, 310
Action plan implementation: announcing retreat outcomes and, 307–308; avoiding post-retreat letdown, 309–310; changing cynicism to support, 311–312; critical leadership actions for, 313; importance of following retreats with, 305–306; looking ahead/planning ahead and, 314–315; making the plan stick, 312–314; senior management role in, 310–311; translating decision into action, 308–309. *See also* Change
Action planning: assuring implementation of, 305–315; benefits of using, 146; described, 112; on measuring successful results, 147–148; organizational strategy for, 200–203; on overcoming obstacles to complete actions, 152–153; on required resources to achieve results, 150–151; on requirements for achieving results, 148–149; on setting objectives/goals, 147, 201–203; on timing of actions, 152; on who will perform required actions, 149–150
Activities. *See* Facilitator activity manual
Administrator role/duties, 16–17
Allen, W., 56
Announcing retreat outcomes, 305–306
Appreciation activity, 296–297
Appricative Inquiry retreat, 34
Archilochus, 179

B

Background processes, 199
Beamer, L., 127
Behavioral assessment: KEYS by Center for Creative Leadership, 75; Kirton Adaption Innovation Index (KAI), 74–75; Myers-Briggs Type Indicator (MBTI), 73; skillful use of, 75–76; Thomas-Kilmann Conflict Mode Instrument (TKI), 74; value of using, 72–73
Berlin, I., 179
Beyond the Wall of Resistance (Maurer), 166
Block, P., 66
Board retreats: described, 13; designing corporate, 86–87; designing nonprofit, 83–85; special design considerations for, 83–87
Body language: meanings of, 130–131; reflecting on what you read in, 133–134
Boyatzis, R., 52
Brainstorming, 270. *See also* Creativity retreats
Breach of confidence, 170
Breakout group discussions, 103–105
Business Week, 7

C

Categorization decisions, 144
Celebrating milestones, 310
Argyris, C., 117
Associations/member organizations retreats, 14
Center for Creative Leadership (CCL), 75
Center for Creative Leadership and Discovery Learning, 33
Change: convenor's goal for positive, 52–53; exploring how individual behavior can, 262–265; leadership as being open to, 58–59; realistic guidelines provided by leadership for, 55; recognizing/removing obstacles to, 231–233; resistance to new ideas and, 165–168; reward structures to help shape culture, 228–229. *See also* Action plan implementation; Culture change retreats
Client selection strategy, 175–176
Closing retreats: activities for, 290–300; allowing enough time for, 112; important role of, 289; writing follow-up report after, 301–302
Closing Thoughts activity, 294
Co-facilitators, 123–125
Collages, 109–110
Collins, J., 178
Communication: How We Communicate activity on, 254–256; strengthening, 253
Compromise decision making, 141
Conference centers, 45
Confidence breach, 170
Conflict: interdepartmental, 266–268; probing for sources of, 259–262; recovering strategies in case of, 168–170; understanding cultural differences to prevent, 128–132
Consensus, 138, 141–142

Considering Risk activity, 286

Consultative executive authority decision making, 139

Content facilitator, 117–119

Content segments: applying theories to real situations, 108; asking/answering questions, 105–106; breakout group discussions, 103–105; drawing/writing verse/performing songs/making collages, 109–110; envisioning possibilities/generating new ideas, 109; the importance of timing, 110; learning about what has happened elsewhere, 108–109; listening, 105; making up and presenting skits, 108; using metaphor to express thoughts/feelings, 109; observing other people's actions/discussions, 106–107; overview of, 100–102; participating on improvisation/role play/storytelling, 107; physical activities, 110; reflecting back on experiences, 107; whole group conversation, 102–103

Controversial/sensitive issues, 224–227

Convenor leadership behavior: awareness of impact of your presence, 53–54; being open about feedback on self, 56; being open to change, 58–59; being there, 56–57; carefully expressing your opinion, 54–55; don't dominate discussions, 54; knowing when to hold back, 55; letting facilitator lead the retreat, 58; managing your emotions, 57–58; minimizing differences among participants, 56; providing realistic guidelines for change, 55; working with entire group, 55

Convenors: assuring implementation of action plan, 305–315; cooperation between retreat designer and, 63–66; facilitator feedback given prior to, 98–99; information to help prepare, 60; leadership behavior during retreat by, 53–59; positive change goal of, 52–53; role/duties of, 15; unclear agreement regarding retreat expectations with, 80. *See also* Retreat leadership; Senior management

Cooperrider, D. L., 34

Corporate board retreats, 86–87

Creativity retreats: cultivating creativity habit, 279–284; described, 14; letting go of judgment, 285–287; minimizing "Groupthink," 276–278; stimulating creative thinking during, 269–275. *See also* Ideas

Cross, E. Y., 127

Cultivating creativity habit, 279–284

Cultural differences: on comfort with physical closeness, 129–130; on comfort showing emotion, 129; on direct and candid expression, 128; language and, 130; on levels of formality/respect, 128; managing, 131–132; on orientation toward individual/group, 129; on perspectives on time, 129

Culture change retreats: challenges of, 213–214; feedback for senior executives/others, 234–237; how individuals foster change, 230; recognizing/removing obstacles to change, 231–233; reward structures helping to shape culture, 228–229; what can realistically be accomplished at, 214–223; working with sensitive/controversial issues, 224–227. *See also* Change

Customer retreats, described, 14

D

The Dance of Life: The Other Dimensions of Time (Hall), 1219

Decision by default, 140

Decision making: action planning and, 146–153; methods of, 137–142; process of participant, 111; translating into action, 308–309; types of retreat, 142–146

Decorations Factory activity, 247–249

Differentiation strategy, 176

Distinctive Competencies activity, 196–197

Diversity issues: awareness of cultural/racial, 126–128; resources on, 127

Drawing activities, 109–110

E

EdgeWork, 33

Elektrixx, 29

Emotional leadership task, 52

Emotional responses: by boss, 164–165; cultural differences regarding, 129; facilitator intervention during, 121–122; handling overt hostility, 161–162; leader management of own, 57–58; leading to participant walking out, 163–164; metaphors used to express, 109. *See also* Feelings

Encouraging participation, 132–134

"Energy voting," 145

Esty, K., 127

Executive authority decision making, 138–139

Executive retreats, 12–13

Executive Team instructions, 250

Expectations and Outcomes activity, 298–299

Experience: learning about other's, 108–109; reflecting on, 107

Expert Opinion activity, 284

Exploring Strategic Purpose activity, 180–181

F

Facilitation resources: on diversity, 127; on retreat facilitation, 125

Facilitator activity manual: Appreciation, 296–297; Closing Thoughts, 294; Considering Risk, 286; Decorations Factory, 247–249; Distinctive Competencies, 196–197; Expectations and Outcomes, 298–299; Expert Opinion, 284; Exploring Strategic Purpose, 180–181; Glimpses into the Future, 186–188; How Conflict Affects Us, 260; How We Communicate, 254–256; for identifying organization identity/priority processes, 200; Impressions, 277–278; Isolated Words, 280–281; Letter to Myself, 295; Looking at Our Values, 183–184; The Messy Room, 290–292; Metaphorical Management, 235–237; Multiple Perspectives, 282–283; Obstacle Busters, 232–233; Our Stable of Clients or Resources, 191–193; Prioritizing Constituencies, 194–195; Rating Resources, 189–190; Really Bad Ideas, 275; Resource/Impact Matrix, 207–208; The Road We've Traveled, 300; on setting goals, 202; Significant Stories, 223; Silent Dialogue, 225–227; Snowball, 257–258; Star Performers, 263–265; suggested activities for peers-only retreat, 267; Taking Responsibility, 261–262; Targeting Core Priorities, 204–205; Timeline of Our History, 221–222; Top Priorities, 293; Vehicle for Change, 242–244; Visit Our Village, 216–220; What Gets Rewarded Here?, 229; Wide Open Thinking, 271–273

Facilitators: ability to change the retreat plan, 134–135; allowed to lead retreat by convenor, 58; being transparent with group, 122; clarifying charges/fees of, 23; confirming availability prior to scheduling retreat, 43; effect on the group by, 116; feedback given to group by, 97–100, 122–123; follow-up report by, 301–302; giving convenors feedback prior to group, 98–99; ground rules established by, 93–94; individual check-in overseen by, 95–97; introduction given by, 92–93; more resources for, 125; outlining for participants role of, 37–38; partnering with another facilitator by internal, 125–126; pre-retreat checklist, 86; process or content, 117–119; provocative mode of, 119; recovering strategies for, 155–170; role/duties of, 15–16; selecting, 22–25; working with co-facilitators, 123–125. See also Retreat facilitation

Facilitator's toolkit, 88

Fast Company, 7

Feedback: being open about received, 56; exploring importance of, 256–258; "Giraffe Awards" as signal for candid, 52; given by facilitator to group, 97–100, 122–123; guarantees of non-

repercussions for, 24; for senior executives/others, 234–237

Feelings: leader's management of emotions and, 57–58; metaphors used to express, 109. *See also* Emotional responses

Fifth Discipline Fieldbook (Senge, Roberts, Ross, Smith, and Kleiner), 147, 185

Financial objectives, 202

Financial resources strategy, 176

"Five Whys" exercise, 147

Fixed format retreats, 14

Fixed-format retreat pitfalls, 36

Flawless Consulting (Block), 66

Folklore processes, 199–200

Follow-up report, 301–302

Following-up. *See* Action plan implementation

Foxes/hedgehogs, 179

Free/informed choice value, 117

"Fresh awareness," 119

Future Search retreat, 14

Future Search (Weisbord and Janoff), 31

G

The GE Way Fieldbook (Slater), 33

General Electric's Work-Out program, 14

"Giraffe Awards," 52

Glimpses into the Future activity, 186–188

Goleman, D., 52

Good to Great (Collins), 178

"Good-natured teasing," 160–161

Griffin, R., 127

Ground rules: establishing, 93–94; when senior manager violates, 159–160

Group intervention, 121

Groups: formation of, 104; formation of subgroups, 102; making up/presenting skits in, 108. *See also* Participants

"Groupthink" minimizing, 276–278

Grove Consultants International, 71

H

Hall, E., 129

Hamel, G., 29

Hammond, S. A., 34

Hedgehogs/foxes, 179

Hostility, 161–162

Hotel locations, 46

How Conflict Affects Us activity, 260

How We Communicate activity, 254–256

Human Synergistics, 34

Humor misused, 160–161

I

Ideas: generation of new, 109; participant resistance to new, 165–168; pulling together participant, 134. *See also* Creativity retreats

Identity processes, 198, 200

Impressions activity, 277–278

Improvisation, 107

Individual check-in, 95–97

Ingvar, D., 185

Intercultural Communication in the Global Workplace (Varner and Beamer), 127

Interdepartmental retreats: to call cease fire in turf battles, 266–268; described, 13

Internal commitment to choice value, 117

Internal management objectives, 202

Interpersonal intervention, 120

Interviews (pre-retreat), 66–69, 81

Introduction to Appreciative Inquiry (Cooperrider), 34

Introduction to retreat, 92–93

Isolated Words activity, 280–281

J

Janoff, S., 31

Jossey-Bass/Pfeiffer, 34

K

Katz, J. H., 127

Keen, P., 198

KEYS (Center for Creative Leadership), 75

Kirton Adaption Innovation Index (KAI), 74–75

Kiser, A. G., 115

Kleiner, A., 147, 185

Koosh ball exercise, 96

L

Language: cultural differences and, 130; meaning of body, 130–131, 133–134

Large system interventions format, 31
Lassiter & Tompkins, 101
Leadership. *See* Convenors; Retreat leadership; Senior management
Leading the retreat. *See* Retreat facilitation
Leading the Revolution (Hamel), 29
Learning objectives, 203
Lessons from the Field: Applying Appreciative Inquiry (Hammond and Royal), 34
Letter to Myself activity, 295
Letting go of judgment, 285–287
Level 1 Resistance, 166
Level 2 Resistance, 167
Leyland, F., 64
Limiting issues decisions, 144
Listening, 105
Logistics checklist, 49
Looking at Our Values activity, 183–184

M

McKee, A., 52
Majority rule decision making, 139
Management. *See* Senior management
Mandated processes, 199
Masterful Facilitation (Kiser), 115
Maurer, R., 166, 167
Mead, M., 116
Meals, 47–48
Meetings vs. retreats, 19*t*
The Messy Room activity, 290–292
Metaphorical Management activity, 235–237
Metaphors, 109
Milestone celebrations, 310
Miller, F. A., 127
Mini-retreats, 310
Minority activism decision making, 140–141
Mission statement, 178–179
Moving right along decision making, 140
Multiple Perspectives activity, 282–283
Myers-Briggs Type Indicator (MBTI), 73

N

Nametags, 79
Nevis, E., 119

New ideas: generating, 109; participant resistance to, 165–168
Nonprofit board retreats, 83–85

O

Observation, 106–107
Obstacle Busters activity, 232–233
Open Space retreat, 14
Open space technology format, 31–32
Open Space Technology (Owen), 32
Organization Consulting: A Gestalt Approach (Nevis), 119
Organization strategies: checking against resources, 206–208; for clients selection, 175–176; devising, 209; for differentiation, 176; elements of, 174–175; evaluating work processes, 198–200; for financial resources, 176; planning for action, 200–203; prioritizing among goals, 203; for scope of work, 177; testing, 210–211; understanding environment of, 185–197
The Organization Workshop: Creating Partnership, 33
Organizations: checking resources for, 206–208; discerning values of, 182–184; prioritizing among goals by, 203–205; reviewing mission/vision/purpose of, 178–179
Osborn, A., 270
Oshry, B., 33
"Other Topics" flip chart, 157
Our Stable of Clients or Resources activity, 191–193
Outdoor experiences format, 33
Owen, H., 31–32

P

Paper Planes, Inc., 33–34
Paraphrasing, 132–133
Participant selection: cautionary tips regarding, 28; cross section representatives, 27; open offer vs. competition in, 28–29; of part-time participants, 29–30; revolutionary voices as part of, 29; sources of, 26; by titles/positions, 27
Participants: application of theories to real

situations by, 108; behavioral assessments of, 72–76; confirming availability prior to scheduling retreat, 43–44; cultural differences of, 128–132; decision making by, 111, 137–139; decisions regarding who to invite as, 25–30; encouraging participation by, 132–134; facilitator feedback given to, 97–100, 122–123; giving retreat mementos to, 309; improvisation/role play/storytelling by, 107; from intact work group/invited outsiders, 27; involved in retreat planning, 37–38; minimizing differences among, 56; notifying, 48–50; observation by, 106–107; outlining role of facilitator for, 37–38; post-retreat resignations by, 59–60; pre-retreat interviews with, 66–69, 81; pre-work for retreat, 76–77; reaching understanding about authority of, 51–53; role/duties of, 17–18; types of possible, 26. *See also* Groups
Peers-only retreat, 266–268
Personal intervention, 120
Personal space, 129–130
"Personality differences," 240–241
Physical activities, 110
Planning retreat: flow of, 177; to review mission/vision/purpose, 178–179; to review organization strategy, 174–177
Porter, M., 200
Post-retreat letdown, 309–310
Power & Systems, 33
Pre-retreat checklist (facilitator), 86
Pre-retreat interviews: design mistake in not holding, 81; sample questions for, 69; value of conducting, 66–69
Pre-work (participants), 76–77
"Primal Leadership: Realizing the Power of Emotional Intelligence" (Goleman, Boyatzis, and McKee), 52
Prioritizing actions decisions, 145
Prioritizing Constituencies activity, 194–195
Prioritizing goals, 203
Priority processes, 199
The Process Edge (Keen), 198

Process facilitator, 117–118
Production Team instructions, 252
Products/services objectives, 202
The Promise of Diversity (Cross, Katz, Miller, and Seashore), 127
Provocative facilitator mode, 119

Q

Questions: clarifying, 132; participant asking/answering, 105–106; pre-retreat interview sample, 69

R

Ranking importance decisions, 143
Rating quality decisions, 143–144
Rating Resources activity, 189–190
Really Bad Ideas activity, 275
Recovering strategies: listed, 155–156; when boss gets furious/bursts into tears, 164–165; when few participants dominate discussions, 156; when group keeps wandering off task, 156–157; when group's energy is flagging, 158; when intense conflict breaks out, 168–170; when participant breaches another's confidence, 170; when participant is overtly hostile/refuses to participate, 161–162; when participant keeps plowing same ground, 158; when participant repeatedly disrupts conversations, 159; when participant walks out, 163–164; when participants resist new ideas, 165–168; when people misuse humor, 160–161; when senior manager violate ground rules, 159–160. *See also* Retreats
Redefining Diversity (Thomas), 127
Reflecting back on experiences, 107
Religious retreat houses, 46
Reporter role/duties, 17
Resistance to change, 165–168
Resource/Impact Matrix activity, 207–208
Resources: on diversity, 127; on retreat facilitation, 125
Retreat agenda, 92–93
Retreat design: convenor involvement with, 63–66; guiding principles for,
7–8; non-custom, 30; pitfalls of fixed-format, 36; for series of retreats, 87–89; special considerations for board retreats, 83–87; using specialized format for, 30–36
Retreat design components: action planning, 112; closing, 112; content segments, 100–110; decision making, 111; giving feedback to group, 97–100; ground rules, 93–94; individual check-in, 95–97; introduction, 92–93; listed, 91
Retreat design mistakes: not allowing for spontaneous changes to plan, 81; not being transparent when changes occur, 82; not forcing hard choices, 82; not interviewing participants in advance, 81; not leaving adequate time for action planning, 82; not letting go of control during unstructured time, 82; not making opportunities for thinking before speaking, 81; not providing appropriate close, 83; not providing enough variety, 81; unclear agreement regarding retreat expectations, 80
Retreat facilitation: changing the plan for, 134–135; encouraging participation, 132–134; feedback as, 97–100, 122–123; to meet desired objectives, 115–117; partnering with another facilitator, 125–126; three values underpinning, 117; when intervention is needed, 120–122; working with co-facilitators, 123–125. *See also* Facilitators
"Retreat fatigue," 88
Retreat follow-up. *See* Action plan implementation
Retreat leadership: behavior during retreat by, 53–59; emotional leadership task of, 52; ground rule violations by, 159–160; how to ensure successful retreat, 53; reaching understanding about participants' authority, 51–53. *See also* Convenors; Senior management
Retreat length: ideal, 42; planning, 40, 42; sample formats on, 41*fig*
Retreat location: desirable characteristics
of, 46–47; planning for, 45–46; sleeping rooms/meals available at, 47–48; sports/recreation available at, 48
Retreat logistics: checklist for, 49; importance of, 39; on length of retreat, 40–42; on notifying participants, 48–50; on scheduling retreat time, 42–45; selecting location, 45–47; sleeping rooms/meals, 47–48; for sports/recreation, 48; thinking about, 78–80
Retreat plan: using behavioral assessments in, 72–76; capturing work product, 70–72; facilitation by changing the, 134–135; identifying scope of issues/creating, 70
Retreat planning: involving participants in, 37–38; regarding goals for retreat, 21–22; regarding the uninvited, 18–20; selecting facilitator, 22–25; on who to invite as participants, 25–30; who's who in, 15–20
Retreat values, 117
Retreats: achievements of well-run, 18; announcing outcomes of, 305–306; differences between meetings and, 19*t*; diversity issues at, 126–132; issues to consider when thinking of holding, 3–4; kinds/types of, 12–14; nine reasons to hold, 5–7; notifying participants about, 48–50; resignations by participations following, 59–60; ten reasons not to hold, 9–12; using "white space" time during, 77–78. *See also* Recovering strategies
The Road We've Traveled activity, 300
Roberts, C., 147, 185
Robert's Rules of Order, 79
Role play, 107
Ross, R. B., 147, 185
"Round robins," 133
Royal, C., 34

S

Sales Team instructions, 251
Scenarios: The Art of Strategic Conversation (van der Heijden), 185

Scheduling retreats, 42–45
Schön, D., 117
Schorr-Hirsch, M., 127
Schwarz, R. M., 125
Scope of work strategy, 177
Seashore, E. W., 127
Senge, P. M., 147, 185
Senior management: action plan implementation and role of, 310–311; culture change and feedback for, 234–237; ground rule violations by, 159–160. *See also* Convenors; Retreat leadership
Sensitive/controversial issues, 224–227
Sequencing actions decisions, 146
Series of retreats design issues, 87–89
Services/products objectives, 202
Setting objectives: action planning for, 147, 201–203; prioritizing among goals, 203; Targeting Core Priorities activity for, 204–205
Significant Stories activity, 223
Silent Dialogue activity, 225–227
Simulations, 32–34
Single Department retreats, 13
The Skilled Facilitator: Practical Wisdom for Developing Effective Groups (Schwarz), 125
Skits, 108
Sleeping rooms, 47
Smith, B. J., 147, 185
Snowball activity, 257–258
Song performance activities, 109–110
Specialized retreat format: advantages of using, 30–31; Appreciative Inquiry, 34; large system interventions, 31; open space technology, 31–32; outdoor experiences, 33; simulations, 32–34; Work-Out, 33–34
Sports/recreation, 48
Star Performers activity, 263–265
Storytelling, 107
Strategic framework model, 175
Subgroup formation, 102
Suggestions: asking for, 132; for group procedures, 133; for options by participants, 133
Summarizing agreements/proposals, 134

T

Table arrangement, 79
Tahiti rule, 44
Taking Responsibility activity, 261–262
Targeting Core Priorities activity, 204–205
"Team-building experiences," 240
Teamwork retreats: being asked to lead, 239–241; clarifying individuals' roles/responsibilities, 245; described, 13; exploring how things are/how they should be, 241–244; exploring how to change individual's behavior, 262–265; exploring importance of feedback, 256–258; for improving work processes, 245–252; peers-only, 266–268; probing for sources of, 259–262; strengthening communication at, 253–255
Theory application activities, 108
Theory in Practice: Increasing Professional Effectiveness (Argyris and Schön), 117
Thomas, R. R., 127
Thomas-Kilmann Conflict Mode Instrument (TKI), 74
Timeline of Our History activity, 221–222
Timing considerations, 110
Top Priorities activity, 293
Two-day retreats, 40, 41*fig.* 42

U

Unanimous consent, 138, 142
Uninvited, 18–20

V

Valid information value, 117
Values: discerning organization, 182–184; underpinning retreat facilitation, 117
van der Heijden, K., 185
Varner, I., 127
Vehicle for Change activity, 242–244
Vendor retreats, described, 14
Visit Our Village activity, 216–220

W

The Wall Street Journal, 7
Weisbord, M., 31
What Gets Rewarded Here? activity, 229
Whistler, J. M., 64
"White space" time, 77–78
Whole group conversation, 102–103
Whole system retreats, 14
Wide Open Thinking activity, 271–273
Work processes: evaluation of, 198–200; retreat plan capturing product of, 70–72; teamwork retreats for improving, 245–252
Work-Out format, 33–34
Work-Out program (GE), 14
Workplace Diversity (Esty, Griffin, and Schorr-Hirsch), 127
Writing activities, 109–110